Developing a Leadership Role within the Key Stage 1 Curriculum
A Handbook for Students and Newly Qualified Teachers

Edited by

Julie Davies

The Falmer Press

(A member of the Taylor & Francis Group)

London • Washington, C.D.

UK   The Falmer Press, 4 John Street, London WC1N 2ET
USA   The Falmer Press, Taylor & Francis Inc., 1900 Frost Road, Suite 101,
Bristol, PA 19007

First published in 1995

A catalogue record for this book is available from the British Library

Library of Congress Cataloging-in-Publication Data are available on request

ISBN 0 7507 0422 5 cased
ISBN 0 7507 0423 3 paper

Jacket design by Caroline Archer

Typeset in 10/12 pt Bembo by
Graphicraft Typesetters Ltd., Hong Kong.

Printed in Great Britain by Burgess Science Press, Basingstoke on paper which has a specified pH vaiue on final paper manufacture of not less than 7.5 and is therefore 'acid free'.

Contents

Contents

Introduction

This book sets out to help students and newly qualified teachers to understand the complexities of being a coordinator of a national curriculum subject at Key Stage 1. Since 1989, initial teacher training courses in England and Wales have incorporated in their programmes preparation for taking a lead in a subject area in their first appointment. There is no longer a place for a teacher (newly qualified or not) in primary schools whose sole responsibility is his or her class. In addition, a teacher must have specific specialist knowledge and expertise in particular subjects which he or she must disseminate to the staff. A teacher also needs the skills of communication, leadership and persuasion. This book contains individual chapters on each national curriculum subject as well as two opening chapters on the general skills needed to be an effective coordinator. Each chapter is written by someone who has been, or is still, a coordinator. The authors have written from personal, successful experience. Their enthusiasm for their particular area shines through their writing as does their practical, pragmatic approach to coordination.

Julie Davies
Manchester Victoria University,
January 1995

Chapter 1

Developing Skills to Become an Effective Key Stage 1 Subject Coordinator

Mike Harrison

Effective curriculum coordinators have a significant opportunity to improve children's learning in their schools. That primary teachers need support does not seem to be in doubt (Harrison, 1994a). The challenge of working with colleagues to produce an effective programme in any subject area is one which will contribute to personal development and enhance the image of the profession.

The key to quality in primary education lies in the skills of the class teacher (see for example Wragg's excellent report on the Leverhulme Primary Teaching Skills Project, 1993). Indeed David McNamara (1994) argues that 'at the heart of educational process lies the teacher' and all tasks other than imparting subject knowledge are merely a distraction for the teacher. In Professor McNamara's *Classroom Pedagogy and Primary Practice*, a book of 145 pages arguing the primacy of teaching and teachers, no mention of curriculum coordination is made. Steve Harrison and Ken Theaker (1989) set out to acknowledge that the role of the teacher is at the very heart of British primary education. At its best 'it concerns itself with the whole child . . . provides for secure relationships and covers all aspects of a child's development' (p. 5). However the increasing complexity of the primary curriculum and society's expectations makes it difficult for the class teacher to keep up to date. Within traditional subject areas there has been an explosion of knowledge and new fields such as science, technology, design, problem solving and health education – not to mention the uses of computers – are now considered entitlements for primary children. Furthermore, we now expect all children to succeed at these studies – not just the fortunate few

> On learning that a curriculum development role (dealing with adults) is expected of you, fear maybe the predominant feeling: 'It may result in a temporary questioning of ability and suitability for leadership, throwing up all manner of doubts and insecurities' (Day *et al.*, 1993, p. 26).

who passed the eleven-plus (Harrison, 1994b): 'We have learned that we are no longer prepared to accept an education service in which only a minority prosper' (Barber, 1994). All this has overwhelmed an education system largely unchanged since the inception of primary schools after World War II. For children to be inducted into some of this knowledge without the use of specialist teachers, who many of us believe would damage the very nature of primary education, we need to exploit the talents of those within schools in a process of mutual support. As Harrison and Theaker point out 'a great deal of enthusiasm and expertise in specific curriculum areas has been locked into individual classrooms. It is only when we share knowledge and skills that the true potential of the professional teacher is realised' (p. 5).

What you can do:
- articulate your feelings about your doubts;
- accept that this is a challenge;
- declare your need for a clear definition of what is expected of you;
- allow yourself to be less than perfect.

How can curriculum development (and by implication improvement in teaching) come about? It does not appear to be high on the list of the way headteachers spend their time. Blease and Lever (1992) examined the detailed diaries kept by twenty-five primary headteachers. They comment, 'None of the evidence supports the view that the headteacher fulfills the role of curriculum developer whilst the school is in session. There is little to suggest this takes place out of school either' (p. 193). By contrast, Campbell and Neill (1994) show that by 1991 nearly nine out of every ten primary teachers had such responsibility and the average number of subjects each was between 1.5 and 2.2 (depending on the size of school). You as a coordinator are being asked, therefore, to join in a team by sharing your talents and expertise with your new teacher colleagues. You may wish to see this as an exchange. As a new entrant to teaching you will find yourself continually asking questions. You will hear yourself asking daily about ordering stock, handling parents' evenings, the school's procedures, times, dates and practices. You *do* have something to offer in exchange – though you may not realize it. Your initial training in, say, the use of computers possibly amounts to more than the training received by the rest of the staff put together. Your work in science or in methods to teach reading will possibly be far more up to date than many other teachers with whom you are working. The fact that you have recently been in as many as four different schools, examined their teaching and learning or subject area policies, seen their different methods in organizing classrooms, witnessed whole school discipline practices, the ways in which children's special needs were met or the ways textbooks are used, means you do have a contribution to make. The discussions you had with your tutors and fellow students about their experiences will fit you to discuss educational issues with your new colleagues. This is, of course, not to deny that you still have much to learn and many skills still to develop, but the task before you is not impossible.

The jobs associated with being a subject coordinator are described in many ways with an even wider variation in the aspects of the role which a newly qualified member of the profession can or should play. Here are two jobs as advertised in one week in the *Times Educational Supplement*:

> Required a newly qualified reception class teacher. Candidates should possess a sound philosophy of education based on a child centred approach within a well organised, aesthetically stimulating classroom structure. We seek an excellent teacher who can demonstrate an affinity with reception age children. Experience in and enthusiasm for the following curriculum areas would be an advantage: English, Art and design, Music.

> Required for this expanding urban primary school, an enthusiastic, flexible, well qualified teacher to promote technology and related areas throughout the school. You should have wide curricular interests including possibly games. Newly qualified . . . full-time permanent post at KS 2.

Such descriptions indicate expectations, give a clue to the range of responsibility and help applicants to get a feel for the environment in which they would be working. They do not usually specify the way in which results may be achieved. We argue that this has to be done by teachers working through each other and agreeing together the basis for changes they want to make. Curriculum coordinators are the means for promoting and implementing these agreed changes and monitoring their development. One way for newly qualified teachers to make sense of all this is to look for the *givens* in their situation and then later consider the range of choices one is left with.

The Givens

In his influential work *Management Teams: Why They Succeed or Fail*, Meridith Belbin (1981) shows that a successful team needs people with specific skills, knowledge, aptitudes, interests and personalities which interlock in order to make a workable organization. You have to accept that part of what you are given is the presence or absence of such ideally interlocking personalities. You must also appreciate that the headteacher, who, to newly qualified staff may appear all knowing and all powerful, also has to suffer the same mix of personalities. He or she has probably inherited staff the headteacher would not have chosen. Those appointed ten years ago were selected to fit the situation of that time. Now new skills and attitudes are needed but not everyone can change so easily. Therefore the first of the givens is the nature of your teacher colleagues. You have to work with them and appreciate that however enthusiastic you are about your proposals, coordination, like politics, is the art of the possible.

Teams of all sorts need leaders. Recent research has shown that the quality of the leadership of the headteacher is probably the most important single factor in the effectiveness of the school (Mortimore *et al.*, 1988). Remember your headteacher (the second given) has chosen you and may have a great deal of hope pinned on your contribution to the school. The headteacher deserves your support and help and in turn you will deserve his or hers.

The third great area of givens is the particular culture of management that you will find in the school. What is expected of you as a coordinator will be better understood by thinking about whole school issues than trying to fathom the import of words written on a job description, which really only serves any purpose in times of dispute. When the going gets tough, the tough reach for their job descriptions! In *The Developing School* Peter Holly and Geoff Southworth (1989) discuss several whole school concerns which will affect the work of subject coordinators. They show that teachers need to be receptive to a collaborative approach and to respect and acknowledge curriculum expertise from within their own ranks. Such an ethos goes hand in hand with an enabling and supportive structure where job descriptions are not highly prescriptive, leaving little room for individual enterprise and initiative. Ideally newly qualified teachers should see that their own job specification shows that the school has different expectations of a newly appointed coordinator from one who has been in post for some time. To make any system work, managerial responsibility and support for the coordination of the coordinators must be made explicit. Headteachers have to monitor their work as managers and offer guidance at critical times.

Time available for curriculum coordinators to do the paperwork will affect the degree of consultation possible and hence its quality. Time for coordinators to work alongside teachers in their classrooms will be necessary in order to change practice. Time to allow curriculum coordinators to see teaching and learning in parts of the school with which he or she is unfamiliar will be required for staff development. You may find headteachers agreeing with these sentiments and still providing you with little or no non-contact time to allow you to do your work. In this

A study of the practice of mathematics coordination in primary and middle schools investigated how time was created for these teachers to undertake their roles effectively.

'Time during the school day was usually made available . . . through headteacher, part-time or floating teacher cover. Other ways . . . included supply and peripatetic teacher cover, student teachers cover, exchange and doubling up of classes' (Stow and Foxman, 1988)

case it will be necessary for you to consider just how much personal time you need to devote to this role and how much to your task of providing for the children in your class. Campbell and Neill (1994) show that above the directed time of thirty-three hours per week teachers generally believe it is reasonable to spend an additional nine hours per week on professional tasks. However, this research of teachers' work from four differently selected cohorts of schools and each using different sampling methods shows that they appear to have been spending a total of fifty-two hours per week in 1991. Thus conscious decisions about how long to spend on each aspect of your workload need to be taken before you can sensibly plan its extent.

The school has to actively promote acceptance that the nature of this devolved responsibility implies emphasis upon managerial skill as well as upon curriculum expertise. Thus teachers selected to become curriculum coordinators will need to develop skills in areas such as the implementation of change, curriculum planning, evaluation and school development, in addition to attending subject based courses.

Harrison and Gill (1992) set out to show that the degree to which any particular primary school has developed such policies may be indicated by:

- the nature of the decisions curriculum coordinators feel confident in making without recourse to the headteacher;
- the mechanisms by which the work of coordinators is monitored;
- the choice of particular teachers to be coordinators and the way they are managed;
- the strength of the systems in place to support coordinators (e.g. class release time, training);
- whether coordinators are respected as models of good practice in their specialist areas;
- the ways in which coordinators are encouraged to learn personnel management skills from one another;
- the degree to which coordinators are able to work in harmony with the school's stated aims.

Activity 1
Consider each of the listed points as they may apply to your school. Discuss with your headteacher or in-school mentor the validity of these statements as indicators of the strength of an effective coordination system. How do such issues define what is expected of you?

Activity 2
What defines the ethos of your school? Consider the ways colleagues relate to one another, the school's symbols and customs, the leadership styles and values on display. What does this tell you about the way to influence other teachers?

Making It Work for You

The importance of understanding and working with the culture of the school will recur again and again in the following chapters. Cultures are born and grow; 'Culture is the way we do things and relate to each other around here' (Fullan and Hargreaves, 1992). Thus the crucial factor in the development of an ethos is the people working in and around the school. You are now one of these people. Whether your influence is for good or ill, and the strength of your sway will depend on the way you personally approach the task. Hence, whether your school situation is ideal or not, by considering your actions carefully you can determine the most appropriate way to ensure progress.

Cross and Harrison (1994) suggest a strategy for this to begin to happen:

> Coordinators therefore need to persuade, cajole and affect the attitudes of staff toward:
>
> 1   the need for change;
> 2   the focus of the change (the curricular area, or an aspect of it);
> 3   the change process itself.

Change will never be achieved solely as the result of your plan, government legislation or incidental INSET. Change only occurs when teachers believe in the need for it, know where it is going, are committed to it and have some ownership of it.

Key personal skills which coordinators will therefore need to develop in order to promote curricular change include an ability:

- to act consistently;
- to maintain hope, belief and optimism;
- to want success (although not necessarily public approval);
- to be willing to take calculated risks and accept the consequences;
- to develop a capacity to accept, deal with and use conflict constructively;
- to learn to use a soft voice and low key manner;
- to develop self awareness;
- to cultivate a tolerance of ambiguity and complexity;
- to avoid viewing issues as simply black and white;
- to become an active listener. (adapted from Everard and Morris, 1985)

Getting Your Message Across

Some newly qualified teachers may find that their opportunities to influence colleagues are limited. Hence the method they use to get their message across may be just as important as the content itself. It may help to establish some guidelines for effective communication. The following list is based on the principles in Joan Dean's (1987) book *Managing the Primary School*:

- Teachers are more likely to be responsive to the advice of coordinators if addressed personally rather than anonymously in a staff meeting or by memo.
- Coordinators will need to learn that with teachers, just as with children, rousing the interest of the listener is necessary in order to get your message across.
- Information is more likely to be valued if it gives an advantage in power or status to the listener.
- No one likes to be seen as letting down their team or working group. It is desirable therefore sometimes for coordinators to present their information in such a way that it requires action upon which others will rely.
- Teachers charged with the responsibility of promoting curricular areas to their colleagues may find an advantage in choosing an appropriate messenger. The status of the source of the information is often seen to indicate its importance.
- The situation (surroundings, time of day etc.) should be chosen carefully in order to predispose the listener to be receptive.

Meetings are the most common method that coordinators use in an attempt to get their message across, but they are not always a success. Just having a meeting is not enough. The prime consideration must be 'What do you want to happen at the meeting?' This point is seldom addressed, for many meetings need never happen at all.

You may need to call a meeting in order:

- to communicate information;
  Subject coordinators will often need to give information to their colleagues, such as the dates and location of a local history and geography book exhibition, the list of computer programs bought by the PTA, and so on. Often this information can be given out in written form with only a brief explanation, possibly without having a meeting at all. The skill you will need to develop is to ensure that the information is read and acted upon. Wasting everyone's time for an hour to compensate for your lack of foresight in not preparing a briefing sheet, however, does not go down well with busy teachers.
- to discuss issues publicly;

If you want teachers to discuss issues, they need to have been properly prepared beforehand by being given the relevant information. You may need to arrange the seating in such a way that everyone can see each other in order to encourage participation. A brainstorming session recorded on tape can generate ideas or possible solutions. The key to success for this type of meeting is to create an atmosphere which encourages staff to share ideas and perceptions. They will not do this if early statements (however odd) are not accepted, at least as starting points for the generation of further ideas.

- to make decisions together. If coordinators are organizing a meeting to reach a decision on a key topic it is vital that everyone is made aware that the meeting has this purpose. Time has to be allowed beforehand, such that small group meetings can already have aired some of the issues. Make sure teachers have had time to read and absorb printed material. Decide before the meeting if you intend to take a vote, or whether it would be more appropriate to continue the debate until a consensus is reached.

An impetus for change may come from:
- changes in staff;
- preparation for an inspection;
- perceived inconsistencies across the school;
- an OFSTED report;
- the influence of a respected advisory teacher;
- an INSET course;
- new resources available;
- new national curriculum orders;
- poor SAT or standardized test results;
- change in pupil roll;
- parents' or governors' comments.

Coordinators will be more effective if they understand the difference between the various purposes of these staff meetings and realize what can go wrong. They need to consider a variety of strategies for organizing and chairing meetings. In *The Primary School Management Book* (Playfoot, Skelton and Southworth, 1989) further useful information can be found on the conduct of effective meetings in school.

What You Can Do Now

Find Out How Much Work Is Going On In Your Subject Area

Look at displays around the school. What do they tell you? For example do they show that maths is seen as more than just sums in books? Can you see a variety of games and sports being played? Does children's artwork feature in assemblies? Do teachers talk about progression in technology skills at breaks or in staff meetings? Does the teaching of reading feature prominently in work labelled under another subject? Identify where teachers place information technology (IT) in their curriculum planning forecasts. By considering such questions you may begin to develop a feel for the task ahead.

Look Further and Ask Questions

Listen if (and how) colleagues talk about work in your area. Will they talk to you about it? Talk to the headteacher to determine his or her attitude. Examine school documentation of all kinds. Has there been a recent inspection report (OFSTED or LEA)? What does this say about the quality of work in your subject area? Are there reference books in the school library in your subject? Find out whether there have been previous initiatives. How have colleagues responded to change in the past?

Find Out About the Latest Advice

Make sure you have read the latest advice from the School Curriculum and Assessment Authority (SCAA) and the most recent subject guidelines for OFSTED inspectors as set out in the handbook. Make contact with a local adviser, advisory teacher, school, college or university where advice may be available. Take note of any courses which might help you or your colleagues. Enquire about any national association for teachers of your subject. Do they have a primary section? Do they have local meetings? How does the local community fit in? Are there people within your community with interest or expertise?

Keep a Record of Your Activity

Start a portfolio where you keep:

- your notes;
- relevant documents;
- a diary.

This will help you to show development and progress over time and to demonstrate your success.

Talk to the Headteacher

- discover the headteacher's thoughts and commitment to your subject area;

- determine its current priority within the school development plan;
- establish a professional dialogue between you and the headteacher;
- register your interest and commitment;
- work out the next step;
- emphasize your priorities;
- formulate a rationale and targets for your work.

Subsequent to such a meeting, start to think in terms of a plan of action. Consider who can help us. How can we help ourselves?

Arrange to Go into Other Teachers' Classrooms to Work with Them, if Possible

You will need to consider the reasons you will need to give teachers for your presence. Are you to be there as a critical friend; to focus on an area the teacher has identified; to discover the quality of the work in your area or to give you an idea of progression in children's skills across the school? Should you report what you find in other teachers' classrooms? Is this information for your headteacher, deputy, the governors, senior management team or for the class teacher only? Is the decision yours? Clarify

> You may be able to create a climate for change by:
> - showing off some aspect of good practice;
> - inviting a speaker into school;
> - displaying articles and reviews;
> - running a workshop;
> - asking a colleague to trial a new approach or recently published material;
> - reporting back to colleagues on a course you have attended.

this in your own mind before you start. The very worst situation is one in which gossip about any particular teacher's practice should spread from such an activity. Up to now primary subject coordinators have often proved reluctant to direct colleagues and enforce ideas. Many teachers see their coordinating role restricted to writing paper policies and offering tips. Traditionally, primary teachers do not offer comment on colleagues' teaching styles, approach and lesson plans, or act as critical friends. A genuine whole school commitment to improving standards of teaching performance would help acceptance of this role for all.

Ask to Control and Account for a Small Budget to Support Your Area

You will then be able to buy and use resources without continual recourse to your headteacher. Arrange to find a method of gaining agreement amongst the staff for the use of this money in your area. Record the results of any meetings (formal and informal) you have had to determine spending of this fund and include this record with an end-of-year account of what the money was spent on. Hand this in to the headteacher even if she or he doesn't ask for (or want) it.

The willingness of your colleagues to accept your advice in part depends on their perception of your ability in the classroom. Teachers will also make judgments as to the value of the advice based on the coordinator's range of experience, ability to organize resources, knowledge of the subject and range of interpersonal skills.

Conclusion

Since the introduction of the national curriculum, teachers have made many changes. Unfortunately this has led to the idea that making change is always personally stressful, that it regularly leads up a blind alley and that it always results in wasted effort. We also have to recognize that externally imposed, centrally directed innovation has led to a disempowerment of the teaching profession. This has led in turn to concentration on the first two of Bredeson's (1989) metaphors of leadership, survival and maintenance, at the expense of the third, vision. Teachers' reaction to innovation overload has been some retrenchment and a wariness of more 'good things'.

Despite everything most teachers will accept change, especially if they believe it will benefit their children rather than merely enhance the reputation of the proponent. They want to maximize the effect of their efforts and teach as effectively as possible. They would like to see their work built upon in future classes.

If we accept that because of outside pressure, teachers' horizons have been lowered, it follows that those who will be the most successful in the next few years will be the leaders who can raise the sights again of those with whom they work. It is the attitude of the participants towards change which appears to be the most influential factor in its successful implementation.

Newly qualified teachers have the energy, enthusiasm and idealism to help schools maintain that vision and affect those attitudes. As Barber (1994) puts it

> the best teaching depends on an intoxicating mixture of pedagogical skills, love of learning and anger at the disadvantage so many young people suffer. If pedagogical skill is allowed to fade, teaching loses its charm. If love of learning dies, then curiosity among pupils dies too. If the fire of anger is extinguished, cynicism . . . emerges from the ashes. (p. 104)

Motivated by a vocation to do their very best for the children in their care, new entrants are every bit as capable of infecting their colleagues with enthusiasm and a willingness to develop in their chosen subject area as their more experienced colleagues. That is the essence of curriculum management.

References

BARBER, M. (1994) 'Keep the new light burning brightly', *Times Educational Supplement*, 9 September.

BELBIN, R.M. (1981) *Management Teams: Why They Succeed or Fail*, Oxford, Butterworth-Heinemann.

BLEASE, D. and LEVER, D. (1992) 'What do primary headteachers really do?' *Educational Studies*, **8** (2).

BREDESON, P.V. (1989) 'An analysis of the metaphorical perspectives of school principals', in BURDIN, J.L. (ed.) *School Leadership*, London, Sage Publications.

CAMPBELL, R.J. and NEILL, S.R. (1994) *Primary Teachers at Work*, London, Routledge.

CROSS, A. and HARRISON, M. (1994) 'Successful curriculum change through coordination', in HARRISON, M. (ed.) *Beyond the Core Curriculum*, Plymouth, Northcote House.

DAY, C., HALL, C., GAMMAGE, P. and COLES, M. (1993) *Leadership and Curriculum in the Primary School*, London, PCP.

DEAN, J. (1987) *Managing the Primary School*, Beckenham Kent, Croom Helme.

EVERARD K.B. and MORRIS, G. (1985) *Effective School Management*, London, PCP.

FULLAN, M. and HARGREAVES, A. (1992) *What's Worth Fighting for in Your School?* Buckingham, Open University Press.

HARRISON, M. (1994a) (ed.) *Introduction to Beyond the Core Curriculum*, Plymouth, Northcote House.

HARRISON, M. (1994b) 'Time to debunk the glorious past', *Times Educational Supplement*, 24 June.

HARRISON, M. and GILL, S. (1992) *Primary School Management*, London, Heinemann.

HARRISON, S. and THEAKER, K. (1989) *Curriculum Leadership and Coordination in the Primary School*, Whalley, Guild House Press.

HOLLY, P. and SOUTHWORTH, G. (1989) *The Developing School*, London, Falmer Press.

MCNAMARA, D. (1994) *Classroom Pedagogy and Primary Practice*, London, Routledge.

MORTIMORE, P., SAMMONS, P., STOLL, L., LEWIS, D. and ECOB, R. (1988) *School Matters*, Froome, Open Books.

PLAYFOOT, D., SKELTON, M. and SOUTHWORTH, G. (1989) *The Primary School Management Book*, London, Mary Glasgow Publishers Limited.

STOW, M. and FOXMAN, D. (1988) *Mathematics Coordination*, Windsor, NFER-NELSON.

WRAGG, E.C. (1993) *Primary Teaching Skills*, London, Routledge.

Chapter 2

Developing a Key Stage 1 Policy for Your Subject Area

Mike Harrison

Developing a Key Stage 1 policy for your particular subject area is often thought of as being the most daunting of tasks, the cause of many restless nights. It should not be so. The point of developing a whole school policy is that it is owned by the whole staff, describes what is actually happening on the ground and gives some indication of the direction the school is going with regard to your area. A whole school policy can:

- publicly demonstrate the school's intentions in your subject;
- help make a case for funding;
- give information to governors, parents, inspectors;
- provide a framework for planning;
- aid coherence, continuity, progression and shape priorities, and;
- assist in achieving uniformity and consistency in school decision making.

It may also:

- help focus the minds of various decision making groups toward common aims;
- improve the effectiveness of meetings by helping us all broadly to share each other's understanding of the situation;
- help participants understand teaching and learning strategies employed by other staff;
- help create a team spirit in making public the school's goals;
- offer a means of evaluation;
- help clarify functions and responsibilities of staff, and;
- help new staff settle in.

> **Activity**
> Look at the school's policy statement for your own or another subject. Does the statement satisfy any or all of the purposes listed here? Could it be made to do so?

The seven sections of the prototype policy presented here are offered to give you a skeleton on which to hang your own ideas and suggestions. Most areas will need discussion and agreement with staff to be meaningful but it is sometimes useful to have a starting document if only to give you something to knock down.

Introduction

You should start with a general statement of the school's agreed intent in this area, which is suitable for teachers, school governors, the LEA and OFSTED inspectors. It needs to be based on national curriculum requirements and to declare that every child should have access to learning in area X and that the school is dedicated to achievement in that area. The statement should reflect the school's ethos and overall aims. For example:

> The school's aims in the English Curriculum consists of teaching children to read, to write accurately and neatly and to express themselves with fluency and confidence.

> Work in IT at Key Stage 1 will cover the five strands of capability, namely: communicating information, handling information, measurement and control, application and effects and modelling.

> In line with the document *History in the National Curriculum* (1991) we shall. . . .

In my opinion this vital opening section must be drawn up jointly by the headteacher and coordinator and agreed by staff and governors before detailed work on guidelines can begin in earnest.

The next step is how the policy has been prepared or what state it is in at present. For example:

> After a year of study by the school's KS1 science working parties and discussion with other staff, this document represents staff opinion and practice agreed at a special meeting held on 23/3/95 and subsequently agreed by governors on 12/10/95.

At this point the contents of the rest of the document might be listed with page numbers.

Implementation

Experiences you intend, as a school, to give children through each Key Stage (or listed in other ways) in order to achieve the above aims should appear here. This may take the form of an interpretation of the national curriculum programmes of study and attainment targets which takes into account the circumstances of your school. This section is not the scheme of work but the document does require sufficient detail to ensure continuity of approach and progression of work throughout the school.

Next list the equipment and materials to which children will have access (are entitled to) by means of this policy. For example:

We use *Cambridge Maths* as our base book in the following ways:
Year 3 Module 4
Year 4 Module 5

Every child will have experience of using a programmable robot and/or turtle linked to LOGO by the time they reach year 2.

We take children to the swimming baths for two terms in Y3 – where they benefit from the instruction of qualified swimming teachers.

Curriculum maps, software maps and definite plans can help to ensure that the policy is adhered to rather than vague promises – such a stance is however more easily assessed by inspectors.

This may be a suitable point to remind readers that gaining knowledge is not the only outcome of your teaching in this subject:

We set out to help children to consider themselves as historians seeking evidence and evaluating what they have discovered.

All children will be encouraged to develop positive attitudes towards work in music.

Our curriculum is designed to promote confidence and enjoyment in using the mathematical skills they have learnt.

There is also a place for helping to gain agreement in the methods which will be used to promote learning in your subject area. If this can be done it may be recorded at this point in your policy document. This will help to remind everyone on what they agreed:

Children will work individually, in groups and as a whole class in geography. This will ensure that . . .

Each child will have the opportunity to change his or her library book each week.

Children normally work in pairs at the computer under the guidance of their teacher.

Children working with programmable robots, such as the ROAMER, will normally be engaged in problem solving activities in groups outside the classroom or elsewhere.

Do not forget to include an equal opportunities statement and any subject specific multicultural issues.

All children regardless of race, gender, physical ability . . . will be given equal access to physical education.

In IT, classroom management will take account of such issues, and classroom materials free from bias will be positively sought.

We respect the religious convention of all groups represented in the school and recognize the needs for flexibility in dress regulations including those for swimming and physical education.

The names and roles of persons responsible for overseeing or coordinating the implementation of the policy need to be recorded here along with the various responsibilities of head and classteachers with regard to it.

Finally, include methods for monitoring the implementation of this policy. Who is responsible for seeing that the agreed practices are being carried out in all classes? Who is to ensure children's entitlement? It may be covered above but still might need saying so here. How will this be done?

Schemes of Work

Whole school or Key Stage 1 schemes of work may be included here or as a separate document. It should fit in with everyone else's method of handling such matters.

Themes or topics to be handled may be listed next by year groups. This list represents long term planning from which individual teachers will create forward, medium and then short term work plans. Whatever the method is in your school it is a good idea to state it here – then everyone knows where they stand.

Next, describe the way information technology (IT) will be used to support learning in your area.

Children will be introduced to the use of databases to support their work in geography in Year 2.

Three different word processing packages are used to help children practice the process of writing. Each package has been chosen to give children access to more sophisticated features as they progress though the school.

Cross-curricular links can also be emphasized, for example: 'Every lesson is an English lesson'.

Finally, a synopsis of work covered in the first year of the high school may be usefully included here.

Assessment of and Recording of Pupils' Progress

List here the purposes of assessment and uses to which records of children's achievement will be put. Include agreed methods of record keeping and times at which such assessments will be made.

> Teachers' record of children's experiences are those kept in annotated forecast books.
>
> Children's work is recorded in their exercise books which are carefully stored to maintain a record of their progress in X.
>
> Example sheets of work in X are kept systematically throughout the year. A summative record is complied to pass to the next teacher.

This section should not be at variance with the school's assessment and recording policy and certainly not at odds with reality! It should state how, what, where and how often. It might even say why records are kept, what the real purpose of plotting pupils' progress is in your school.

How do you report progress to parents? It may be desirable to demonstrate in the policy document what is meant by progression.

> As children progress they will be able to write stories with more complex themes, write in different styles and for different purposes, and their handwriting will appear more mature.
>
> IT progression will be demonstrated by children carrying out more complex tasks, applying more advanced skills, becoming more independent and confident using IT, and by using more sophisticated software.

The location of examples of children's work which exemplifies levels of attainment and progression between them might be stated here along with any other germane information.

Resources

Here include a comprehensive list of equipment (with serial numbers if appropriate), books in stock, books in the library to support learning in this area, software, posters, videos, working models etc. available for teachers to use.

Make sure to write a policy for who gets to use what when and how, where they are stored, and any security features to help in the efficient deployment of resources.

A future purchasing policy is helpful:

> The school development plan sets out an objective of complete renewal of the maths scheme within four years.

> We are committed to replace all BBC computers with A40000s by September 1996.

> Physical education will be a priority area in 1995–96 and at that time . . .

It is crucial to include repair arrangements for equipment (with telephone numbers and necessary forms) and arrangements for safety checks on large PE apparatus.

Finally, if available, include a list of appropriate television and radio broadcasts.

Staff Development

The successful implementation of the policy will probably need INSET, both school based and using outside agencies. The policy document will appear more complete and credible if such arrangements are included here.

Also, the following may be included:

- Targets for INSET may be a feature of your school and expressed here as a spur to achievement.
- A list of recommended books for teachers personal reading would be useful.
- The job description or agreed targets for the curriculum coordinator might be published here.
- Names and addresses of support agencies which may offer advice or materials for teaching in your subject area can also be listed.

Review/Evaluation of This Policy

The headteacher and staff will need to review this policy to take account of changing circumstances. The date for its reconsideration may be stated in this final section.

You might consider discussing with staff the inclusion of measures by which the success of the policy and its implementation may be judged. These may include teachers and children's perceptions; children's work and other written evidence; SAT or standardized test results, a review of teachers' forecasts, parents' and governors' responses or classroom observation.

Chapter 3

Reading at Key Stage 1

Rita Ray

Key Stage 1 teachers are acutely aware of the need to establish basic skills of literacy and numeracy. In the early stages the aspects of literacy – speaking and listening, reading and writing – are for the most part undifferentiated and taught through a whole language approach. However there are specific issues in reading to be discussed and agreed upon by school staffs when compiling a curriculum policy.

Every Key Stage 1 teacher is to some degree an expert in the teaching of reading and within the whole school policy there should be flexibility for teachers to put their own beliefs into practice, provided they accord with those of the school. There should be consideration of children as learners and the teacher's role in facilitating learning and providing a reading environment.

Attainment in reading is fundamental to the learning process, not only in English but across the curriculum. The national curriculum has set out areas to be developed and assessed in reading, highlighting the basic skills and targets that primary schools have always fostered. Teachers have definite ideas about the standards that need to be achieved in reading in order to facilitate attainment in English and in other subjects.

What Are the Central Skills and Strategies to Be Developed at Key Stage 1?

The plan for Key Stage 1 usually includes early years and occasionally even nursery, since teachers in these classes are keen to help children to work towards the requirements of the national curriculum. This may mean something as simple as introducing the characters from a main reading scheme, using introductory big books at storytime or just making sure that children handle books and hear well-known rhymes and stories. In other words, how the normal business of the early years curriculum can mesh with the national curriculum programme of study for reading.

The programme of study sets out the aims of the reading curriculum under the following headings: Range, Key Skills, and Standard English and

Language Study. Under the heading of Range are set out the different kinds and genres of text that children should have experience of at Key Stage 1. Key skills may be summarized as those aspects of a reading programme which build up fluency and accuracy: phonic knowledge, graphic knowledge, word recognition, grammatical knowledge and contextual understanding.

Ellay (1989) reports that the single most important activity for building knowledge and skills required for successful reading is reading aloud to children, though it is the child's active involvement in sharing the text that supports development. Storytime can be planned as a more interactive session, taking place at times other than the end of the day slot.

The Role of the Reading Specialist in Key Stage 1

The HMI report (1990) stated that where reading standards were good, the coordinator had played an effective role in helping the school to achieve, by consulting and advising staff and helping to train non-teaching staff and parents. Where possible they worked alongside colleagues but for many lack of non-contact time ruled out this kind of support. Clear, well-formulated policies for reading were also strongly associated with good standards.

An obvious factor in successful subject leadership is good communication and the maintenance of open dialogue with colleagues about concerns and issues in reading. Most of all, as a subject specialist, you must quietly assert your own standards by presenting a good model and by putting beliefs about what are the best and most effective ways for children to learn to read into practice. Becoming a subject specialist should improve your own expertise and classroom practice.

Everyone likes to feel valued as a person and as a professional and, as a subject specialist, you will have to deal with colleagues sensitively. It is as well to separate personal and professional issues so that it is possible to tackle needs for development in teaching reading while maintaining good relationships. As with children, focus first on something positive before leading into discussion of the areas to be improved. There is a whole literature on the management of people and change, but no specialist knowledge is required to be courteous and considerate in dealings with colleagues.

New ideas will be more readily received if they are presented as accepted models of good practice rather than as your own personal preferences. Find a school that has a good example of the practice you would like to promote in your school and arrange a visit by members of your staff. Colleagues and advisers in your region may know of a school with similar storage space to your own that has, say, a good way of storing and accessing central reading resources or an exciting way of organizing and displaying books that has motivated and improved reading in the school. Publishers' representatives can usually give you the name of a school that presents a good model of using their reading scheme or other materials.

Where to Start

It helps to start with structured targets to match against outcomes when trying to evaluate effectiveness.

Make a plan identifying areas of change and desired outcomes in the long term, for two years, and in the short term, for six months. The plan should address the school's individual needs which may lie in some of the following areas:

- management and organization of reading at whole school level and/or class level;
- agreement on a whole school policy for reading;
- beginning reading;
- resources for reading;
- staff expertise in teaching reading;
- highlighting of awareness of reading in other subjects;
- monitoring and assessing reading;
- providing for special needs in reading;
- home reading/shared reading.

In consultation with the headteacher and a close colleague identify realistic goals, within the constraints of time, resourcing and teacher–pupil ratios.

The targets you set should be specific, measurable and achievable. You may wait to discuss them further with the working group (see below) and together you can decide what the targets should be, who should be involved in achieving them, how they can be achieved and what the criteria for success should be.

Here is an example.

Target:	To introduce home reading
How:	Provide book box, organize meeting, make a booklet for parents.
Who:	Booklet and other materials for meeting to be prepared by specialist. Meeting to be organized by specialist and reception class teacher. Reception class only to be involved in first instance.
Criteria for success:	Sustained interest on part of parents, children and teacher. Any observed improvement in early reading skills, familiarity with a wider range of books that can be attributed to the home reading project. The specialist and teacher may produce a checklist as well as keeping records of the number of books borrowed and going through the comments in the 'take home' record.

Updating Expertise

Membership of an association such as UKRA (United Kingdom Reading Association) will provide information on conferences and workshops as well as reports of recent practical research. The Centre for Reading at the University of Reading provides useful resource lists and books, such as the Moon individualized reading list, mentioned below. Get together with colleagues who are also subject specialists to discuss common strategies for updating expertise. Ensure that you have lists of courses offered by the LEA and other providers.

Staff Development

It is likely that you will be expected to lead staff training sessions in school. There are several ways of organizing staff development time, according to the purpose of the sessions. Here are some examples:

- to pass on information from conferences attended and to share any recent developments in reading that you have noted and summarized;
- to acquaint staff with new materials – either to have a preliminary demonstration by a publisher's representative before ordering materials *or* to allow staff to look at and organize new materials. This is a valuable area for INSET. Teachers appreciate time and space to investigate and organize existing materials, to step back and see the materials as a whole, how they work throughout the school and how they might be used more effectively. Teachers often discover aspects and possibilities they were not aware of and find they can fulfil needs with the school's existing resources;
- to spend time on an identified INSET need, such as assessment of reading in the classroom. This may be run by the subject specialist or an appropriate visitor, such as an LEA adviser.

The OFSTED report on English (1993) stated that in more than 50 per cent of schools there were clearly identifiable INSET needs which were not being met, 'in particular, where reading was concerned, how to include the teaching of phonic skills in a broad approach to reading development' (p. 18).

Working Groups

Subject specialists form a working group to discuss issues as part of the decision making process. It helps to have others to share and discuss but bear in mind that you are the group leader and the end result must reflect your view of good practice. The size of the working group will depend on the number of staff available. Two members of staff should be sufficient. Structure meetings by having a briefing note to focus discussion and end with an action note which records decisions and opinions and provides material for the next briefing note.

Compiling a Curriculum Document

Compiling a curriculum document constitutes a major task for the specialist, with the help of the working group. You can arrange to collaborate with other specialists to evolve a flexible format for whole school policy in each subject. It is possible to extend this collaboration to other schools, exchanging ideas and modifying documents to suit particular schools.

The reading policy forms part of the curriculum document for reading. Although the school document is often referred to as 'the reading policy', the policy itself is simply a statement of the school's beliefs, rationale and aspirations in the area of reading. It is necessary to explain *how* this policy can be translated into action effectively throughout the school and this is what the rest of the document is concerned with.

The curriculum document should be a working document. Members of staff should be able to refer to it for information about the school's resources and how to use them to the full. A useful way of organizing the document is to place the information in clear plastic envelopes in a ring binder. In this way information can be changed or updated and the contents list adjusted accordingly. The use of a word processor will also aid updating. An example list of contents for a curriculum document, with comments on each area, is suggested below.

Statement of rationale

Example of a statement of rationale for Key Stage 1:

> The school policy for reading reflects the consensus of opinion of the whole teaching staff and has the full agreement of the governing body. The policy was approved at the [date] meeting of the governing body. The implementation of this policy is the responsibility of all teaching staff.
>
> We believe that reading is not simply the decoding of marks on a page but involves the ability to read with understanding a wide range of different types of text including fiction, non-fiction, everyday texts such as labels, captions and lists and print in the environment. Competence in reading is the key to independent learning, therefore the teaching of reading will be given a high priority. Success in reading has a direct effect on progress in most other areas of the curriculum and is crucial in developing children's self-confidence and motivation.

Methods of teaching reading used in school

The main approaches to teaching reading:

- the 'real' books approach, in which children learn to choose and share books and by an 'apprenticeship' experience gradually join in the reading and eventually become independent readers;
- the use of graded, commercially published reading schemes;
- the teaching of a phonics programme in which children learn to decode and build words by putting together the sounds of the letters.

The OFSTED report on English (1993) found that in most schools there was a mixed approach to the teaching of reading. There was widespread use of reading schemes, as well as teaching of phonics and shared 'real' books. In practice, teachers usually prefer a consistent reading programme backed up by phonic teaching and expanded by a choice of children's fiction. It should be borne in mind too that up-to-date schemes have many of the characteristics of good children's books. Children treat the scheme books as 'real' books and frequently choose a book more than once rather than simply being anxious to move on through the scheme.

One way to ensure the provision of good quality fiction at different levels is to order, or make up, book boxes. The boxes contain a selection of fiction sorted into different levels. For teachers who want to make up their own book selection the booklist *Individualised Reading*, compiled by Moon and Moon (1989) (Reading and Language Information Centre, University of Reading) is useful.

As well as boxes of fiction, some suppliers, such as Madeleine Lindley Ltd, make up packs on particular subjects or themes – history, equal opportunities and so on. Most libraries used to make up topic boxes for loan but in some areas this service is now limited or has been cut.

It is not so easy for teachers to judge the readability level of non-fiction books. For children the task of taking in new information can be complicated by the kind of language structures they meet in some non-fiction texts. Non-fiction can be harder to read than fiction because:

- there is no narrative to lead the child through;
- there are no fictional characters to identify with;
- the child has no clues to predict the content;
- the language structures may be unfamiliar.

Care must be taken too when showing what we assume to be factual pictures and photographs to young children. They do not bring prior knowledge to the pictures and can often take them very literally. For example, an excellent colour photo of moth eggs was thought to be a plate of jelly, despite the context, and the photo of a butterfly in this same beautifully produced 'big book' was believed to be some kind of monster, because of the size of the picture. These factors should be borne in mind when choosing information books.

Management of reading

Management of reading includes

- organizing book area and information sources;
- group and individual reading;
- managing time to monitor reading.

This section should describe how scheme books, resource materials, tapes, library books, book boxes and home/shared books are organized, stored and loaned.

There will be guidance on monitoring reading, by hearing children read or by providing resources that will check understanding. Some schools state that hearing reading is a skilled task that should be undertaken by teachers rather than classroom assistants.

Home reading/Shared reading projects

It is a common practice to send books home, often a scheme book and a chosen library book, to reinforce reading done in school and for children to get praise and reassurance, rather than expecting carers to teach reading. A more structured approach is to invite parents/guardians into school and talk to them about shared reading – how to sit, how to help the child follow the book and join in, and so on. There are videos that show examples of children and carers enjoying reading together. Many schools produce booklets for carers giving guidance on sharing books with children.

Resources for reading

You can start by checking any existing resource lists in school and making an audit of reading materials. The way in which materials are stored and organized will depend on the design of the school buildings. For reasons of economy many reading resources are stored centrally in cupboards, on shelves or in custom-made sections at child level.

Children should be able to access materials in order to choose and change books. Photocopied sheets may be stored in a low level filing cabinet. The children should take responsibility for the materials they use and keep them tidy. However, take into account that it is difficult to keep track when the resources are shared and not continually in sight of the class area.

Teachers are often reluctant to discard old materials and you will need to agree on criteria for throwing out spoiled or out-of-date resources. There may be relatively new resources which are under-used simply because they do not slot easily into the reading schemes and schedules. Some of these may be matched to specific purposes or put out for use by the children in the class literacy centre or on the writing table.

Assessment and recording

Assessment and recording includes

- the school's method of recording and passing on records;
- reporting to parents and others;
- list of tests used in school;
- national curriculum assessment.

Some teachers like to use national curriculum statutory assessment materials as a starting point for discussion. You can study a range of record keeping systems, including the school's existing method, to find an efficient and manageable one. Record keeping should be kept as simple as possible. There are several recommended ways of keeping reading records which are worthy and valid in themselves but unrealistic when placed in the context of all the other records teachers have to keep.

As far as reading is concerned it is sufficient for everyday purposes to keep a book or file containing a list of names (which can be used with several pages), a space for the name of the book, noted errors to be worked on and comments by the teacher and child. Other test results, class and individual, can be kept in the same file for reference. Many schools have a system of recording which dates each attainment so that rate of progress can be logged.

In view of current changes from statements of attainment to level descriptions record keeping systems are being revised. The first reaction may be to unpick the level descriptions and turn them back into statements of attainment. A more productive course of action is to work from the programme of study to evolve 'learning objectives', setting out the key skills and knowledge that are crucial to all-round reading attainment at each stage, and which will remain so despite any more modifications to the English document. The important difference between statements of attainment and level descriptions is that we do not have to count up statements of attainment to place a child at a level. The teacher can judge whether or not the child has worked through the requisite parts of the programme of study to be described as, say, 'working within level 3'.

The basic format of record keeping agreed on by the staff should be manageable and give the required information. Those who wish to can keep more detailed notes in addition to this basic format.

For children who have special needs in reading or who are making slow progress it is useful to keep an extra check, possibly in the form of an 'action file'. It may be that the children are undergoing a process of recording in relation to the DFE Code of Practice for children with special educational needs. If, however, a child is just making a slow start and may improve with a little help the action file may be sufficient to keep a regular check on progress. This may be done by regularly observing the child to see whether he or she is progressing at a reasonable pace for that individual in learning the basic skills such as early sight words and letter sounds. Use a more objective test at the end of each term. Review the file and decide, if necessary, on action to be taken to help the child.

List the tests currently in use in the school. In consultation with the headteacher, adviser or a more experienced colleague, discard any out of date and inappropriate tests and order new ones. Most schools use a variety of tests for different purposes.

Norm referenced tests, such as the Young Test (Young, 1980) or the Salford Sentence Reading Test (Bookbinder, 1976) have been standardized on large and varied groups of children and are useful for monitoring standards as they give a 'reading age'. The Young Test can be given to a whole class, while the Salford Sentence Test is administered to one child at a time. (The Salford Sentence Test is somewhat dated but is often used as it is difficult to find a test which serves the same purpose.)

Diagnostic tests, such as the Neale Analysis of Reading Ability (revised version), are used to give individual profiles and show where a child's strengths and weaknesses lie.

Criterion referenced tests are tests in which a child is checked for a particular skill, e.g. 'knows all letter sounds'. In criterion referenced testing children are simply required to be able to do something. They are not assessed against other children of their age as they are in norm referenced testing.

In the context of national curriculum *formative assessment* and *summative assessment* have been highlighted. Formative assessment is carried out by the teacher in the classroom. In the case of reading it will consist of ongoing monitoring of the child's progress, for example, hearing the child read, noting errors and growth points and using this information to plan the next steps of teaching. It is the specialist's job to make sure that staff are using the same kind of standards to assess children's reading. Summative assessment means that assessments are summarized, especially at the end of a Key Stage, as in the assessments at the end of Key Stages 1, 2 and 3.

Miscue analysis and *informal reading inventories* give a picture of individual reading attainment and comprehension. These forms of assessment also accord well with the requirements of the national curriculum.

In miscue analysis children's reading errors are categorized and used in planning the pupil's teaching programme. The system may look complicated at first but teachers soon internalize the process and find themselves looking for patterns in errors automatically. Errors are categorized into syntactic (grammar), semantic (meaning) and graphophonic (letters/sounds).

Informal reading inventories are reading passages on which miscue analysis is carried out, but which also have questions to test different kinds of comprehension:

Figure 3.1: Miscue analysis

MISCUE TYPE	ORIGINAL TEXT	ACTUAL RESPONSE	CODING SYMBOL
Non-response (refusal)	prairie	no attempt to say any part of word	<u>prairie</u>
Substitution	which crept between his toes	which kept between his toes	which c̶r̶e̶p̶t̶ ^kept between his toes
Omission	I feel like a grease-spot	I feel like grease-spot	I feel like ⓐ grease-spot
Insertion	and then found he couldn't stop	and then he found he couldn't stop	and then ∧^he found he couldn't stop
Reversal	so tightly was he pinned down	so tightly he was pinned down	so tightly was⌐he pinned down
Self-correction	then the laughing turned	then he-the laughing turned	then t̶h̶e̶ ^he laughing turned
Hesitation	so wide that	Hesitates for some time then supplies word. Oblique stroke shows where hesitation occurs.	so wide/that
Repetition	Thomas tried to break the threads	Thomas tried to tried to break the threads	Thomas <u>tried to</u> break the threads

(*Source*: Arnold, 1984)

- literal understanding – the answer can be found in the text;
- inferential understanding – there are clues to the answer in the text.

Teachers can prepare their own reading passages but it is easier to use those which have already been placed at a reading level and have appropriate questions. Such passages may be found in *Independence in Reading* by Don Holdaway (1979). Informal reading inventories can be time consuming for the teacher but no more so than most diagnostic tests. They need not be administered very often, nor to all pupils, but informal reading inventories can be especially useful in pinpointing less obvious difficulties in order to plan programmes.

Children should contribute to their own assessment. They will feel that they have more insight into the control over their own development as readers if they have a say in their assessment. Although they may find it hard to express any difficulties they are experiencing, the act of consulting can be beneficial.

Figure 3.2: Informal reading inventory

B   A Birthday Surprise

One day a little boy said to his father,
'Soon my birthday will come.
Will you give me a big present?'
'Yes,' said his father.
'Do you want something fast or
something slow?'
'I want something fast,' said the boy.
'A car is fast.
A boat is fast.
But what is slow?'

At last the birthday came.
'Here,' said the father. 'Happy
Birthday!
Here is your surprise present.'
'A puppy,' the boy laughed.
'He is fast when he is running
and he is slow when he is sleeping.
Thank you for a good surprise.'

(*Source*: Holdaway, 1979)

An Informal Prose Inventory

Level B (6–7 years)

Name: **Age:**   **Date:**

Set: This is a story about a boy who gets a very pleasant surprise.

A Birthday Surprise

One day a little boy said to his father,

'Soon my birthday will come.

Will you give me a big present?'

'Yes,' said his father.

'Do you want something fast

or something slow?'

'I want something fast,' said the boy.

'A car is fast.

A boat is fast.

But what is slow?'

Oral — IL: up to 3 errors

Q1   Why did the boy think his father would give him a present? (L)
     R1   It would soon be his birthday. ☐

Q2   What did the boy want for his birthday? (L)
     R2   Nothing in particular. Something fast. ☐

Q3   What puzzled the boy when his father asked him if he wanted something fast or something slow? (L)
     R3   What present might be slow? ☐

Jottings:

Block 1

29

Figure 3.2: (cont'd)

Silent:

At last the birthday came.

'Here,' said the father. 'Happy

Birthday!

Here is your surprise present.'

'A puppy,' the boy laughed.

'He is fast when he is running

and he is slow when he is sleeping.

Thank you for a good surprise.'

Recall:

R4 When his birthday came . . .
    Q4   *When did he get the surprise?*

R5 Father said 'Happy Birthday!'
    Q5   *What did the boy's father say
        as he gave him the present?*

R6 The boy was given a puppy.
    Q6   *What present was the boy
        given?*

R7 The boy said the puppy would be
    fast when it was running and slow
    when it was sleeping.
    Q7   *How did the boy think the
        present was both fast and
        slow?*

R8 The boy laughed.
    Q8   *What did the boy do when he
        saw the puppy?*

R9 The boy thanked his father for the
    good surprise.
    Q9   *What was the last thing the boy
        said to his father?*

Q10 Why did the boy laugh? (1)
    R10 *Because he thought it was
        funny that the puppy could be
        both fast and slow.*

Comprehension — IL: 7 correct responses

Reaction: How did the boy feel about his present?

Imagery: What kind of puppy did you see in your mind?

Block 2

Informal Reading Inventories

What can the IRI tell us that a standardized reading test does not?
In a standardized reading test we may see how well a child scores in relation to other children of his or her age. However, it does not tell us much about that particular child or how we can help him or her to get more out of reading.

The miscue analysis pinpoints particular kinds of errors as well as showing us what percentage of a text the child can read and whether or not he or she is achieving independent reading. We also note *how* a child reads, whether he or she finds it stressful or enjoyable, etc. and the IRI allows us to assess comprehension. It's a common observation that two children in a class may have the same reading age yet have a totally different approach to reading as well as experiencing widely differing problems.

When we have the results of the IRI what do we do with them?
First, we establish at what level the child is reading. (The passages in *Independence in Reading* by Don Holdaway (1979) have comprehension questions and an instant assessment of reading level.) Then the errors are analysed to see if they form any coherent pattern. If the child is reading at frustration level, for example, there may be many different kinds of errors and although there is no consistent pattern it is not difficult to conclude that the passage was not matched to the child's ability. If accuracy is better than comprehension the child may be a 'word caller' who sees reading as a performance skill. He or she should be encouraged to read silently for self-satisfaction. If comprehension is better than accuracy then the child is not correcting himself or herself independently. Diagnosis of specific word recognition skills and appropriate instructions are required.

Plan a programme with long term objectives and short term aims. Find suitable teaching materials to implement the programme. The time-scale for achievement of aims will vary according to the child.

CRITERIA FOR READING LEVELS

Level	Word Recognition	Comprehension	Related Behaviour Characteristics
Independent	99%	90%	Rhythmical expressive oral reading Accurate observation of punctuation Acceptable reading posture Silent reading more rapid than oral Response to questions in language equivalent to author's No evidence of lip movement, finger pointing, head movement, vocalisation, sub-vocalisation, anxiety, tension
Instructional	95%	75%	(as above)
Frustration	90% or less	50% or less	Shows one or more of the following: unusually loud or soft voice, arhythmical or word by word reading, inaccurate observation of punctuation, finger-pointing, lip movement, head movement, subvocalisation, frequent requests for help, signs of tension (e.g., nailbiting), lack of interest, yawning or fatigue, refusal to continue, anxiety.

References and booklist

This section consists of books and journals available in the staff room as well as other relevant material, for example, reading scheme manuals.

Appendix

The appendix will contain more detailed explanations of methods, materials and resources used in school. For example:

- publisher's information/chart on reading scheme and other resources;
- instructions for administering miscue analysis and informal reading inventories;
- how to organize a book week and visits from authors;
- information on school procedures and materials for children who need extra help;
- home/shared reading booklet.

How Can the Reading Specialist Monitor Change and Evaluate Outcomes?

The first term as reading specialist will most likely be spent in observing, making relationships and gathering information rather than in attempting to initiate any substantial change. A common piece of advice to any new appointee is to leave things as they are for a while but use the time to find out what is going on and to gauge colleagues' feelings and opinions.

In order to improve something you must be clear about the existing state of things and able to identify areas of strength and weakness. Look at any recent reports in the school (HMI, OFSTED, LEA inspectors) and relate the reports' findings to your own observations and key points identified for development.

Evaluate outcomes against initial aims and long and short term plans. Keep a short weekly diary noting, for example, small achievements, changes in whole school approach or differences in the staff's way of working together. You may be surprised at the way achievements build up and at the improvements attained when looking back over the diary entries.

Check results of tests to see if measured standards have improved. This could present some difficulty. In order to be fair you should use the same test each time, preferably using a different form of the test. (The Salford test has three forms, A, B and C.) If you have radically changed the approach to reading in the school then the test may no longer be testing what you set out to teach. For example, if you have introduced an approach which relies on reading for meaning then a word decoding or phonics test may not yield the best results.

If an approach is balanced and takes into account all the dimensions of reading attainment then any up-to-date and well-constructed standardized measure should be fair and objective. Miscue analysis should be used in an ongoing way to give a profile and help to plan next steps in the child's programme.

Finally, curriculum leadership hinges on the ability to gain the trust of colleagues and to carry them along with you. Organizing an effective whole school reading policy will do much to contribute to positive relationships.

References

ARNOLD, H. (1984) *Making Sense of It*, London, Hodder and Stoughton.
BOOKBINDER, G. (1976) *Salford Sentence Reading Test*, Sevenoaks: Hodder and Stoughton.
ELLAY, W.B. (1989) 'Vocabulary acquisition from listening to stories', *Reading Research Quarterly*, **24** (2) pp. 174–87.
HMI (1990) *The Teaching and Learning of Reading in Primary Schools*, London, DES.
HOLDAWAY, D. (1979) *Foundations of Literacy*, London, Ashton Scholastic.
HOLDAWAY, D. (1979) *Independence in Reading*, London, Ashton Scholastic.
MOON, B. and MOON, C. (1989–) *Individualised Reading*, Reading, Reading and Language Information Centre, University of Reading.
OFSTED (1992–93) *Report on the Teaching of English, Key Stages 1, 2, 3 and 4*, London, HMSO.
YOUNG, D. (1980) *Group Reading Tests*, Sevenoaks, Hodder and Stoughton.

Useful Addresses

Madeleine Lindley Ltd
79 and 90 Acorn Centre
Barry Street
Oldham OL1 3NE
Tel.: 0161 620 3001
　　　0161 627 5820
Fax: 0161 620 0454

United Kingdom Reading Association (UKRA)
UKRA Office
C/O Warrington Road CP School
Naylor Road
Widnes
Cheshire WA8 OBP

Chapter 4

Coordinating English at Key Stage 1

Jane Birch

Introduction

A confident and competent grasp of English both spoken and written is one of the main aims of primary education. Children need to achieve a basic competency in English to enjoy their entitlement to all other subjects in the primary curriculum. Schools are most often judged by the standards of literacy of their pupils. Parents, especially in the earliest years of schooling, judge their child's progress in school by how well they are able to read. In the longer term, an enjoyment of language in both the spoken and written forms is a means of pleasure and relaxation both in school and for life. This is why I believe coordinating English is the most important coordinating role in the primary school.

You as an effective coordinator will enable pupils, parents and staff to be clear in their aims and to understand what they are trying to achieve, why they are trying to achieve it and how they intend to do it. You will do this by providing a multidirectional system of communication so that children benefit from the provision of educational experiences which are carefully structured to provide continuity and progression.

This chapter will look at the many responsibilities of the English coordinator's role using communication as a theme. The first section will concentrate on your role within the curriculum, the second on your extracurricular role. As a new coordinator who is also in the first few years of teaching, addressing some of the ideas in the second section may help with easing into the role and achieving some early successes.

Your Role Within the Curriculum

The Audit

It is not possible to suggest a complete course of action for all new coordinators to follow as every school will be at a different stage in their provision of English. Unless you have been specifically directed to undertake certain tasks by the headteacher, it will be worthwhile spending some time information-gathering before you complete an action plan.

You need to find out as much as possible about what has been done in the past. Has the school been involved in any LEA initiatives? How much work have the parents been involved in? What sort of in-service training has been provided for the staff and how much? You also need to assess the attitudes of the staff at this point. How do they feel about the provision of English at this time? How open are they to accepting new ideas and how willingly do they participate in in-service training?

Gather together as much documentation produced by the school as possible. As a coordinator you should always keep copies of anything you produce or present to the staff and details of any in-service training you provide. If you are lucky this will have been done in the past and you will have a good base to work from. Even if this does not exist make sure you start a box or file with all the information relevant to English collected together. Find out how much teacher reference material the school possesses and ensure this is collected together and available for all staff to use.

It would be a good idea to carry out an audit of both resources and staff opinions at this stage as this will give you the necessary information to make decisions about your own action plan for English. Published material such as Guidelines for reviews and internal developments for schools (GRIDS) by the Schools Council can be used to give you an idea of how to construct your questionnaires.

When you have collected information from your audit, from talking to the headteacher and the staff and from visiting classes, you should be in a position to produce your own action plan. This should include general long term aims and more specific short term aims which have a timetable for their implementation. Remember to take very small steps, especially at first; you still have a full time teaching commitment and probably very little non-contact time. Once you have your first aim in front of you, for example, provide some information for parents on helping their children with reading, get help. There is an enormous amount of published material in this sphere so get hold of a good selection of it. Try and look at literature provided by other schools, talk to some of the parents and ask what they would like and how they would prefer it to be presented. Contact the LEA adviser for English. When you have collected all this information sit down and try to write your letter, booklet or whatever you have decided to produce, and then give it to the headteacher, staff and a few parents to see if they like it before you distribute it generally. It is not seen as a sign of weakness to be asking for help; the more help you can get and the more people you involve in your projects the more successful you will be.

Writing an English Policy

One of your tasks as English coordinator will, no doubt, be to write an English policy or to revise an existing policy document. This is a means of communication. Your school is stating its aims and procedures for the teaching of English at Key Stage 1. You should not, however, try to describe what to do down to the very last detail as you will be left with very little room for creativity and originality within individual classrooms.

Your policy should describe what you do, not what you think you should be doing or what you would like to do. It should describe common approaches and systems which benefit the children's learning by achieving both continuity and progression.

If possible, look at the policies produced by other schools and read any information you can find on writing policies. Use Chapter 2 of this book. Then put these documents away, give yourself a series of headings; parents, assessment, record keeping, reading, writing, speaking and listening, transition, special needs, equal opportunities, cross-curricular links, resources etc. and set to work.

Your English policy should be a whole school policy which means all staff should have contributed to it in some way and should be fully aware and in agreement with its contents. You may work on a section at a time at staff meetings and from questionnaires you have previously given to the staff. However you wish to approach this will depend on the management of your school. In reality you often end up writing most of the document yourself, but you must always let the staff agree to it before you produce your final draft. It is also advisable to let parents and governors read through it.

A suggested format for an English policy would be one A4 policy statement, containing a general summary of your aims for the teaching of English in your school. Then a description of aims, objectives, methods and resources under the headings already mentioned and finally a scheme of work describing what is taught in each area of English at each age level in Key Stage 1. You should also include any examples of common recording and assessment sheets with clear instructions on how and when they should be completed. Lists of resources and where they are located are also necessary.

In-service Training

Once you have begun to gain more confidence as a curriculum leader you may wish to try and provide some in-service training for the staff. Again, do not be afraid to ask for help. Have a word with the headteacher or deputy head who will have had experience of providing these types of activities, or any other member of staff who has successfully provided in-service training that you have attended and enjoyed. The adviser for English should be able to help you or may even be able to provide courses within schools themselves. Local lecturers are often available for in-service sessions for schools. These last two ideas will usually involve a cost to the school but may actually be more cost-effective than only one member of staff attending a course outside school and the school having to pay not only the course fees but also travelling expenses and supply cover costs too. If you know staff in other local schools who are knowledgeable on the area you are looking for they may be willing to come to your school and provide some informal training. If you are in the position of having to provide the session yourself make sure you are well prepared and well rehearsed (even if you have to practise in private into a tape recorder or in the bath). Make sure you have all the resources you need prepared well in advance. Make lists in advance and a timetable for your session and keep to it or you may find you have only covered half of what you wanted to say or, worse still, you might get to the end of your material with the session only half over.

The style and format of your sessions will vary according to the aims and objectives of your session. Sometimes you may be asking staff to share their ideas or experience. For example, if you were putting together your policy document and you were working on developing writing you would want all the staff to contribute their ideas about their existing good practice. These sessions are valuable and you should try to encourage all staff to contribute and make them feel that their ideas are valued and will be included in the resulting policy. You should chair these sessions tactfully to ensure that one or two people do not dominate by spending the whole session describing what happens in their classrooms. Although it is important to have these sessions, it is even more important that staff are introduced to new ideas and are asked to think about areas or issues in different ways. If for example, you were concentrating on speaking and listening you may choose to use one session to share ideas of good practice and to discuss examples of children's work in this area (transcripts of what they have said or tapes) and you may use another session actually to teach the staff some new speaking and listening games, by playing them yourselves. You may also use your in-service time to report back to staff about courses you have attended. You should provide a written report of these activities for staff to take away with them so they can refer to it and use ideas in their own classrooms.

Another useful INSET activity is to plan displays cooperatively throughout the school. You could choose a literary theme for your displays for a term. The work which is then produced throughout the school can be used to demonstrate continuity and progression in the children's work.

Open days or evenings are a good way to get parents involved in their children's learning and give staff a more informal opportunity to chat about the curriculum. These can be organized with not too much effort if all the staff are willing to participate. Decide which areas of the school you will use. It may be better to restrict yourselves to the hall and a few classrooms rather than involving the whole school or producing enough work will become a difficult task. Then get the staff to work together across the Key Stage rather than alone in individual classes. This means the task is not quite so daunting and people will not feel they are being scrutinized as individuals but rather that they are part of a collective team. A range of the children's work should be available over the Key Stage, including all aspects of English work, remembering that much of this may be cross-curricular. Textbooks and reading materials should also be available as well as booklets or sheets with information for the parents to take home. These might explain how things are taught in school and, more importantly, they should suggest ideas for parents to try at home.

If this type of event is successful in your school, parents may then express a wish for more specific workshops such as helping their child with handwriting or spelling. These could be organized either after school, in the evening or during the day if you are able to be released from your class. You may need help from the adviser for English to put together enough information for a workshop of this type. The adviser may even be willing to run a workshop for you or at least take part with you on the first occasion. Materials available include commercially produced videos, such as those done by the BBC from their INSET broadcasts. Some authorities have a department where such materials are available for loan.

Monitoring

Part of your role as English coordinator is to monitor the provision of English in your school and to ensure the children are reaching their full potential and receiving their full entitlement to the English curriculum within each classroom. At the moment this is a relatively sensitive area, especially as in the past teachers have been used to working alone in their classrooms and are not too used to commenting on or about other members of staff. This is, however, a requirement of OFSTED and needs to be addressed.

Care should be taken to place monitoring within a positive approach to improving the provision of English and building upon existing good practice. Staff should not be made to feel that they are being spied upon! If possible coordinators should try to work alongside class teachers, perhaps by jointly planning English activities. They should also look at samples of children's work to ensure that standards are as high as possible.

Record Keeping and Assessment

You should ensure that as part of your whole school approach to planning (both short and long term) everyone is planning for English to ensure that all elements of the programme of study are taught. For long term planning, for example, on a half termly topic web, you should indicate the main areas of each attainment target that you intend to teach and the main areas to be assessed should be identified. Some of these objectives will be cross-curricular and linked to the half term topic; others will be subject based and will be taken from your year group scheme of work. Over a year teachers should have undertaken assessment activities for each attainment target. Also, in

cooperation with the teacher responsible for special needs, individua
programmes should be prepared for those children who are either w
or below average in English.

For shorter term planning, for example, weekly lesson plans, ... staff
should indicate what is being taught in each area of English and should indicate how this is being differentiated for each attainment group. Teachers should
also indicate how lessons will be delivered – individual, group or whole class
teaching. If help from another adult in the classroom is used this should be
recorded and whether the lesson is a teacher focused activity. More often
than not, in Key Stage 1 classrooms, the children will either be working in
small groups with their activities teacher directed or, in a wholly integrated
approach, they would be selecting their own work schedule for the day.

Teachers should be clear about what they are teaching in their English
activities, why they are teaching it and what they expect the outcomes to be.
The children also benefit from being aware of this! Expectations should be
high at all times and children should always be expected to do their best.

Assessment is still very much a developing area and many staff may feel
unsure and in need of support in this area. Often they feel that they know
their own children's attainments well enough and it is not necessary to do
specific assessment activities or keep records on paper. You must encourage
them to build assessment into their normal classroom routines and to develop
a portfolio of evidence of assessed pieces of work for each child. It is then a
good idea for staff within the Key Stage to get together to compare and
moderate levels of work. If, in addition, you can do this with coordinators
from other schools this would be even more useful.

You may need to provide ideas for assessment activities which staff can
use. These could be taken from previous years' SATs. You may also need to
devise sheets for record keeping and assessment so that the whole school will
adopt a uniform approach. You may decide to build commercial testing into
your scheme of work, for example, many schools use reading tests at the end
of each year. Baseline assessment has also developed and commercial tests are
available although they are rather complicated and time consuming and it
would probably be best to devise your own assessment by selecting carefully
from a range of tests or by collecting together evidence of children's work on
entry to school. You will then be in a position to clearly demonstrate children's progress by the end of the Key Stage when they are taking their SATs.

Reading

Coordinating reading alone is a massive undertaking (see Rita Ray's chapter
on reading in Key Stage 1) and, in the current educational debate, a difficult
task to undertake because there is so much uncertainty about methodology.
Your role is to ensure that staff and parents are aware of the ways you have
chosen to teach reading in your school and to ensure that everyone sticks to

this way so that there will be structure, progression and continuity for the children. You must ensure that all teachers keep records of the children's reading progress in a similar manner so that continuity is maintained through the school (an example of a recording sheet is given in Figure 4.1). You must also agree on the amount of times a child will be expected to read to the teacher in a week for example, and also the other kinds of activities that will be provided to support the development of reading skills. These can all be described in the school's scheme of work for reading, but it is your task as coordinator to see that they are being carried out and to provide help and support to make it possible for all teachers to do this.

It is not possible here to go into detail about the different methods of teaching reading; suffice it to say that no one method will be successful on its own, neither will relying on one reading scheme. Most advice now suggests that a mixture of methods will succeed the best so that children receive both phonic training and a gradual acquisition of basic words and also access to real books. Children do need to be taught the skills of decoding new words, they do need to be told to learn new words from memory and they do need a structured way of tackling more difficult books. Because reading is so complex to teach, it is essential that teachers keep records of children's progress. These should include the books they have read, the dates they have read to the teacher, an assessment of their performance and suggested action to improve their skills. Most schools also provide some sort of booklet which goes home with reading books so that parents and teachers can share together in their child's progress.

Skills in reading are not only in learning to read; they are also in comprehension and in being able to use non-fiction books to find out information, for example, for class or individual topics. These skills should begin to be developed in Key Stage 1. If you have a school library containing non-fiction books classes will enjoy weekly visits to this with work being focused on how the library works and how to use books to find out information. Most new reading schemes also now have non-fiction written specifically for Key Stage 1.

Developing Writing

Children's writing at Key Stage 1 should always have as its underpinning theme an awareness of audience and purpose. Children need to understand why they are writing and who the writing is for. They are much more enthusiastic about writing a birthday card for a relative or answering a letter they have received than practising a skill in isolation. This again comes back to the main theme of communication. Children need to understand that, after speech, writing is our main way of communicating with one another. What they have to say is important and therefore must be in a form which can be understood by its intended reader.

Figure 4.1: Example of a reading recording sheet

| Name | | | | | |
D.O.B					
Date	Home Language	Development of reading skills	Attitude	Action	
Title	Terms in School	Strategies used	Child's response, enjoyment		
Page No.			confidence		

Teacher completes this sheet at regular intervals with a child and this record is passed on through the school.

*

Dearing's new national curriculum programme of study (1994) states that, 'Pupils' early experiments and independent attempts at communicating in writing, using letters and known words, should be encouraged.' Writing centres or tables should be in existence in all classrooms and opportunities for writing should be included in structured play areas. For example if a post office were to be created the children should visit a real post office and collect a range of forms and other materials that are available. Often the teacher or another adult needs to work in this area with the children, especially in the initial stages of its development so that the children have a model to show them the writing opportunities that are available. In the writing centre, activities need to be carefully structured and introduced to stimulate the children's imaginations and encourage them to participate in a meaningful way. For example, to develop the post office theme the writing centre could be used for letter writing with the teacher leaving letters to be answered by the children. They could then move on to looking at addresses for their letters. Often writing centres and structured play areas disappear or have a lower profile the further up the Key Stage you go. This should be addressed as children are able to write more and concentrate for longer so that activities in these areas can actually be more fruitful.

Some schools promote independent writing as their means of children learning to write and others prefer a more formal system where children start writing by first copying over the teacher's writing, then they copy underneath it and then perhaps from a separate paper. Both systems end up with the children then writing independently using their own or a shared word book and using as many words as possible from memory or using skills of word building that they have been taught. As is the case with reading, a variety of approaches is probably the best as not all children will learn in the same way. What is necessary however is a very careful system for planning for the teaching of writing to ensure that each child receives a systematic approach to learning to write. For example, children need to be taught to hear and identify the letter sounds of the alphabet and to be able to name them and they then need to be able to recognize them in print. They need to be taught how to build up words from their letter sounds and from blends, digraphs and vowels. They need to learn many commonly used words by heart as they cannot be built up from their sounds and they need to look at words which belong to families with similarities in their spellings. They should know strategies such as 'look, cover, write, check' for learning spellings. Children need to be taught how to form their letters correctly, otherwise they will have problems later when they are learning joined up writing. Teachers need to begin the basics of grammar work and look at Standard English from reception level. This can be done very effectively by using big books for story sessions and talking about capital letters, full stops, question marks, describing words etc. Children should also write creatively, making their own books, and factually, making newspapers or reports.

Your role as coordinator is to ensure that all children are receiving this carefully structured approach. You will be able to do this by looking at the planning of other teachers and by working with them in their classrooms. There is an enormous amount of literature available to give ideas and advice about the actual content of lessons. You must ensure they are being delivered and of a high quality. It is particularly important that teachers keep a careful check on children's progress when they are relying on a developmental approach to writing because there must come a cut-off point when it is decided that a particular child has special needs in this area and needs extra help or a different approach which is much more structured (see Figure 4.2).

Developing Speaking and Listening

Planning for speaking and listening can often be neglected as it is often assumed that it is occurring all the time in all classrooms. One way to overcome this is to use a planning sheet such as the one shown in Figure 4.3 which enshrines Attainment Target 1 as of equal status in the planning stage. It is of course true that speaking and listening are occurring all the time, but there is no planned acquisition where there is no specific target setting and a stated sequence of development in this area. It becomes clear how difficult it is actually to teach well in this area when you try to set up and assess activities. Your assessments should include activities in a range of contexts and settings such as individual and group discussions in a variety of lessons. Classroom organization and management issues are very relevant here as you need to stay with the activities to listen to the discussion. The use of a tape recorder is essential and you should ensure that all classes have access to one, preferably one each. The use of story tapes, either commercially produced or home-made is important, as are tapes which contain other kinds of listening activities such as directions to follow to draw a picture or perform a particular task. It is useful to get the children used to a tape recorder actually taping their discussions as you can then leave an activity and listen to the results later.

Drama activities feature prominently in the new orders for the national curriculum. This is an area with which the staff may need help as many people feel unsure about how to set up activities, especially with early years. You need to try and attend a course yourself as it is probably easier to learn practically rather than from reading a book.

As with reading and writing you should ensure that all teachers are of keeping records of progress in speaking and listening (see Figure 4.4). You need to assess the capabilities of the staff and either provide relevant in-service training yourself or try to direct them to relevant courses or literature. You cannot expect to immediately become an expert yourself when you become coordinator for a subject. Your skills should be in assessing needs and trying to ensure that they are catered for. The National Oracy Project is a good place to start to look for help and advice.

Figure 4.2: *Example of a writing recording sheet*

Name .... D.O.B	Home Language	Development of understanding of written language conventions	Action	Attitude Child's response, enjoyment, confidence	Context Type of writing, independent shared, guided, strategies used, complete or extract	Date

Figure 4.3: Language planning sheet

Week N°	Speaking & Listening AT1	Reading AT2	Writing Spelling Handwriting AT3	Vocabulary

Figure 4.4: Speaking and listening profile (formative)

Name ....   Home Language ....
D.O.B ....

Social Context	Learning Contexts							
pair	collaborat-ive reading/ writing activities	Play/ drama and story telling	Env. Studs & Historical research	maths/ science invest	design copst art craft projects			
Small group								
Child with adult								
Small/large group with adult								

Date	Developments, contexts, attitudes.

Special Educational Needs

You will find that the majority of requests for help for children identified as having special educational needs (SEN) because they are either well above or below average, tend to be in the subject of English. You will need to work with the SEN coordinator within your school to help teachers plan individual programmes of work and find the resource they require. You should ensure that all staff are aware that records should be kept of all work programmes etc. so that they can be passed on to the next teacher or used as evidence of what the school has done if outside agencies become involved.

Equal Opportunities

It is the responsibility of all curriculum coordinators to promote an awareness of equal opportunities issues within their curriculum area. You should always ensure that any resources you use or new resources you purchase are free from bias of any description and show all races, disabilities and genders in a positive light. English is an area which generates discussion and controversy on a number of equal opportunities issues. The whole area of Standard English required by the national curriculum generates cause for concern. All children are entitled to full access to the national curriculum. As English coordinator you could become involved in ensuring access where children need extra provision because English is not their mother tongue or where they have a disability which means they need access to computers or word processors to aid their writing. You should be aware of issues such as research into the progress of boys and girls in reading and ensure suitable materials are available to stimulate the interests of all children.

Using Information Technology (IT) in English

In conjunction with the IT coordinator you should ensure that staff are planning specifically to teach the skills of word processing including drafting and editing using computers. It is essential that these skills are developed in Key Stage 1. Special stickers can be purchased from Northwest SEMERC in Oldham (address given at the end of Chapter 11) to cover the keys and make them into lower case letters. You should also ensure that staff are introducing children to the skills of information storage and retrieval. If you are lucky enough to have a CD ROM on your school computer there is some superb software available for this purpose. Dorling Kindersley for example produce good quality children's software. If you have enough computers in school to be able to station one in your school library, you would be able to catalogue your books on it and children would then be able to look up information they required. This is quite an ambitious project and would be one where the extra help from parents would be invaluable.

Communication with Parents

Developing a good relationship with parents is not only essential as a classroom teacher but also vital as an English coordinator. It has been stated in HMI reports that children who read regularly at home make much better progress. Parents can help their children's progress in English enormously and they are almost all willing to help at home in some way. What is most important about your role as coordinator is to ensure that the ways they are helping are similar to those you are adopting in school. Obviously it is up to individual class teachers to do much of the explaining but you must provide suitable literature for them to send home and maybe workshops or open evenings for parents to come into school. Most of all you need to be approachable and available! Parents should feel able to come and speak to you on a one to one basis. As English coordinator it is now time for you to become involved in more than just your own class. A suggestion is to swap classes with another teacher for a story session each week. You may also need the help of parents for certain occasions such as workshops or for helping set up and maintain a library or put together booklets you have made. You could try and build up a group of parents or even grandparents who are willing to come into school and share books on a regular basis. Some schools have successfully targeted retired people to come in and help as they often have more spare time on their hands than busy parents. You thought running your class was a full time job up to now, so how are you going to find time to be a coordinator as well?

Extracurricular Activities

A good way to make a successful impact as a new English coordinator is to organize events or activities which could be described as extracurricular. These tend not to be as controversial as introducing a new reading scheme or altering the recording system for speaking and listening. They also tend to be quite high profile in the eyes of the children, staff and parents. A big success in this area will give you a positive image in your new role and also boost your confidence to tackle other issues.

Book clubs and book fairs in particular are not so difficult to organize and will be popular with the children. They are also a way of earning extra books for the school by gaining commission on what is sold. Scholastic, for example, will deliver a book fair which is contained in four metal cases. These remain in your school for one week so that your selling times can be quite flexible. They provide leaflets and posters to publicize the fair and will give you a range of ways to take your commission. These include taking 50 per cent in value from your total sales figures in books from the fair. These can then be chosen by the staff for their classrooms or can be added to the school library. Extra commission is also given if you book another fair. This can be used to provide prizes for any competitions you might like to encourage to build up interest in the event. Letting classes visit the fair during school time to listen to some of the stories or just to browse also helps the sales. Once the fair is over you do not need to count the books; you just close up the cases and wait for them to be collected. You bank the money and send a cheque for your total sales to Scholastic Book Fairs. Even the phone calls to arrange the fair or ask for advice are free. Other publishers and independent booksellers also provide these kinds of activities, although the rates of commission do vary considerably. Publishers also run book clubs which have regular magazines from which the children can purchase books. They also have a system of saving whereby children can purchase stamps on a weekly basis towards the cost of books. This system is much more time consuming for both the organizer of the scheme and also the class teachers who are involved in collecting the money.

Visits to local libraries are relatively easy to arrange, especially if the libraries are within walking distance. Most libraries will provide story sessions for the children. Often block loans are available to teachers so the children are able to select books to take back to school or they may be encouraged to return to the library with their parents and join for themselves. Librarians are also sometimes able to visit schools and provide story sessions, although these days the time available for librarians to work with schools is becoming more and more limited. Some authorities still have school library services and it is well worth talking to them to see what they are able to offer. Making use of public libraries is also a golden opportunity for children to work with non-fiction if your school library is lacking in this area. Libraries will sometimes have visits from poets or authors to which you may be able to take groups of children.

Projects you could organize within school, perhaps to coincide with a book fair, are book weeks or visits from authors, story tellers, poets, theatre groups or drama students. The main drawback to these events is the cost. It may be an idea to link up with another local school and pay for half a day each. Your local teacher training establishment may be interested in joining you in a project as it would be a valuable opportunity for their students to gain experience.

Resources

As English coordinator you should really have your own budget for English to order new resources where necessary. You should try to look at catalogues which arrive in school and if you are interested in anything send for evaluation packs or invite the representative to come into school. You will then be able to decide in conjunction with the other staff and the headteacher if you want to spend your money on these goods. LEA advisers also often obtain samples of new materials such as reading schemes and may have evaluated them already, so it is worth contacting them if you are considering investing large amounts of money. Try to keep staff aware of new resources as they are introduced, but also be very wary as publishers often relaunch older materials in new covers. Before you complete your requisition for English, always ensure that you ask staff to let you know if they require anything in your area, as people will use things more effectively if they have chosen them themselves or if they have already found them useful.

You should ensure that all English resources in school are kept together where possible, especially teacher reference materials. Much of the other materials will probably be in individual classes so it is a good idea to collate lists of resources and their whereabouts and distribute these to all staff. You should try to set yourself a target of auditing resources at least once a year to ensure that they are all in working order, especially items such as tape recorders, which are infamous for not being used because leads are missing, or games which cannot be played because pieces are missing.

Acknowledgment

The figures used in this chapter have all been used at Harpur Mount Primary and were adapted from Manchester's Early Literacy Project and ILEA's Primary Language Record.

Useful Literature/Reference

BLOOM, W. *et al.* (1988) *Managing to Read: A Whole-School Approach to Reading*, London, Mary Glasgow.

CARTER, R. (1990) *Knowledge about Language and the Curriculum*, London, Hodder and Stoughton.

ILEA (1989) *The Primary Language Record: Handbook for Teachers*, London, ILEA/CLPE.

ILEA (1990) *Patterns of Learning: The Primary Language Record and the National Curriculum*, London, CLPE.

MANCHESTER CITY COUNCIL EDUCATION DEPARTMENT (1992) *English in the National Curriculum: Key Stage 2*, Manchester, MCCED.

MANCHESTER CITY COUNCIL EDUCATION DEPARTMENT (1993) *English in the National Curriculum: Key Stage 1 Resource Pack*, 2nd edn, Manchester, MCCED, October.

MOON, C. (1994) *Individualized Reading*, Reading, Reading and Language Information Centre, University of Reading.

SCHOOL CURRICULUM DEPARTMENT COMMITTEE (1984) *Guidelines for Review and Internal Developments for Schools (GRIDS)*, York, Longman.

SMITH, F. (1985) *Reading*, 2nd edn, Cambridge, Cambridge University Press.

Magazines

Some useful magazines include ILEA/CLPE's *Language Matters* and the *GNOSIS* publications.

Also of use could be *Primary English* published by The English Association, University of Leicester, 128 Regent Road, Leicester.

There are regular articles in both *Child Education* and *Junior Education* on the teaching of English.

General Resources

There are a huge range of English resources available on the market.

The Scholastic range of books include many on English and develop themes into useful practical activities which children can do. The *Teacher Handbooks* and the *Inspirations* series are especially recommended. See also the *Blue Prints* series by Stanley Thornes, Cheltenham.

Amongst the reading schemes which you may find useful are Oxford *Reading Tree*, Ginn (especially *All Aboard*), *New Way, Badger, Sunshine, Letterland* and Collins' *Jets*.

For handwriting you might try Nelson Handwriting or the Charles Cripp's books. Egon Publishing produces *Spelling Made Easy*.

For word processing, Phases from SEMERC and Pen Down from Longman Logotron are recommended.

There is a huge variety; evaluation and inspection packs are a useful way forward as they can be returned if you decide the resources don't meet your needs. Alternatively invite the publishers to provide a short talk for your staff.

Chapter 5

Directions in Mathematics: The Coordinator Effect

Barbara Stewart and Ian Hocking

Introduction

Coordinating mathematics is one of the major tasks in primary schools. As, perhaps, a newly qualified teacher or experienced teacher new to such a role, you will need a knowledge and enthusiasm for the subject that is matched by the ability to work with colleagues (with a variety and different levels of talents) in a sensitive way which will, nevertheless, challenge and assist them to produce quality learning experiences for their pupils.

In order to gain your colleagues' confidence and commitment to this vital area it will be necessary to hold discussions on their understanding and beliefs of why they think mathematics should have a permanent place in the primary curriculum. An activity such as this will make a productive start to the INSET you will need to provide in your school, and may be a profitable way towards developing a unified, collaborative, working school policy on the teaching and learning of mathematics.

Why Teach Mathematics?

Why ask the question, especially since the advent of the national curriculum which has firmly placed a legal framework for mathematics within the curriculum for 5–16-year-olds? Even before the Education Reform Act of 1988 few would have questioned the considerable emphasis placed upon mathematics. Today even greater emphasis is attributed to the subject by post-16 education, commerce, industry and, not least, parents. However, it is worth reiterating some of the most significant reasons for the inclusion of mathematics in the compulsory years of education.

Mathematics is:

- a powerful means of communication – to represent, to explain and to predict;

- an increasingly powerful tool in many commercial and industrial environments;
- a discipline which, with others, can contribute to the development of logical thinking skills;
- finally, but not exhaustively, worthy of study for intrinsic interest, beauty and enjoyment.

To summarize:

Mathematics is taught not only because it is useful. It should be a source of delight and wonder, offering pupils intellectual excitement and an appreciation of its essential creativity (NCC, 1989 and 1991).

These beliefs, as already noted, need to be developed from whole staff discussions and so the above suggestions can be given to start a discussion or as a comparison against which a school can match its own ideas.

Since the 1980s the traditional role of the primary teacher has been greatly affected by, among other things, 'Teachers' Conditions of Employment' (DES, 1988) and the implications of the national curriculum. Teachers have not only to be good classroom practitioners but have to accept that they will be expected to help the professional development and practice of their colleagues and influence the learning of the children. Thus, schools 'seek to exploit the talents of those within the school', for 'it is only when we share skills and knowledge that the true potential of a professional teacher is reached' (Harrison and Theaker, 1989, p. 5).

Profile of a Mathematics Coordinator

What attributes might a governing body be looking for in a mathematics coordinator? A mathematics coordinator should have the following qualities:

- credibility (qualifications and knowledge of subject and experience, enthusiasm for the subject);
- good communication skills (a good listener; approachable; assertive but non-threatening; open; sensitive; patient);
- good organizational skills, including the ability to see priorities, having clear ideas and being determined (seeing things through) as well as opportunistic and analytical;
- flexibility;
- positive attitude;
- self-motivation;
- realism;
- energy;
- ability to stimulate;
- commitment to own professional development;
- and, not least, a sense of humour.

You have been appointed as a mathematics coordinator so what factors will enable you to be an effective coordinator? You need to be aware of three key areas of the role: good leadership skills, time and school support structures.

Skills to lead colleagues effectively include:

- demonstrating personal good practice;
- holding effective staff meetings – planned ahead, timed, with a set agenda, keeping and acting upon minutes, chairing meetings and leading discussions and encouraging and valuing the contributions of others, and so on;
- gathering information – through talking to colleagues and pupils, classroom observations, analysing pupils' work and school policies, auditing resources;
- organizing effectively, including arranging special events such as mathematics fairs and activities, visiting and initiating colleagues' visits to other institutions; organizing resources; providing INSET; raising finance;
- interacting with parents – informing them of the school's work, approaches to teaching through special events, workshops, talks for them, displays and encouraging parental involvement in their own child's work through, for example, activities such as those developed by a project that is a pact between teachers, parents and children in mathematics (Bringing School Home; IMPACT);
- interacting with governors and informing them of developments through policy documents, reports, development plans, displays, talks, 'fairs' and special events.

The absence of non-class contact *time* is a major constraint in the effectiveness of a coordinator. Time to observe the teaching of the agreed curriculum and to work alongside colleagues in the classroom will have to be negotiated with the headteacher. However, the effective management of your time will play a key part in determining how successful you are in your role and this is where having and setting clear targets to achieve within a realistic time scale are vital. This can be expressed formally within a school development plan (SDP) which clearly identifies targets, costs and evaluation criteria.

The SDP also requires other *supportive structures*. These include:

- the headteacher showing support for the coordinator of mathematics and enabling discussion and the exchange of ideas;
- clear lines of communication;
- a team spirit among the staff;
- whole staff acceptance of responsibility to implement agreed policy;
- a self-evaluating whole school philosophy;
- available time for certain activities;

- a whole school commitment to professional development;
- a management implication for a budget and funding – a negotiated and recorded financial allocation for resources.

However, always remember that these structures, as with many other things, need to be evaluated as to their effectiveness in meeting needs.

If you are to become a mathematics coordinator what will your role, duties and concerns be? They will include:

- *administration*: communication; finance; managing resources–materials, apparatus, books, human resources; internal and external assessment; record keeping of the staff and pupils;
- *implementing the curriculum*: policy with scheme of work; planning; evaluating; monitoring and reviewing; continuity; progression and differentiation;
- *working with colleagues*: teacher attitudes and expectations; teamwork; handling diversity; arrangement of INSET; provision of INSET guidance; support arrangements of INSET monitoring; appraisal;
- *pupil concerns*: gender and equal opportunities; self-esteem; grouping; classroom organization; diagnosis; transition;
- *outside (and inside) the classroom*: parents; governors, LEA; DfE; professional bodies; sources for help; liaising with other schools; working with other professionals.

Let us now look in more detail at some of these responsibilities. It is essential for a school to have well-documented policy statements which both influence and reflect the classroom practice. The OFSTED *Handbook for the Inspection of Schools* defines a policy as 'an agreed School Statement relating to a particular area of its life and work'. What does this mean in practical terms? According to the national curriculum Non-Statutory guidance,

A school policy statement in mathematics will describe the purposes, nature and management of the mathematics is taught and learned in a school . . . It will form part of the overall curriculum policy of the school (NCC, 1989; 1991, p. B4 para 4.1).

We suggest that the policy should leave the reader with a clear flavour of a school's philosophy – a particular set of beliefs and guiding principles which give a school's view of mathematics and the opportunities that should be provided for the pupils. This should be accompanied by a short statement or suitable quotation giving reasons for teaching mathematics in the context of the whole curriculum of the school.

It would also include, at least, title and date of inception, aims, broad, general statements on concerns such as teaching and learning strategies, including grouping and classroom organization, equal opportunities, gender issues and support for special needs pupils and second language learners, cross-curricular issues such as marking pupils' outcomes, pupils' personal and social development and parental involvement. It would also include the coordinator's job specification and statements on transition and liaison procedures.

Let us begin by looking at our proposed aims for the teaching of mathematics. The teaching of mathematics should assist the pupils:

- to become aware of the mathematics that is all around;
- in developing confidence in their mathematical abilities, and in developing interests, attitudes and aesthetic awareness;
- to be aware of mathematics as an essential element of communication – to represent, explain, predict – verbally, graphically, written;
- by providing opportunities for an in-depth study in mathematics;
- to acquire an awareness of the fascination of mathematics e.g. appreciation of pattern, feel for number;
- in developing an enquiring mind and a mathematical approach to problems, developing imagination, initiative and flexibility of mind in mathematics, working cooperatively;
- in developing basic concepts and logical thinking, working in a systematic way, developing general strategies;
- to see mathematics as a powerful tool, e.g. in planning a school trip, executing a design;
- in acquiring knowledge and learning skills, asking and answering own questions;
- in their appreciation of relationships within mathematics;
- to see the purpose in mathematics – in that it deals with people and life.

These suggestions can be used by you, the mathematics coordinator, either as a starting-point for whole school staff discussion or as a list against which you can compare your own suggestions.

It is not enough to state only the aims connected to skills, facts, understanding and knowledge of mathematics but to note also attitudes and personal qualities, social skills, manipulative and study skills, and communication skills that you hope that all your pupils will develop. An integral feature of any policy document is a well-considered and clearly articulated set of aims, without which it is difficult for schools to deliver a coherent, relevant and stimulating mathematical curriculum. The coordinator will be required to review periodically, or indeed, to initiate the statement of aims for mathematics teaching within the school.

The following list of aims were suggested by the Mathematics Association and modified as a result of several hours of staff meetings at one particular school. They should not necessarily be regarded as an exemplar with universal application. None-the-less, they are presented in the expectation that they may serve as a checklist of existing aims or as a starting point against which ideas may be evaluated.

Aims: A pupil should:
Attitudes and Personal Qualities
- enjoy mathematics;
- enjoy a sense of achievement;
- have a positive attitude to mathematics;
- be confident and flexible of mind when facing new problems;
- be able to challenge ambiguity in text, media, etc.;
- persist, even when things go wrong;
- be creative and imaginative – able to determine own methods and pose own questions;
- develop good work habits;
- understand the part that mathematics plays in the world;
- undertake sustained periods of mathematical study.

Social Skills
- cooperate with others – sharing materials and ideas;
- work as a member and leader of a team, respecting different views.

Manipulative Skills
- make appropriate and accurate drawings;
- work to appropriate degrees of accuracy;
- write clearly, recording in statements clearly and systematically;
- use symbols and terminology logically;
- use instruments, e.g. ruler, compass, scales, calculator, etc.

Study Skills
- read and comprehend mathematics books and use appropriate reference skills;
- plan independent work, be organized, logical and systematic;
- retrieve, use and return appropriate resources.

Communication Skills
- explain, discuss, describe and listen;
- communicate with clear expression and fluency;
- record findings by means of real objects and diagrams and present them to others using tabular, graphical forms applying suitable scaling and labelling of axes;
- interpret and analyse critically mathematical information, e.g. use of statistics in the media.

Mathematical Process Skills
- sort, match, discriminate, classify;
- look for patterns and relationships;
- analyse a problem, simplify difficult tasks, select suitable strategy;
- apply appropriate techniques;

- make and test a hypothesis, generalize, prove and disprove;
- reason, enquire;
- apply combinations of mathematical skills and techniques;
- estimate and approximate and develop a feel for number ('at homeness');
- recall, apply, interpret mathematical knowledge;
- make logical deductions from given mathematical data;
- select appropriate data, interpret results;
- decide *when* it is sensible to use a calculator – and *how* to use it sensibly!;
- carry out mental calculations;
- appreciate the relationships between concepts;
- understand the need for standardization, e.g. in measurement;
- recognize and use spatial relationships in two and three dimensions;
- understand mathematical principles.

A collection of aims will be of little value, however, unless there is a corporate and committed ownership of those aims. Enacting a practical interpretation and expression of the aims is of the essence but is more likely to be the case where such an ownership exists. Therefore, where a school spends several hours in compiling its agreed aims and objectives this is time that is well spent. Who leads these sessions? It is a role of the coordinator.

Equal Opportunities

An important aspect of the coordinator's role is to build into the policy a clear commitment to the highest possible achievement of all pupils, regardless of sex, race, social class or disability. Expectations have been shown to have a marked impact on the levels that pupils achieve. Often, unwittingly, teachers have preconceived expectations of particular groups of pupils which then influence the way pupils are treated.

Attitudes and expectations related to race may include the notions that Asian pupils work harder than white pupils do or that Chinese pupils have better computational skills. Clearly such notions have the propensity for reenforcement by the teacher (through the work offered to the pupils and the interactions between teacher and pupils).

Similarly, the teacher may have stereotypical views of boys as mathematicians. They may be regarded as more interested in (because they may ask more questions) and competent at mathematics than girls are. Thus the teacher may allow boys greater access to technical Lego and the computer. Boys may receive more questions and be set more challenging problems whilst girls are encouraged to be neat and to work independently. However, such skills may well have contributed significantly to the recent phenomenon of girls out-performing boys in GCSE, particularly with respect to coursework elements.

Expectations related to home background of pupils may manifest itself within the classroom. For example, creating a predominantly 'middle-class' style within the classroom may favour those pupils whose background is similar so that they are then perceived to be more able mathematically simply because they appear to have greater skills of articulation.

Teacher attitudes towards, and expectations of, pupils with disabilities may impede the achievement of those pupils. If, for example, the pupil has limited communication skills this should not be allowed to prevent that pupil from having the opportunity to work with his or her peers. Similarly, gross motor difficulties should not inhibit a pupil's progress in mathematics.

The coordinator should help all colleagues to become alert to some of the above attitudes and expectations and then to overcome them. Within this chapter it is not possible to give full treatment to such a crucial area of teaching but simply to raise the issues which are more comprehensively covered in other texts (e.g. ILEA, 1988b). Appropriate reference to the national curriculum document *Mathematics in the National Curriculum*, and, in particular, issues raised in the non-statutory guidelines (NCC, 1989 and 1991) must also be included.

Cross-curricular Mathematics

Cross-curricular links or mathematics across the curriculum are noted in the non-statutory guidelines which promote the starting points of a mathematical trail and the use of the environment; a problem (e.g. planning an outing or party); a general theme, topic or project (e.g. Ourselves, which is a broad-based topic); a topic in mathematics (e.g. pattern).

Mathematical skills can be applied and developed in science (especially those of measurement – linear, area, volume and data handling), geography (bearings, directions and data handling are necessary skills), PE (a good vehicle for demonstrating number, sequencing, shape and space abilities), and history (e.g. time lines). When planning such links it is vital to consider questions such as:

- Have I identified and determined the specific skills, knowledge, processes, areas of content that are to be included (during the half-term, week, etc.)?
- Are there sufficient opportunities for the pupils to use the mathematics they have already learned within the activities?
- Will the pupils be encouraged/need to learn new mathematical skills within the activities?

The above considerations are very important from the point of view of progression and differentiation. In addition, further questions include:

- Have I regarded the pupils' interests, skills and experiences in selecting the topic/starting points?

- Have I provided opportunities for the pupils to use computers, calculators and information technology skills?
- Have I identified the cross-curricular skills, such as problem-solving skills, communication skills, study skills, which can be developed with the mathematical activities?
- Will the pupils have time to develop their own lines of enquiry?

Although there are advantages all round in the thematic cross-curricular approach, which includes planning that provides for progression in skills and knowledge and processes as the thematic work develops, there is no point in artificially bringing in mathematics. It is still perfectly respectable and desirable to do mathematics as mathematics!

The 'new' national curriculum orders are due for implementation from August 1995. It is proposed that the number of attainment targets are reduced to three in Key Stage 1: Using and Applying Mathematics; Number; Shape, Space and Measures. Sorting and Classifying (part of the previous orders, Handling Data, Ma5) are now in both Number and Shape, Space and Measures whilst aspects of recording and interpreting data are now in Number. The Number patterns of the previous orders Algebra Ma3 are now in Number. Measurement areas previously in Numbers Ma2 and Shape and Space Ma4 are now brought together in Shape, Space and Measures.

Another feature of the new national curriculum is a move away from statements of attainment to level descriptions. The level descriptions describe the types and range of performance which the pupils working at a particular level should demonstrate.

By the end of Key Stage 1, the performance of the great majority of children, it is suggested, should be within the range of levels 1 to 3. The School Curriculum and Assessment Authority (SCAA) suggest that in deciding on a pupil's level of attainment at the end of Key Stage 1, teachers should judge which level description best fits the pupil's performance, and each description should be considered in conjunction with the descriptions for adjacent levels.

This process of making rounded judgments should accommodate the balancing of a child's strengths against any weaknesses. However, these judgments need to be consistent throughout (and beyond) a school. Each level description refers to a range of achievements, so interpretation will depend upon the weight individual teachers give to these different aspects. Thus a process of moderation within a school (and, at least, throughout a cluster of schools) backed up by some examples of assessed work is one way of gradually building a professional consensus on how to interpret the level descriptors. SCAA intend to publish (forthcoming, 1995) some examples of assessed work.

The second element of the national curriculum, the programmes of study have become Key Stage programmes of study, so that there are separate Key Stage 1 and Key Stage 2 programmes. These programmes, SCAA suggests, are made up of sections which should interrelate. Developing mathematical language, selecting and using materials and developing reasoning, they say, should be set in the context of the other areas of mathematics. Sorting, classifying, making comparisons and searching for patterns should apply to work on number, shape and space and handling data. The use of number should permeate work on measures and handling data.

The new national curriculum orders for mathematics will mean that a school has to begin to plan transition to the new curriculum. Therefore, the creation of a climate for change is again very necessary. It is essential that, for effective change, there is a whole school commitment and effort. This means that you as coordinator have to ensure that your colleagues – who are going to put the change into practice – are aware of educational developments and are prepared to be evaluative and analytical. Your climate for change is helped by having regular, well-organized staff meetings; your developing aspects of good practice in your class and displaying the results, as well as inviting colleagues into your classroom to observe or to work with you; you valuing your colleagues and their ideas; organizing workshops and relevant visits; inviting a local inspector to talk with staff about current issues and so on. However, when implementing any change, it is necessary to do a curriculum review to establish where you are now and to be careful not to 'throw the baby out with the bathwater'.

The Scheme of Work

An actual policy usually covers only a few A4 sheets of paper. However, a vital part of a policy is the scheme of work. A scheme of work expresses the policy in practice and is the blueprint for achieving it.

Why Is a Policy With a Scheme of Work Necessary?

Its functions are:

- to provide a measure of agreement – a framework within which to work. This is especially helpful in the induction of new colleagues;
- to help to promote continuity and progression;
- to create security and give confidence – of staff and external agencies;
- to help to ease negotiation about practice and provide a template through which you can determine whether what you are doing fits in with agreed policy;
- to confirm the staff in their beliefs and in their day-to-day activities;
- to allow for creativity – looking ahead to the future with room left to include new ideas.

What Should a Scheme of Work Contain?

A scheme of work is derived from the policy and gives detailed plans for teaching and learning that readily translate into classroom practice. The teaching and learning plans should be stated clearly so that continuity, coherence and progression are provided for whilst allowing, within the framework, a teacher's creativity and pupil's interests to be catered for through each Key Stage.

Other areas to be included are:

- record keeping procedures;
- assessment and evaluation procedures, including examples of children's work to indicate development and level of attainment;
- links within other curriculum areas;
- suggestions for use of commercial schemes;
- resources to be used and their location, including computer software;
- list of recommended books for teachers' personal reading;
- list of appropriate television and radio broadcasts, including videos;
- suggestions for display;
- suggestions for marking pupils' work;
- content – guidelines, an indication of the main knowledge, concepts, skills and attitudes to be addressed in each year;
- approximate amount of time to be allocated each week;
- forms of presentation;
- suggestions for work with the least and most able children.

In the mathematics non-statutory guidelines it is suggested that the programmes of study set out the basis of what should be taught during each Key Stage and will be used by schools in framing their scheme of work along with work outside the programmes of study.

How Should Mathematics Be Taught?

Whilst the content of the curriculum is largely defined through the national curriculum programmes of study, the way in which it is delivered is left very much to the discretion of individual schools. However, the majority of schools take cognizance of the major recommendations of the Cockcroft report and, more recently, OFSTED criteria (OFSTED, 1994a). Paragraph 243 of the Cockcroft report states that:

mathematics teaching at all levels should include opportunities for:

- exposition by the teacher;
- discussion between teacher and pupils and between pupils themselves;

- appropriate practical work;
- consideration and practice of fundamental skills and routines;
- problem solving, including the application of mathematics to everyday situations;
- investigational work (DES, 1982).

It is neither sensible nor justifiable to be too prescriptive about which of the above strategies ought to be adopted at any given time. Rather the choice will be influenced by the skills and confidence of the teacher and of the pupils. Teacher confidence is a potent force in determining the direction and attitudes of the learner. Coordinators have a key role here both in raising awareness and in providing leadership by example, INSET and support. Many texts (see references and further reading section) are available which provide practical suggestions to assist teachers in, for example, investigative ways of working in the classroom.

Resources

In order to implement the national curriculum and to aid teaching and learning, resources for mathematics need to be considered carefully. An audit of current resources is usually a vital first task of a newly appointed coordinator. You need to know what resources are already available in the school before a carefully considered judgment can be made on gaps to be filled, future needs and new purchases. In making judgments the following factors, at least, need to be considered:

- the aims stated in the school's policy (so that resources support them);
- the national curriculum requirements;
- the essential attributes you will look for in resources.

Resources include apparatus, materials and commercial schemes. The establishment of criteria for choosing resources that are clear, justifiable and known by all need to be established. These can include the statement that a commercial scheme is a servant not a master and questions such as:

- Does the commercial scheme have a teacher's manual with a clear philosophy, especially for the teaching and learning of mathematics and does its philosophy match our school's beliefs?
- Is the format suitable for our classrooms (pupil work books, photocopiable sheets, textbooks, cards, games, equipment-based schemes and so on)?
- How costly is the scheme initially, and to replace 'expendable' materials?
- Is the curriculum content suitable for our policy and scheme of work and how far does it meet the national curriculum requirements?

- Is the content logical, practical and progressive – does it cater for differentiation?
- Is the content relevant to the pupils' interests and experiences?
- Would the commercial scheme meet our school's equal opportunities, anti-racism, etc. requirements?
- Are evaluation and assessment activities part of the scheme?
- Does it include a helpful source of reference material for teachers?

Knowledge of where resources are stored is vital for *all* teachers. Storage issues need to be discussed and decided upon as the deployment of resources is an important area of the coordinator's responsibilities. The issues of centralization versus distribution of resources needs to be considered by the school and sometimes a practical compromise may be achieved. There are several potential difficulties associated with distribution:

- expensive items are not necessarily used economically;
- all colleagues need to be informed as to what exists, should they need to borrow it from another class;
- storage space should be available within a class so that the resource may be readily available.

Similarly, some practical difficulties can arise from the centralization of resources:

- expensive resources (e.g. ROAMER) need to be secure;
- efficient retrieval, when needed, is dependent upon careful organization of the resource area;
- colleagues need to be aware of the need to return items to the central area after use;
- colleagues need to be aware of the existence of all items.

The debate can be argued on either side but several key points emerge:

- whatever storage system is deployed, all colleagues need to have an up-to-date list of resources and further, should be aware of how to use them;
- each class should have ready and immediate access to: counters, die, calculators, multilink, etc.;
- certain resources can be regarded as age-specific, and therefore held in those classrooms, for example, laces and beads, in reception and year 1;
- generic items such as ROAMER and DIME solids which might be used by a range of ages could be stored centrally.

Teachers often say that they themselves are not always confident in terms of their own knowledge and understanding of mathematics and so as part of the coordinator's role it is necessary that he or she provides resources for the teachers' professional development. This may include a reference library as well as holding workshops on the effective use of, say, a piece of structural apparatus.

At some time or another a school team led by a mathematics coordinator will need to address all of the above issues and the other noted ones. Issues need to be talked about but must be acted on.

Facing the Inspection

Quality of learning is a key area of an OFSTED inspection. As part of the evidence gathering process the mathematics coordinator will be interviewed. In what direction may the questions lie? Possibly they will be similar to the following:

1. How clear are your stated responsibilities as a mathematics co-ordinator? Do others know exactly what your responsibilities are?
2. Is there any further written guidance to expand the school mathematics policy? Is there a scheme of work?
3. What is done about planning across the Key Stage?
4. Do you know how much time is provided within overall subject planning in mathematics to meet national curriculum requirements?
5. How do you attempt to monitor and evaluate the mathematics curriculum in the school (i.e. take responsibility for performance, plan improvement, etc.)?
6. Is there a common format applied to assessment and recording procedures? What about marking of written work in mathematics?
7. Have you engaged in any 'agreement trials' in mathematics? If so, across which year groups and at which levels?
8. Was there any follow-up to the mathematics issues discussed at the staff meeting? Was one meeting sufficient?
9. Where do you feel staff need the most support in order to maintain and improve their effectiveness in teaching mathematics?
10. Have any of you attended a 20-day mathematics course? If so, what has been its impact upon you? upon the school?
11. What do you feel about the level of resourcing for mathematics in the school – including reference books and facilities?
12. What use do you make of the school site for the teaching of mathematics, such as trails, etc.? What about visits out of school to enrich the curriculum?

Conclusion

In this chapter we have endeavoured to give a taste of the skills and their implications – managerial, interpersonal and organizational – required of an effective mathematics coordinator, and to discuss aspects of the responsibilities.

Coordinating mathematics is a very active and demanding role but one that is very worthwhile and satisfying. (Remember that your beliefs will influence your practice. Your enthusiasm and energy and how you value your colleagues are strong allies in your role.) You are affecting the teaching of your colleagues and the learning of the pupils, for effective, creative teaching stimulates the pupils' own thinking capability as well as their use of language, ideas and symbols. Enjoy your responsibility.

References and Further Reading

ATKINSON, S. (ed.) (1992) *Mathematics with Reason*, London Hodder and Stoughton.

BEAM Starters: New National Curriculum Edition (1988) This edition revised by PARKIN, S., WORDEN, J. and STRAKER, A., London, Harcourt Brace Jovanovich.

BIRD, M. (1986) *Mathematics with 7 and 8 Year Olds, 8 and 9 Year Olds, 9 and 10 Year Olds, 10 and 11 Year Olds*, Leicester, Mathematics Association.

BOOTH, W., BRITTEN, P. and SCOTT, F. (1993) *Themes Familiar*, Twickenham, Belair Publications Limited.

BURTON, L. (1984) *Thinking Things Through*, Oxford, Blackwell.

DAY, C., HALL, C., GAMMAGE, P. and COLES, M. (1993) *Leadership and the Curriculum in the Primary School*, London, PCP.

DES (1982) *Mathematics Counts* (The Cockcroft Report), London, HMSO.

DES (1985) *The Curriculum from 5 to 16: Curriculum Matters 2*, an HMI Series, London, HMSO.

DES (1985) *The Curriculum from 5 to 16: Curriculum Matters 3*, an HMI Series, London, HMSO.

DES (1988) *School Teacher's Pay and Conditions Document*, London, DES.

DUNCAN, A. (1992) *What Primary Teachers Should Know About Maths*, London, Hodder & Stoughton.

FLOYD, A. (ed.) (1981) *Developing Mathematical Thinking*, Milton Keynes Open University Press.

HARRISON, S. and THEAKER, K. (1989) *Curriculum Leadership and Coordination in the Primary School*, Whalley, Guild House Press.

HMI (1989) *Aspects of Primary Education: The Teaching and Learning of Mathematics*, London, HMSO.

HUME, B. and BARRS, K.(1988) *Maths on Display – Creative Ideas for the Teaching of Infant Maths*, Twickenham, Belair Publications Limited.

ILEA (1988a) *Mathematics in ILEA Primary Schools: Children and Mathematics Part 1*, London, ILEA.

ILEA (1988b) *Mathematics in ILEA Primary Schools: Making it Happen Part 2: Everyone Counts*, London, ILEA.

MERTTENS, R. and VASS, J. (1993) *Partnership in Maths: Parents and Schools*, London, Falmer Press.

MATHEMATICS ASSOCIATION (1988) *Managing Mathematics*, Cheltenham, Stanley Thornes.

MATHEMATICS ASSOCIATION (1987) *Sharing Mathematics with Parents*, Cheltenham, Stanley Thornes.

NATIONAL CURRICULUM COUNCIL (NCC) (1989 and 1991) *Mathematics Non-Statutory Guidance*, York, NCC.

OFSTED (1993) *The Teaching and Learning of Number in Primary Schools*, London, HMSO.

OFSTED (1994a) *Handbook for the Inspection of Schools*, London, HMSO.

OFSTED (1994b) *Science and Mathematics in School: A Review*, London, HMSO.

PURKIS, S. (1993) A Teachers' Guide to Using School Buildings, English Heritage.

RHYDDERCH-EVANS, Z. (1993) *Mathematics in the School Grounds: Learning Through Landscapes*, Crediton, Devon, Southgate Publishers Limited.

SCHOLASTIC PUBLICATIONS LTD (1994) *IMPACT: Maths Homework for Key Stages 1 and 2*, University of North London Enterprises Ltd, Leamington Spa, Scholastic Publications Ltd.

SCAA (1994) *The National Curriculum Orders, London,* HMSO.

SHUARD, H., WALSH, A., GOODWIN, J. and WORCESTER, V. (1990) *Children, Mathematics and Learning*, London, Simon and Schuster.

SHUARD, H., WALSH, A., GOODWIN, J. and WORCESTER, V. (1991) *Calculates, Children and Mathematics, The Prime Project*, Hemel Hempstead, Simon and Schuster.

WILLIAMS, E. and SHUARD, H. (1994) *Primary Mathematics Today*, 4th, Harlow, edn, Longman.

WOODMAN, A. and ALBANY, E. (1988) *Mathematics Through Art and Design*, London, Urwin and Hyman Ltd. (now Collins Educational).

Associations, Monthly Magazines and Other Material

Mathematics Association (MA)
259 London Road
Leicester LE2 3BE

Association of Teachers of Mathematics (ATM)
Shaftesbury Street
Derby DE23 8YB

Claire Publication and Jonathan Press
Tey Brook Craft Centre
Tey Brook Road
Colchester
Essex CO6 1JE

Mrs G. Hatch
Manchester Metropolitan University
Didsbury School of Education
799 Wilmslow Road
Didsbury
Manchester M20 2RR
(Bounce to it; Jump to it)

NORMAC Publications
c/o Mrs M. Stout
Cinnamom Brow C E Primary School
Perth Close

Fernhead
Warrington
Cheshire WA2 0SF

Scholastic Publications Ltd (Central Office)
Villiers House
Clarendon Avenue
Leamington Spa
Warwickshire
CV32 5PR

IMPACT Central Office (for information and assistance)
The University of North London
0171 607 2789 (extension 2658)

IMPACT INSET Pack from IMPACT Supplies Limited
PO Box 1
Woodstock
Oxon OX20 1HB

Strategies Magazine (*Maths and Problem Solving 3–13*)
Questions Publishing Company
27 Frederick Street
Hockley
Birmingham B1 3HH

Manchester LEA Publications
ACORN Centre
Royal Oak Road
Wythenshawe
Manchester M22, S

BEAM Project (1988) *Children and Mathematics*
BEAM (BE A Mathematician)
Barnsbury Complex
Offord Road
London N1 1QH

Chapter 6

The New Science Coordinator

Kathryn Bowe

You are a newly qualified teacher. You have just started your first post and, along with the daunting prospect of a new class, you are also the science coordinator for Key Stage 1. The situation is certainly intimidating, considering you can only just decide how to group the tables in your new classroom. Take heart and know that your feelings of apprehension are nothing compared to those infant teachers' panic attacks when, in 1985, there was a statement of policy made by the DES insisting that science should be taught in all infant classrooms. After 1985, new policy documents landed on school doormats with frightening regularity. Remember, many a science coordinator before you has had pre-curriculum meeting palpitations with the thoughts and fears of how to impress on fellow colleagues the need to implement sixteen attainment targets and their accompanying programmes of study. In addition, assessment, testing and record keeping were important aspects to be addressed.

Science has historically struck a chord of fear, misunderstanding and apprehension in many teachers' and pupils' minds. This may be due to such factors as poor teaching methods in earlier days, the learning of misunderstood facts, the watching of boring demonstrations or the apathetic attitudes of certain teachers. It is interesting to consider that when any adult thinks about a subject that they liked or disliked at school, it is the teacher that taught them that subject who immediately springs to mind. That teacher's enthusiasm, keen or otherwise, has a strong effect on the attitude of pupils. Teachers have the power to foster a love or a hatred of science. Unfortunately, there are still a number of primary teachers in the profession who do not like science, do not particularly enjoy teaching it and feel it is their priority to teach the three Rs and science can come later, taught by specialists. It is in these cases that we are thankful for the national curriculum.

At least when you take up your post, the donkey work has been done. The curriculum has been slimmed down to more reasonable proportions and should stay in its present form for at least five years. Also, those teachers who have survived the impositions of the previous ten years have become accustomed to the fact that science is a core subject that has to be taught and you will find that they are on the whole open and receptive to you and your role. You will find that in most cases teachers are now very familiar with the requirements by law and appreciate your position as coordinator. Don't forget, all primary teachers are coordinators of something. They know you have a job to do and that you are newly qualified and will be surprisingly supportive and helpful.

Prepare to be a Science Coordinator

Initially, consult with both your headteacher and appointed mentor. Both these people should appreciate your difficult position and advise you to take at least the first term to settle with your new class and develop your class teaching routine. Take the opportunity to use this time to prepare yourself for the task of being an active science coordinator. The following list of preparations will help you:

- Make sure that you are fully conversant with the national curriculum requirements for Key Stage 1. When you are writing out your plans for the year, month, week, day, have your document out in front of you so that you are absolutely aware of the parts that you are teaching in your class. Also be conscious of which parts of the national curriculum other teachers in Key Stage 1 are covering.
- Ask for a copy of the existing policy document in school. Read it carefully.
- Make an extra special effort in your own planning, teaching and recording of science. Experiment with different methods, individual work, group work, whole class lessons. Evaluate these methods, improve upon them.
- Show good practice through your displays. Beg and borrow from industry museums, parents, etc. Make your science practical and eye-catching.
- Talk to other, more experienced teachers about science. Actually, do more listening than talking. Time spent in the staff room is very valuable. Do not spend all your lunch-time preparing for the afternoon session in the classroom. Spend some time in the staff room at lunch-times. Also, have twenty minutes there at the end of the day – before you go back to set up for the following day. These times informally chatting with colleagues are an invaluable learning time for you.
- Take note of how curriculum meetings are conducted by other co-ordinators. Watch to see how they handle conflict, how they introduce change, how they present their subjects, whether the staff are interested or not. Measure which members of staff are going to be supportive. Consider how you might like to conduct a curriculum meeting.
- Do an inventory of existing science equipment in school. Is it kept in a central store? Is certain equipment kept in certain classrooms? Is it shared? Is it working? Has it ever been used? At this stage, don't

change anything, just make a note of it. Ask to see the last three orders for science equipment. When was any new equipment last requested? Where is it now? Who is using it?

- Visit the local teachers' centre. Attend any courses on science. Talk to other teachers from other schools (especially newly qualified teachers). Find out the availability of borrowed equipment.
- If possible, ask to see the planning file, which should have individual class plans in it, including science. Try to assess whether these class plans reflect what is set down in the existing policy.
- Look at the school development plan. How high a priority is science? If it is put as high priority follow these points with alacrity! Your time is nigh!
- Above all, be humble. You may be Einstein's great-grandson, but you have only been teaching a matter of weeks. If you have already started, you will be realizing that theory and practice are two very different things. You already know that, as science coordinator, you should be displaying 'good practice'. This comes with experience. Teachers are very defensive, territorial and possessive. If you bowl in, trying to teach your grandmother to suck eggs, you will get a frosty reception. Ask questions, seek advice, listen, try ideas and review your own practice all the time.
- Start to build up a book of ideas, pictures etc. related to science – not just for yourself but for all stages of early years and Key Stage 1. Try to find a way of cataloguing your information so it will be easy to find at short notice. Good sources include *Child Education* magazine and also *Question*. Join the Association for Science Education (ASE).
- Once you have settled into school, see if you can negotiate time with the headteacher so that you can go into other people's classes. Observing other teachers at work is an excellent opportunity rarely taken up. If another teacher does not mind you coming into his or her classroom, discuss first exactly what you are going in to do. Take note of the teacher's approach. Watch how the children respond. Listen to the questioning skills of the teacher, try to assess how and what the children are actually learning. Always discuss your observations with the teacher afterwards and even if you have decided that you now know how *not* to do it, say something positive and appreciative.
- As you become more used to school routine and you develop a feel for how the science is being taught in your school, you will become more ready to take an active role as science coordinator.

Become Active!

By now you will be in sole charge of the science equipment. This is a major job and a very difficult one if certain items are secreted away in selected individual teachers' classrooms! However, worry not, so long as you know where they are. It is not so important that they are under your watchful eye all the time.

Different schools have different systems. Some keep the relevant equipment for the areas of the curriculum being taught in certain year areas. Others have the majority of the science equipment kept and monitored by the science coordinator. Whatever the system, you will need to review it. You have already done an inventory. If you are really unhappy about the stock system or the quality of stock, discuss the issue first with the headteacher, then bring it up as an item at one of your first curriculum meetings. There is nothing teachers like better than listing the things that they need in order to do their jobs properly! In actual fact, KS1 science can be taught with surprisingly little special equipment but it always helps if the following items are easily accessible:

Basic equipment needed to teach science

adhesives
aquarium
bags – paper and plastic
balloons – variety
balls – variety
bucket
balances – variety
candles
colour paddles
colour pyramid
compost
containers – variety
corks
foil
funnels
iron filings
jugs – measuring, pouring
kaleidoscope
labels
lollipop sticks
magnets
magnetizing glasses
magnispector

marbles
mirrors – different sizes, shapes
Petri dishes
pipettes
plant pots
plasticine
posters
prisms
rubber bands – variety
safety goggles
sand glasses (timers)
scales
scales (bathroom)
scissors
stethoscope
stop clocks
straws
syringes
thermometers – variety
torches
tubing – plastic
viewers – variety
watering can

More luxurious equipment

binoculars
electrical equipment: for circuit making
camera

cooker – e.g. Baby Belling
dental mirrors
disclosing tablets
glue gun
skeleton
tape recorder
weatherboard
wind direction indicator
rain gauge

Storage can be difficult. You may be fortunate enough to have a resource room with a science section. You may have a large cupboard. You may be expected to find an area in your own classroom. If you are lucky and teach in a well-ordered, well-budgeted school, you may have access to purpose-built furniture with cupboards, drawers, resource filing cabinets etc. It is more usual to have to produce your own storage area, however.

Science equipment is notoriously bulky and irregular in shape. However, many items may be stored in a series of boxes or containers such as:

- crisp boxes (with hole in the front) piled up and painted and labelled;
- shoe boxes as above;
- cut away soap boxes;
- plastic baskets (from the greengrocer);
- tins (coffee baby milk);
- old book cases or lockers – revamped and relabelled.

Whichever way you store your equipment, other teachers' estimation of you as a science coordinator will go up tenfold if they ask you for an item and you can lay your hands straight on it.

Published Resources

You may find that your school has a published scheme in place. If it has, find out who is working which section, and how it correlates with the scheme of work. If there is not a scheme of work actually written into the existing policy, put that on your list of things to bring up at your science curriculum meetings.

Use the planning files to help you sort the sections of published materials already in school pertinent to each topic covered. This takes a long time. Just do a half term at a time. It is a common irritation to teachers that just as they finish a topic or theme, they find some super pictures, work cards or sections of ideas that would have been just right for their class! Try to pre-empt this by having a section of ideas and resources ready before the start of the new half term.

If there are no published materials in school, go to the local teachers' centre and look at a selection. Consider asking the headteacher to purchase only some or part of published schemes. This could also come up for discussion in your future science meetings.

Science Curriculum Meetings

The time arrives when you have to lead a series of science curriculum meetings. You should have plenty of warning about this as it should be written into the school development plan well in advance. If you are not sure about when it is, ask the headteacher or deputy head because you need plenty of time to prepare. When deciding what to do at your curriculum meetings take into account how long you have, what needs to be done, what the staff want to do, and plan accordingly. It may be that you have a half term of weekly staff meetings; this might mean six or seven one-hour sessions. You might be asked to run one or two INSET days. You may be asked to do one science meeting per half term. All schools have their own way of approaching curriculum development. Whichever it is, by now you should be developing some ideas of your own as to what needs to be done by the school. Make preliminary lists and discuss them with the headteacher first. Always make the point in your first staff meetings that you want to cover the areas that the rest of the staff feel are important. Share your ideas with them and ask if they consider them important too. You will find that mostly they do. Enlist the backup of the headteacher, deputy head and your mentor and discuss the content and structure of the science meetings written before you start.

Try to formulate an agenda. Staff like to know what to expect and what they will need to bring to a meeting. Keep to the starting and finishing times and always make a note of anything that was decided (it may be policy that minutes are kept). Vary the styles of your meetings. Sometimes they will need to be formal and informative. Try to make them stimulating and interesting. Promote discussion, value everybody's opinions (even if you don't agree with them). Use audio and visual aids – videos, children's work. Ask outside speakers to come in from the local teachers' centre or from the university. Some industrial companies have speakers who will come to schools for these occasions. Sometimes they have a hands-on practical workshop. Whatever it is that you do, make sure that it is going to be of *value* to the rest of the staff. Time is short in schools and there is nothing more annoying than spending time in a staff meeting thinking about that pile of marking or that display or those worksheets that need preparing. Teachers like to go away from INSET thinking 'Yes, I'll *do* that tomorrow, next week, next year'. Ask yourself, what will the staff be able to go away and *do* after my meeting?

The Content: Ideas for Staff Meetings

The content of your science meetings depends on the stage of development of your school. Some schools have gone a long way to developing the science curriculum and are at the later stages of refining and reviewing the situation. You have learnt at college about the cyclic stages of curriculum development. What you want to know is 'What do I do?'

The following ideas are by no means a comprehensive list of activities to carry out for INSET. They are one or two tried and tested ideas that show the types of activities that generate science development. Copy other ideas from things you have done at college or on courses. A good booklet to help you has been developed by the National Curriculum Council (1993). It should already be in your school and it is called *Teaching Science at Key Stages 1 and 2*. It is an invaluable resource for the science coordinator to use to improve the quality of implementing science in schools.

Discuss 'What Is Good Science?'

This is a good opening activity. Ask the staff to jot down briefly (on their own) what they consider to be good science, then ask them to pair up and compare notes. Continue to increase the sizes of the groups of staff, increasing and developing their ideas until they come to a whole staff. With you co-ordinating, write a consensus of opinion as to what you and your staff consider to be good science. This activity generates a lot of discussion. Allow enough time for the different sizes of groups to make notes. By the end, you should have an agreed statement designed by the whole staff. At least then you may consider yourselves working towards the same ideals. Encourage the staff to include things that make this particular statement pertinent to *science* rather than a generalized statement that could be true of any area of the curriculum. This statement could be included in your update of the existing policy. Note who contributed (name all the staff) and when it was written.

According to OFSTED (1993):

> Good learning in science means that pupils are acquiring under-standing of key scientific concepts that enables them to be used in unfamiliar situations. They are developing the skills of imaginative but disciplined scientific enquiry including systematic observation and measurement, making and testing hypotheses, planning and carrying out investigations competently and safely and drawing inferences from evidence. They are learning to appreciate the powerful but provisional nature of scientific explanation and the processes by which models are created, tested and modified in the light of evidence. They are study-ing the practical applications of science and how these are changing the nature of society and the economy. They are exploring some

of the moral dilemmas that scientific discoveries and technological developments can cause.

Revised National Curriculum Document

This document has had to be revised on a number of occasions over the past few years! The latest policy should be the final one for at least five years. For this staff meeting, all the teachers need to be able to see a copy of the document, or you could photocopy the relevant pages onto an overhead acetate. Basically you have got to read the document together and discuss the points made. The national curriculum document can be looked at more closely when developing or revising the scheme of work.

Attainment targets
AT1   Experimental and investigative science
AT2   Life processes and living things
AT3   Materials and their properties
AT4   Physical processes

Programme of study

1   Experimental and investigative science

   • plan, predict and recognise when a test is fair;
   • use measurements and senses to obtain evidence;
   • consider evidence and explain results.

2   Life processes and living things

   • life processes: main characteristics of living things;
   • humans as organisms;
   • plants as organisms;
   • variation and classification: similarities and differences, groupings;
   • living things and their particular environment.

3   Materials and their properties

   • grouping materials: explore differences, sort by properties;
   • changing materials: by handling and by heating and cooling.

4   Physical processes

   • electricity: uses, simple circuits;
   • forces and motion: speed, forces, effect on direction and shape;
   • light and sound: sources, recognize that sound travels.

Figure 6.1: Organizing a scheme of work

Reception	ourselves	homes	hot and cold			
Year 1	colour	opposites	books			
Year 2						

Revise or Write a Scheme of Work

Depending on your particular school, the scheme of work could be already in place. Whether it is or not, the latest statements in the national curriculum will probably need to be applied. The scheme of work tells the individual year group teachers what they should be covering. The National Curriculum can be basically cut up and shared out by all the staff.

Bear in mind that many areas of the curriculum (especially experimental and investigative science) need to be returned to time and time again for the children to reinforce and extend their learning. With this in mind, make a series of copies of the programmes of study. Cut them up into workable sections and allocate them to certain year groups or certain topics that are covered.

Make a large chart like that in Fig 6.1 showing the basic topic areas covered by each year group and place the sections on the chart until they have all been shared out. Move the headings around until everyone is agreed which areas should be covered by which year groups. Once people have agreed and know exactly which sections of science they will cover, they will feel much happier about attempting to implement a reasonable amount of content.

It is worth spending a lot of time considering this chart with the staff through developing it further by actually identifying good scientific activities to cover programmes of study at appropriate levels. You can work towards avoiding repetition and yet can build progression into your scheme of work. The other advantage is that you can influence activities to be done at certain times of the year and so prevent overlapping the need for specific equipment.

Look at Experimental and Investigative Science

This is an area of science where primary teachers need a lot of help. They can cope with the general content of the curriculum but getting children to experiment and investigate is a difficult area on which most primary staff groups need to work.

One way to approach this is either to ask the staff to *all* carry out the same investigation with one group of children during the following week, and to try to make time to observe and record everything they say and do. (Yes, they will come out with all sorts of reasons as to how and why they couldn't possibly do this). But calmly suggest that what you might do is give the children the activity to do at lunch-time or during an assembly so that you may observe uninterrupted by the rest of the class. This is a one-off situation and you are trying to see whether the children are investigating or not. Examples of activities you could provide them to do are:

- Give the children a set of corks, a tank of water and access to any other equipment they might want. Ask them to find out all they can about the corks. Sit and observe. Try to note all that is said and done. (If possible video record or tape the children).
- Give the children a selection of toy cars and two ramps (perhaps old shelves or a PE bench). Ask them to find out which is the 'best'. Observe and note.
- In an area where birds are regularly fed, give the children a selection of food, such as bread, raisins, crisps. Ask the children to find out which food the birds like best. Observe and note.

At the next staff meeting ask the staff to look at their notes and to indicate when and where children were involved in the attainment targets set down in the national curriculum. Better still, ask them to consider when and where they as teachers *could* have intervened and developed and taught relevant sections, for example when to introduce making a record; the type of record that may be useful; developing the sense of fair testing etc.

Go on to emphasize to the staff the need to plan for open-ended investigations such as these in advance. If necessary, during a meeting, brainstorm ideas for each other's topics. Note them down for future reference. Teachers always feel better with a list of ideas to work on.

Consider Assessment

By now, teachers should be carrying out assessments as a matter of course (those involved in SATs will be a big support to you here). However, assessment in science can still be quite a bugbear to the average class teacher.

Show the staff a variety of ways of assessing the children, such as question and answer, tick lists, observations (as above), past SAT tests. Again, ask them during the following week to do a science assessment pertinent to the science being currently covered in their class. Ask them to give you one piece of work that they have assessed. Photocopy those and the relevant sections of the national curriculum including the level description sections. At the next staff meeting ask pairs of teachers to assess each other's pieces of work and give levels. Discuss whether teachers make the same judgments about each other's work and how much teachers are influenced by the knowledge of particular children.

What should come out of this activity is that assessment, too, needs to be very carefully planned and linked to the level description. The work needs to be 'levelled' and then that level needs to be noted somewhere in a file or on individual children's records according to the system followed in your school. Sometimes parts of a level description are covered, for example, a piece of work about the organs of the body. At a later date the child would need to be assessed on his or her knowledge on the parts of a flowering plant. This needs to be noted. By reading and discussing the level descriptions section of the document teachers can get more out of deciding on the 'levelness' of a child.

The Written Policy

The responsibility for producing the written policy lies with you. Don't worry – there should already be something down on paper as far as a written policy is concerned. By the time you come to post you should be evaluating, reviewing and adding to it. If the existing policy is so sketchy that it needs rewriting completely, there are certain headings that you need to write statements on. Remember it is not just down to *you* to write the policy; it is supposed to be a joint effort between you, the headteacher and the staff.
    Your statements should:

- Include reference to the main school aims and objectives – linked to science. You could put in here the staff statement of what is good science.
- Show how the policy has been developed. Refer to the existing paper (however flimsy). Mention the whole staff.
- Describe how science is taught in your school (it will include a variety of teaching methods). (NB: This is another good staff meeting idea).
- Explain and refer to the scheme of work and how it came to be produced.
- Refer to cross-curricular links and give examples.
- Emphasize that there will be equal opportunity for all children.
- Stress the safety factors carried out in school. (NB: Another staff meeting session!) Refer to the ABE safety booklet (DES, 1989).
- List the resources in school. State how they are organised.
- Give examples of assessment procedures, also show the current methods for recording science.
- Make a statement as to what still needs to be done, put a time scale on it and mention the people involved.

The policy does not have to be very long and wordy. Show the rough draft to the headteacher and other members of staff before finalizing it. Make sure copies are available for everyone, including governors.

And Finally

Once you have conducted a series of staff meetings, resourced your school, rewritten your science policy and implemented a scheme of work, you will be feeling much more confident – exhausted, but much more confident! You will find that there is much, much more to be done. You could quite easily be science coordinator full-time and still not complete the job. However, remember that you are still a class teacher and you have a serious responsibility to the children in your immediate care. You can only do so much. Each class teacher has to find his or her way of teaching science within their own classrooms. Back at the start of all the national curriculum implementations, the statement of policy by the DES said: 'the school needs to have at its disposal at least one teacher with the capacity, knowledge and insight to make science education for primary pupils a reality' (DES, 1989). Take into account, you are at your school's disposal! Also take into account your own stage of development, however. Above all, enjoy yourself and the children and staff will follow suit.

Reference

Association for Science Education (1990) *Be Safe*, 2nd Edition, Hatfield, Association for Science Education.

Department of Education and Science DES (1989) *The Implementation of the National Curriculum in Primary Schools*, London, HMSO, Summer/Autum.

National Curriculum Council (NCC) (1993) *Teaching Science at Key Stages 1 and 2*, York, NCC.

OFSTED (1993) *Science: Key Stages 1, 2, 3 and 4, Fourth Year, 1992–93*, London, HMSO.

Chapter 7

Geography in the Early Years:
The Role of the Subject Manager

Rosemary Rodger

As a foundation subject of the national curriculum, geography is now firmly embedded within the curricular requirements of Key Stage 1. Nursery and reception aged children, who although not subject to the same statutory requirements, are likely to be included in the whole school curriculum. Geography for these children is referred to as the human and social area of learning (OFSTED, 1994a). As a subject manager you will need to look at the ways in which the foundations of geographical understanding are laid in the early years of schooling and how the study of geography supports learning of the basic skills of reading and writing. This chapter aims to offer a rationale for the teaching of geography in the very early years (3–5 years) and outline a range of strategies to help the newly appointed subject manager for geography in an infant school or the infant department of a primary school support colleagues in the teaching and learning of geography from the nursery through to Year 2. The role of the subject manager as leader, monitor and evaluator of standards, communicator, organizer, gatherer and deployer of resources and writer of the geography policy and scheme of work will be considered.

So what does the role of the subject manager involve? How can he or she ensure children are receiving their basic geographical entitlement and are pursuing activities that are broad, balanced, differentiated and relevant according to the needs of the children? How is progression achieved? How are resources deployed? How can the subject manager devise aims for the geography curriculum which are broadly compatible with the curricular aims for the school? How do you write a policy, plan the geography curriculum, ensure implementation in the classroom and, importantly, persuade colleagues that the study of geography is an essential part of the curriculum? How can you provide for children with special educational needs (SEN)? Is the system of record keeping and assessment manageable? Hopefully, this chapter will answer these questions.

Background

Reports and surveys (DES, 1978, 1989) in the past fifteen years point to a neglect of geography in the early years prior to the introduction of the national curriculum. More recently, surveys by the Office for Standards in Education (OFSTED, 1993a, 1993b) cite an increase in the amount of geography taught. Their surveys concluded that the quality of teaching and learning was better in Key Stage 1 than Key Stage 2, with nearly three-quarters of the lessons based on the study of the home, the local area, the early development of map skills or the recording of weather conditions (OFSTED, 1993a, p. 6). Subject managers were seen to be having a positive effect on the quality of geography teaching (OFSTED, 1993b, p. 18).

According to the guidance offered by OFSTED (1994a, p. 77) into the human and social area of learning for children under 5 it is suggested that this area of learning:

> sets the context for developing geographical, historical, and social and personal skills and understanding . . . Children should learn about their locality and how they, their family and the people they meet relate to each other and the local community . . . The programme of activities should include for example, walks and visits which encourage children to notice and record features in the local environment.

The educational debate which continues to polarize the curriculum for the early years between protagonists of the child-centred approach (Department of Education, 1967; Hurst, 1994; Nutbrown, 1994) and more recently the subject-centred advocates (Alexander *et al.*, 1992; Rodger 1994a) masks what the theoretical debate should be concerning itself with. What is important is the provision of high quality learning experiences and a consideration of what children are learning. One of the most effective ways of doing this is to organize what we want children to know (knowledge) into subjects. Each subject has its own set of concepts and skills, thus providing teachers with a framework on which to base their planning, teaching and assessment of the range of concepts, skills, knowledge and attitudes children acquire as they grow. Geography has a powerful part to play in reinforcing and promoting basic skills in literacy and numeracy (OFSTED, 1994b; Rodger, 1994b) as well as the opportunity it provides to develop geographical knowledge and understanding.

This attention to geographical subject knowledge, skills and concepts which traditionally has been omitted from the curriculum for young children may be the reason for the reluctance that some teachers have shown, in the past, in relation to the study of geography. The national curriculum is a statutory framework and one which reception class teachers have turned to for support (Rodger, forthcoming) What is clear from my own research is the need expressed by these teachers for a clearly identifiable curriculum for the under-5s. One of the aims of this chapter is to show that the study of places and people is essential to the development of young children and should be included within the early years curriculum.

As subject manager for geography it will be important for you to persuade colleagues that the study of geography in its widest sense has a fundamental role in the early years curriculum. A basic requirement of learning in the early years is that it is practical and initially involved with the here and now. Indeed, the following principles coined by Tina Bruce from the work of the early pioneers in early childhood education and the Early Years Curriculum Group could form the overarching aims for your geography policy statement: 'The child's education is seen as an interaction between the child and the environment including, in particular, other people and knowledge itself' (Bruce, 1987, p. 30). And from the Early Years Curriculum Group (1990, p. 3): 'In the early years children learn best through first hand experience.'

The Role of the Geography Subject Manager

I want to offer a likely scenario at this point. You are a recently qualified teacher, not a geography specialist, but you have been given responsibility for geography in the infant or primary school where you are responsible for the reception class. This is not an unrealistic picture. On a recent in-service course for geography in the early years there were eight out of twenty teachers delegated to the role of subject manager for geography and of these seven were reception class teachers. I will try to offer a pragmatic, rather than an idealistic, portrayal of the way in which you can become effective in your role. You will be expected to demonstrate a range of skills not readily acquired or enhanced through the role of the class teacher or student. Can you lead colleagues effectively? Is your own knowledge and understanding of geography secure? Join the Geographical Association (GA) and receive regular information about teaching geography in schools as well as a wealth of practical ideas. Read *Geographical Work in Primary and Middle Schools* (1988) by D.W. Mills. This book has been updated by the GA. It does provide an excellent theoretical and developmental justification for the teaching and learning of geography with young children.

I now want to expand on the key tasks of the subject manager for geography and offer a range of practical measures which will assist you in your newly delegated role as subject manager.

Writing a Scheme of Work

What exactly is a scheme of work? Are you able to purchase a scheme of work or do you prefer to use your finances to increase resources such as maps, aerial photographs, globes and atlases? Whatever decision is taken you will

Figure 7.1: What to include in a scheme of work for geography

A scheme of work is designed to help teachers plan in the medium and the short term.

A scheme of work will reflect the long term planning processes agreed by the school.

A scheme of work contains:

- aims and objectives for the subject linked to the school's overall aims and objectives;
- content linked to national curriculum knowledge, skills and understanding from the programme of study for each Key Stage;
- outlines of continuing and blocked units of work, where appropriate;
- time allocated to each unit and the subject as a whole across the year;
- links with other subjects;
- resources to support learning;
- contributions to cross-curricular themes and dimensions;
- assessment, recording and reporting procedures;
- procedures for identifying INSET needs;
- consideration of issues of equality of opportunity.

(Adapted from NCC, 1993)

need to look at the route through the scheme or devise a scheme of work which ensures the children cover national curriculum requirements. Some published schemes do this (Hughes, *et al.*, 1992). The National Curriculum Council (NCC, 1993) outlined what is to be included in a scheme of work (Figure 7.1).

Further guidance on what to include in a scheme of work for geography is described in an OFSTED report outlining geography in Key Stages 1, 2 and 3 (OFSTED, 1993b). This report is based on inspections by Her Majesty's Inspectors (HMI) of ninety-six primary schools, eight middle schools and ninety-three secondary schools. One hundred and twenty lessons were seen in Key Stage 1. The definition of a scheme of work outlined below has been altered to accommodate the new requirements for the study of geography in Key Stage 1.

A scheme of work provides detailed guidance and good support to the class teacher by:

- setting out the content to be covered in each Key Stage and including reference to the relevant sections of the programme of study;
- ensuring that the geography subject is not fragmented by integrating geographical skills, knowledge of places and themes;
- the integration may take the form of topics, such as 'My Home' or 'The Seasons' in Key Stage 1. Discussion with colleagues about the selection of topics to be included within the scheme of work for geography should take place to avoid overlap with other subject managers.
- the best geography in topic work in Key Stage 1 occurs when the geographical element is clearly identified by the teacher.

As an example OFSTED described the following practice in a reception class:

> Among the most effective lessons were several that focused on directions and routes. In one class, containing reception pupils, a teacher took a group of pupils for a walk and related the features they saw, such as conspicuous buildings, to a simple plan of the route and to photographs she had taken previously. On returning to the classroom, the pupils made use of the plan and photographs to explain the route and describe the features to the rest of the class. The teacher produced an enlarged street plan on which the key buildings had been coloured, and the route was then followed on this plan. The pupils responded well to the teacher's open-ended questions, and showed a good understanding of the map skills involved (OFSTED, 1993a, p. 7).

The scheme of work should be included within the geography policy (see Figure 7.2). An important first step in your role as subject manager is to begin writing a policy for geography that is agreed upon by all members of staff. Figure 7.2 offers a checklist of tasks required to be undertaken as you begin to devise your policy. It looks daunting, but don't feel you need to have this in place the first term you are in your role. Set yourself targets and try to have the policy in place within a term. The amount of work required will vary depending upon whether you have inherited a post vacated by someone who has moved to another post of responsibility or you are the first person in the school to have this responsibility.

Figure 7.2: Writing a geography policy

1 Writing a geography policy needs to be part of the whole school planning process – is it included in the school development plan?
2 The policy should be formulated and agreed upon by the whole staff.
3 As the coordinator you may wish to present the outline suggested below for consultation at a staff meeting.
4 The policy needs to contain:
   a) a brief definition of geography. There is no need to reinvent the wheel; there are definitions which are suitable in national curriculum documents;
   b) the aims of teaching and learning geography. These need to reflect the overall aims for the school curriculum;
   c) teaching and learning approaches – the enquiry process, key questions, fieldwork, role play, simulations, issues, geography through stories;
   d) a statement regarding time allocation;
   e) a scheme of work/curriculum plan to cover national curriculum requirements;
   f) reference to geographical vocabulary;
   g) links with other subjects;
   h) links with cross-curricular themes and dimensions – particularly equal opportunities;
   i) provision for children with special educational needs;
   j) resource lists and their availability, including the use of IT;
   k) assessment and record keeping procedures;
   l) the role of the subject manager;
   m) health and safety guidelines on fieldwork;
   n) in-service needs;
   o) provision for monitoring, evaluation and review.

Planning the Geography Curriculum

Methods of planning vary between schools. There is no one system. Many primary schools, particularly in Key Stage 1, have adopted 'broad-based topic work involving the study of wide-ranging themes which draw on a large number of subjects' (OFSTED, 1994b). What is essential however is that you are aware of the way in which children progress through the statutory requirements for national curriculum geography (Figure 7.3) What is being taught and when? Are your colleagues well-informed about progression and continuity and how to achieve this?

Figure 7.3: National curriculum requirements in Key Stage 1

Time allocation KS1	36 hours per year
English through other subjects	36 hours per year
IT through other subjects	27 hours per year

Key Stage 1 programme of study: Attainment targets – Geography

All pupils are required to carry out three geographical investigations:
1 the locality of the school,
2 a contrasting locality,
3 a particular geographical theme (the quality of the environment in a
    locality).

Geographical Skills
1 **In studying places and a theme**, pupils should be taught to:
   a) observe their surroundings from different viewpoints, examine photographs, pictures
       and pictorial maps of places, and use an increasing range of geographical terms in
       describing what they see;
   b) use relevant information from material provided by the teacher to investigate particular
       places and themes;
   c) develop their geographical skills through work both in and out of the classroom.

2 **In studying places and a theme**, pupils should be taught to develop and use the following
   geographical skills:
   a) observing, communicating and recording information about places by asking and
       responding to questions about their surroundings;
   b) following directions, including the terms up, down, on, under, behind, in front of, near,
       far, left, right, north, south, east, west;
   c) using and making different kinds of maps and plans, both real and imaginary, at a
       variety of scales, using pictures/symbols and other aspects of a key;
   d) following a route on a plan or a map;
   e) using maps and a globe to identify major geographical features.

Places and Themes
Pupils should have the opportunity to investigate:
1 the locality of the school,
2 a contrasting locality, either in or beyond the United Kingdom,
3 the quality of the environment in a locality.

3 **In studying the physical and human features that give places their identity**, pupils
   should be taught:
   a) about the main physical and/or human features of the localities;
   b) about the effects of weather on themselves and their surroundings;
   c) how land and buildings are used;

Figure 7.3: (cont'd)

   d)   about similarities and differences between localities;
   e)   that the localities studied are set within a broader geographical context.

4 **In developing an awareness of places other than those studied directly**, pupils should
   be taught:
   a)   to give the address of their home;
   b)   to name the country in which they live;
   c)   that their own country is part of the United Kingdom, which is made up of England,
       Wales, Scotland and Northern Ireland;
   b)   to locate on a map the constituent countries of the United Kingdom;
   e)   to mark on a map of the United Kingdom approximately where they live.

5 **In investigating the quality of the environment in a locality**, pupils should be taught:
   a)   to express their likes and dislikes about the environment concerned;
   b)   about changes in that environment;
   c)   about ways in which the quality of that environment can be sustained and improved.

(Source: SCAA, 1994)

Do you know what is meant by progression and continuity? The definition below is taken from the Royal Society of Arts Report *Start Right* (1993):

> Continuity and progression are interlinked concepts relating to the
> nature and quality of children's learning experiences over time. Pro-
> gression is essentially the sequence built into children's learning through
> curriculum policies and schemes of work so that later learning builds
> on knowledge, skills, understanding and attitudes learned previously.
> Continuity refers to the nature of the curriculum experienced by chil-
> dren as they transfer from one setting to another . . . Continuity occurs
> when there is an acceptable match of curriculum and approach, allow-
> ing appropriate progression in children's learning. Effective assessment
> and record keeping systems are the keys to these ends. (Sylva, 1993).

The most effective way of assuring continuity and progression is to collect
a range of geography work – maps, plans, written descriptions of places –
and discuss them with your colleagues against your own knowledge of the
stages which children go through. Weigand (1993) discusses progression in
the development of map skills in his book *Children and Primary Geography*.

National curriculum level descriptions can also be used. The orders for
geography recommend that children in Key Stage 1 study the immediate
locality before moving on to study a contrasting locality. There is now no
requirement to study a locality in an economically developing country, but I
would include this in Year 2 work for the following reasons:

- Children may have knowledge gleaned from the media about the
  poor quality of life and conditions in several economically developing
  countries, which needs to be countered by unbiased information about
  life in, say, India.

- We live in a multicultural society. A consequence of this is the need for all children to begin to develop an understanding of life in other cultures, particularly those which may be a reflection of the lives of children in your schools.
- Many children travel extensively and have a considerable amount of first-hand experience which can be used in the classroom.

There are many themes that offer scope for geography. The list below shows how the geographical strand can be identified:

ourselves – our addresses, how leisure time is used, difference between leisure and work;

people who come to our school – the different activities they carry out;

going shopping – what goods and services are provided in the local shops?

colour – looking at colours on maps and what they refer to;

water – identifying sea from land, forms of water in the environment;

hot and cold – the weather, seasons, comparisons between hot and cold countries;

safety – where we play; is it safe? how could it be improved?

senses – looking around; what is pleasant? how could it be improved?

food – mapwork; where does our food come from? different types of farms;

The seaside – do features reveal the functions? is there a harbour?

How Much Time?

As outlined in Figure 7.3, thirty-six hours a year will need to be allocated to the teaching of geography in Key Stage 1. It will be necessary for you to discuss with the headteacher and colleagues how this time can be most effectively distributed. Are you blocking a period in each term or year for a geography-focused topic and allowing a regular amount of time for ongoing geographical work such as study of the weather and seasonal topics? It is important that you are able to quantify the amount of time and that this allocation ensures pupils are covering all the requirements of the geography curriculum. Are there some English skills, such as information-gathering and referencing which could be promoted through the geography curriculum?

Gathering Resources

Geographical work is dependent upon children having access to a range of resources such as maps, globes, photographs, aerial photographs, pictures and other artefacts which help to develop a sense of place. Is resourcing for

Figure 7.4: Essential resources for Key Stage 1 geography

Maps
Playmats – farm, roadways, streets in a town or village
Large scale maps of the areas around school to be used for fieldwork – you will need to make
    these
A4 base maps of the areas around school for use with older Key Stage 1 pupils
Plastic floor maps of the United Kingdom
Plastic floor map of the world (if your contrasting locality is another country)
A4 base maps of the UK with country boundaries marked
Plan of the school – inside and outside
Plans of individual classrooms
UK outline in the playground – directional arrow for north
Collection of tourist maps, picture maps, trails and so on
Supermarket plans
Atlases and group atlas and picture books
A globe for each classroom

Photographs
A selection of picture maps from *Child Education* and *Primary Geographer*
Oblique aerial photographs of the school and contrasting locality (Ask at your local secondary
    school)
Photographs of street furniture and landmarks around school

geography included in the school development plan? Present a list of costed essentials to the headteacher. The adoption of a published scheme is expensive and may not be suitable for your school's needs. However, do request inspection copies and select the aspects that are suitable for consideration. The range of software to support geography is growing. One of the most comprehensive programs is 'My World' which includes files on the weather and town and village plans for different age groups.

Will resources be centrally stored giving access to all staff? You will need to devise a system for monitoring this. Is there additional material for children with SEN, both the less and more able children? You may need to familiarize yourself with the requirements in Key Stage 2 for those Year 2 children who show particular aptitude for geography. A range of atlases, differently scaled maps and base maps of your own and contrasting localities are essential for the more able child. Figure 7.4 lists the essential resources for geography.

Providing for Nursery and Reception-aged Children

Access to structured play experiences which enable children to develop a sense of place is essential in the very early years and beyond. Structured construction play with a range of wooden blocks will give children the opportunity to create roadways, buildings and other structures seen in the environment. Provide these areas in the classroom with paper and clipboards, encourage the children to draw and display what they have made in the area, and count and sort the blocks that they have used. Can a partner make the same structure from the plan? Devise task cards for use with the playmats. Can the children draw the landmarks passed along the journey from the school to, say, the police station on the playmat? Ask the children to build a town with a church, school, supermarket and so on. Other possible activities include:

- draw a simple base map of the classroom. Mark where the teddy is hiding. Can the children find where it is? Only allow a small number of children to do this to avoid the chaos which might ensue if you have many children searching for teddy in the classroom.

- make a model from construction material and draw the finished product from a bird's eye view. Children need lots of practice at this.

- provide the children with silhouettes of familiar objects. Can they identify them?

It is important for you as the subject manager to emphasize that these experiences will lay the foundations for later geographical learning. As part of your role as manager it will be important that you are able to persuade your colleagues that geography or the human and social area of learning is vital for children's learning. The following section offers a rationale and a range of practical staff development activities you can carry out in school.

Sharing Teaching and Learning Strategies

As a subject manager, planning and leading staff development sessions for your colleagues will increase confidence and provide the opportunity for you to share practices you use in the classroom. Essentially in Key Stage 1 you need to encourage your colleagues to become geographers themselves by engaging in practical fieldwork, map making and reading and looking at the way in which play materials can develop conceptual understanding. Where can you start?

Planning a Staff Development Day
1   Identify, in liaison with the headteacher, a sequence of time for geography staff development to be put on the schools' professional development programme.
2   Start to gather resources. Audit the resources available and also the play materials in the nursery and reception class (see Figure 7.4).
3   Plan a sequence of activities for the staff themselves to engage in which will develop not only their own geographical understanding but also their understanding of the way in which their pupils learn about people and places. These are also examples of the kinds of teaching strategies to be used with the children.
4   Activities (Some examples follow).

Mapping a Route

This activity is suitable for reception, Year 1 and Year 2 classes. Ask teachers to work in pairs or fours.

Provide each group with four sheets of A3 paper taped together, and a series of photographs of landmarks and street furniture of a walk in the school grounds, from the school gate to the local shops or around the park. The task could be given an environmental focus by including pictures of graffitti, rubbish and other environmental hazards. The task is for the teachers to draw a very large scale map of the area depicted by their photographs, find the landmarks and features and mark these on their map. This exercise will involve the teachers in considering scale, plan view, concepts of place and space and the environment. It will also help them realize how difficult it is to draw a map of their own – something children are frequently expected to do. Ask the teachers to match this activity to the programmes of study and discuss the organizational implications of this in the classroom. It is important that children have access to a very large scale map of an area for directional, symbolic and plan view work.

In the classroom

Following group or whole class work with the large scale base map some children will be ready to make their own maps. In a reception class the children are likely to produce something along the lines of Figure 7.5, while in Year 1, they might produce something like Figure 7.6. These map representations will help you to assess your children's conceptual understanding, and help you to plan what they need to do next. Spatial awareness, plan view, orientation, symbolic representations and scale are all concepts which can be assessed from a map drawing.

Using Postcards to Develop an Understanding of Contrasting Environments

This activity is suitable for Year 1 and Year 2 classes. The teachers are to work in pairs for this activity.

Have available a selection of postcards clustered around the themes mentioned earlier: seaside, countryside, Lake District, urban environments, buildings (old and new), transport, rivers, etc. Give the group a list of six key geographical questions (p. 101) an atlas, globe (if appropriate) and writing materials (there may not be time for this). The task is for the teachers to find out as much as they can about the place on the postcard and to consider how to use this activity with their own classes. Have available a list of geographical words which can be introduced (Figure 7.7). Vocabulary related to the physical landscape is difficult for young children to conceptualize, consequently it will need a lot of reinforcement through fieldwork, pictures and photographs.

Figure 7.5: A 4-year-old's map representation of the journey between home and school

When I went to School I saw lamp Post and I saw

In the classroom

This is a very successful activity to develop new geographical language and to assess existing geographical knowledge. Provide children with blank postcard-sized cards to write their own messages home. Encourage the writing to address the key geographical questions. The children can design their own illustrations to include named landmarks. Very often children will draw their own map representation here.

Geography through Story

Using a story as a starting point for geographical investigation is within the grasp of all schools with a reasonable selection of picture and storybooks. For this workshop have available a collection of familiar stories. Ask the teachers

Figure 7.6: *A 6-year-old's map representation of the journey between home and school*

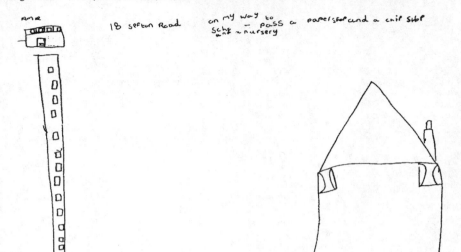

to apply the following criteria to judge how suitable they are for mapping the story, finding out about people's lives, or investigating what damages the environment. Indeed all three activities could be carried out using one story. The Dearing Report (1994) has suggested that English may be taught through other subjects for thirty-six hours a year. Geography-based stories provide a good basis for this as long as the text is appropriate for the reading level of the children. The following list of criteria may help you to judge the appropriateness of reading and interest level:

Is the content of the story within the children's experience?
What are the geographical features of this story – vocabulary, journey?
Can the children apply geographical skills as they record aspects of the
    story?
Does the story cover particular geographical themes?

A list of suitable stories are given at the end of this chapter. This activity could lead in to a planning exercise using one of the stories as a starting point. Give each group of teachers a planning grid (Figure 7.8) and ask them to discuss ways in which elements of the story could be used to provide the basis for work in the classroom. The examples below provides exemplars (Figures 7.9 and 7.10) based on two well-known stories: *Jyoti's Journey* by Helen Ganley (1986) and *When We Went to the Park* by Shirley Hughes (1985).

Figure 7.7: Geographical vocabulary in Key Stage 1

Physical geography	Weather and climate	Settlements	Transport	Economic activities	Locational words
Hill	Season	House	Road	Shops	Map
Stream	Desert wind	Shop	Car	Work	Plan
Slope	Rain	Park	Pedestrian	Jobs	Country
River	Cloud	Settlement	Canal	Farm	Area
Lake	Frost	Village	Railway	Factory	Place
Sea	Ice	Town	Journey	Service	Position
Waves	Storm	City	Transport	Quarry	North
Land	Weather	Building	Bridge	Mine	South
Soil	Spring		Tunnel		East
Pond	Summer				West
Steep	Autumn				Near/far
Gentle	Winter				Left/right
Beach	Snow				Up/down
Valley					
Mountain					
Wood					
Forest					
Rock					

(Source: NCC, 1993)

Discussion Activity Based on a Case Study

Give the staff a copy of this case study (Rodger, 1994a) or talk it through with the staff and discuss the way in which a geography-based activity can be used as a vehicle for the acquisition of basic literary skills in a reception class with the appropriate teacher intervention.

Case study

The teacher identified some expectations of the task based on the authorities' assessment and record keeping guidelines for geography:

1 follow simple instructions;
2 follow simple directions e.g.: around the room/outside;
3 identify familiar features in the local area;
4 make visits locally and talk about this;
5 represent by drawing buildings, roads and so on;
6 know that buildings are used for different purposes;
7 reflect features of the local area in drawings;
8 have an awareness of dislikes/likes in own environment.

To introduce the activity the four-year-old children were shown an oblique drawing of a school playground and encouraged to share with the teacher their perceptions of this picture. The children responded enthusiastically to this activity. The picture had elements with which they were familiar

Figure 7.8: A planning matrix to use in a staff development session: Using story as a stimulus for a geography topic

Curriculum Planning in the Early Years

	THEME		Subject	Geography
Geographical concepts	Geographical skills	Stories	Programme of Study	
	Activities	Resources	Learning Outcomes	Cross-Curricular Links
Discussion area				
Writing area				
Reading area				
Structured play area				
Mathematical area				
Construction area				
Creative area				
Scientific area				
Other first-hand experiences				

Figure 7.9: *Exemplar of planning using* when we went to the Park *by Shirley Hughes as a stimulus*

Curriculum Planning in the Early Years

Theme: Journeys in the local environment
Reception Class
Starting Points:
Talking about familiar journeys
Reading a story

When We Went to the Park
(Shirley Hughes)

Geographical Concepts

Place   river   wood
bridge
wall
pond
hill

Discussion Area

Sheet showing the route to the park   How to get to the park?
Walk, bus

Children to mark the features they
have seen and mark the route with arrows
What would you like in your own park?
Improving the environment

Scientific area

Mathematical Area

wet/dry sand and soil
Using the 3D map the children to   pouring water on to both
devise their own routes from A to B   What happens?
Children to direct each other   Differences between sand
   and soil
What did Grandad and child see as they walked around the
park?

Construction Area

People who work in the park

Make a 3D model of the park
with Lego or wooden blocks

Put the swings, slides, buildings
on the model/plan

Pictorially sequencing objects seen on
the journey and display as a zig-
zag book   Seasons

Reading Area   **Writing Area**

Listening tape or sounds   Language to include   Word bank
in the park   left/right   swing board
     under/on   concept keyboard and
     down/up   overlay link
     over

Creative Area

Children to colour, draw and stick   Paint pictures of the park
objects seen on the route onto a   and observational drawing of
large plan of the journey   features on the journey from
Sequence objects seen on the journey   photographs

Other first-hand experiences

Own park visit
Things to consider when planning own
visit to park
Photos,   map of the route
pre-visit   Features seen on the route to
toilets, undercover   Include buildings
route to follow

     safety aspects
     pictures of various parks and features

Figure 7.10: *Exemplar of planning using Jyoti's Journey by Helen Ganley as a stimulus*

Curriculum Planning in the Early Years

THEME: Journeys across the world   Year 2

Starting Points: *Jyoti's Journey* (H. Ganley)

Geographical Concepts

Place
Settlement
Town
similarity and difference

Discussion Area

Jobs
Local industry and jobs
Migration and
immigration

Housing

House style
Different buildings
and uses
Comparisons between India
and England

Geographical Skills

Observation – differences
between countries, housing,
customs, buildings, behavioural
patterns and clothes
Recording   Social Skills

Communication skills
Intellectual skills
Problem – solving:
how many ways can you
travel to India?

Writing Area

diaries of journeys
accounts of routes
to various places
write a holiday guide
rewrite the story

Reading Area

Read through the story
Show pictures and
discuss the story, using
locational vocabulary

Have a range of maps,
atlases, AA books,
travel guides in your
book corner

Creative Area

Food
Staple foods
In India and England
Make a rice meal

Ask an Indian parent
to come in to school
to make specialist
meal

Other first-hand experiences

Mapwork
studying maps
and globes
Making maps and plans
of journey from India to
England

Cultural and religious customs
Make a collection of cultural artefacts
Talk about these and draw from
direct observation
Talk about families and
differences between large
families and small single parent ones.

Scientific area

Differences in clothing and why
weather changes
Imaginative recollections of
fantasy journeys and real journeys
using other support material, e.g.
pictures, postcards.

Mathematical Area

Investigation of the
differences between
washing clothes in
the river and using
washing machines

Role Play

Indian wedding with all
the costumes

Scrap book of pictures of
India taken from travel brochures
etc.

(children playing, puddles, a football, policeman and a police car). Rather than seeing the policeman as a helpful figure the children suggested he had come, 'in case there is fighting', or 'in case there's been something stolen'. This introductory activity was carried out to help the teacher discover what knowledge and understanding the children were bringing to the activity and create 'a joint involvement episode' (Schaffer, 1992).

The children walked around the school with their teacher and identified a range of features. They saw . . . flowers (Nicholas), trees (Barry), football ground (John), playground (Janet). To assess the children's understanding of following directions each child was invited to touch three features in the playground in the order stated by the teacher. All the children achieved this. There was further evidence of recalling where and what they had seen back in the classroom as the children drew their representations of their walk on a large sheet of paper which they shared. The boys were much more spatially aware and able to record features in the order in which they were seen. The features seen on the walk were listed by the teacher on a flip chart to help those children label features on their own maps. Representations were accepted with encouraging comments from the teacher – usually relating to explanations of a particular symbol. The first hand experience was crucial in enabling the children to locate features in order.

Discussion

This activity can be analysed on two levels. First, it is possible to comment on the attitudes displayed by the children as they completed the task. They were involved, initially working independently, in creating their own mini-map alongside their peers. As the maps began to take shape and include features such as a ladder on the playground, the teacher with a group of children walking up the steps, trees, etc., playgrounds and school buildings began to delineate their boundaries. Several boys were anxious to position the features as they walked the route. The children responded, looking and talking about the picture and showing high levels of concentration. Playtime came and went. Other children were asked to leave the group as they 'are confusing us'. Behaviour and motivation increased. It was necessary for the children to cooperate in sharing resources (the felt pens). This led to high levels of collaboration. The sharing of one sheet of paper was a significant factor here.

At the second level in terms of children's learning, particularly geographical learning there is evidence of children identifying features in their environment, distinguishing between offices and shops: 'I think that's a flat . . . no, it's not, it's offices'. All the children were able to distinguish between the nursery and the school building. The children commented upon the flowers in the beds outside the main entrance, and all the flowers trampled on the field, but no one commented upon the graffiti on the doors and walls around school. The activity provided ample opportunity for the children to develop their speaking and listening skills. Mathematical skills were used to count and record accurately the number of trees and bushes seen on the trip. Positional and directional language was used extensively. Scientific process skills were used to some extent as the children observed closely the bushes and flowers in the playground. A range of language and reading skills were used as appropriate for four-year-old children – some writing labels to stick on to features on their map, others reading the list of features from the flip chart. The task was differentiated by outcome, and for assessment purposes provided an example of achievement in a range of curricular areas and at a number of levels. The activity was not restricted to highly structured closed worksheets, although at its inception planning was detailed and the teacher was clearly aware of the range of possible outcomes for the children. The characteristics of this activity were active involvement by the children, working cooperatively and the chance to critically question and enhance thinking as well as acquiring a range of basic skills.

Equal Opportunities

Stories and studies of children from other cultures can provide children with an understanding of these cultures. Be careful in your selection of material that you are not reinforcing stereotypes. *A Country Far Away* by Gray and Dupasquier is one such example. At one level the story compares the lives of two children, one in the UK living in a detached house somewhere in suburbia where dads and sons wash the cars and garden, while mum and daughter cook and clean the house. In the hot country the family live in a mud hut, run around scantily dressed and sit outside when it is school time, thus reinforcing the stereotype which most young children already hold of life in hot countries (Harrison and Harrison, 1989).

A much more appropriate story is *Somewhere in Africa* by Mennen and Daly, which explores the richness of African life through an African child reading a book borrowed from the library in the city in which he lives. An audit of materials should ensure that the children are getting a balanced view of other countries. There are a range of photographic packs depicting life in other countries, which although produced for older children, do provide a rich secondary resource for classrooms (Action Aid, 1993).

In this section of the chapter I have selected a range of activities that will enable children to be geographers. It is deliberately eclectic. Space does not enable me to cover a host of other activities which can be implemented in the classroom. The use of maps is fundamental to the study of geography, therefore within any geographical investigation have a range of maps, including Ordnance Survey (OS) maps, picture maps and aerial photographs. Children are fascinated by maps and although the study of OS maps is not included in the national curriculum, the display of an OS map at child height will provide endless opportunity for discussion about the meaning of symbols and provide a good support for any work that is being carried out on symbolic representation and map legends with children in Year 2.

Providing for Children with Special Educational Needs

Much of the programme of study for Key Stage 1 is written to enable all children have access to work which is at their level of capability. For example, in the programme of study it is stated that pupils will 'offer their own explanations for what they observe'. Have available a selection of photographs of the immediate environment for children to discuss (Hughes and Thomas, 1994). The area in which you as subject manager will need to ensure adequate provision is for those children at the upper end of the ability scale. Are there opportunities for pupils to develop information-finding skills using atlases? Can some children see the need for a key to the map? Can they invent symbols and see the need for consistency in their use?

All geographical activity is accessible for children with special educational needs. The way in which you expect children to record their findings may need particular attention. Is it possible for children to audio tape or video tape their findings about a specific environment? Humberside County Council (1992) has provided extensive guidelines on the teaching of geography to children with special educational needs in Key Stages 1–4. For example, can you provide taped sounds of seaside and other environments for visually impaired children?

Assessment and Record Keeping

Although the ten levels of achievement are still in place for all national curriculum subjects there has, since the review of the orders, been a change in the way in which assessments will be made of children's achievement in geography. It is recommended by SCAA (1994) that the programmes of study should guide the planning, teaching and day-to-day assessment of pupils' work. The essential function of level descriptions is to assist in the making of summary judgments about pupils' achievement as a basis for reporting at the end of a Key Stage. The introduction of level descriptions will absolve teachers from the need to use elaborate tick lists as the basis for assessment.

Records of the pupil's achievements in geography need to be collated and a matrix of achievement in relation to the national curriculum is required for parents. The most effective way of achieving this is to keep selected examples of children's work annotated with the date and level of achievement against level descriptions in the national curriculum orders. Can there be an element of self-assessment in this, whereby children themselves comment verbally to the teacher on their understanding of a particular activity and the teacher records the relevant parts of this discussion to be added to the annotated record? Can you as subject manager suggest ways in which this can be managed in a busy classroom? Do you have non-contact time? If not can you negotiate it?

Geography and the Early Years Curriculum

One aspect of geography which is central to the early years curriculum is the first-hand exploration of the environment and the acquisition of a range of skills which will help children to understand that environment. Indeed, as the programme of study for geography states, 'much of the pupil's learning should be based on direct experiences, practical activities and fieldwork in the locality of the school' (SCAA, 1994, p. 2). It is necessary to ensure that first-hand investigations will have at their centre the following essential geographical questions which will ensure the acquisition and development of geographical knowledge about the environments or *places*. These are:

What is this place like? – this will involve the collection of information and evidence about places from maps, photographs, and books.

Where is this place? – using locational knowledge and reference and information-finding skills.

Why is this place as it is? – this will encourage curiosity and causal links between, for example, climate and what people wear.

How is this place connected to other places? – this will develop economic awareness in children as they investigate communication networks.

How is this place changing? – a more difficult question for young children, but one which can be successfully addressed in terms of the effects of the environment on familiar places.

What would it feel like to be in this place? – an essential question for young children to enable them to enter the imagined worlds in their storywriting and role play activities (Storm, 1989, p. 4).

An OFSTED report (1994b, p. 14) cites the importance of good questioning skills to assess pupils' knowledge and challenge their thinking as a factor associated with high standards of achievement in more than 50 per cent of lessons observed.

David Mills (1988) discusses the ways in which young children come to terms with the 'real world'. That is, the world in which things have a place (of knowing where things are), of making journeys around and to places for a purpose, of becoming aware of distant places and reading of places. Children come to terms with this 'real world' through play. Their understandings of the 'real world' develops as they make-believe. Children need to fantasize and act out everyday situations to begin to see there are other perspectives than their own. This will lead children to an awareness and an ability to interpret and adapt to the world around them. (Figure 7.11).

Figure 7.11: The importance of geography in child development

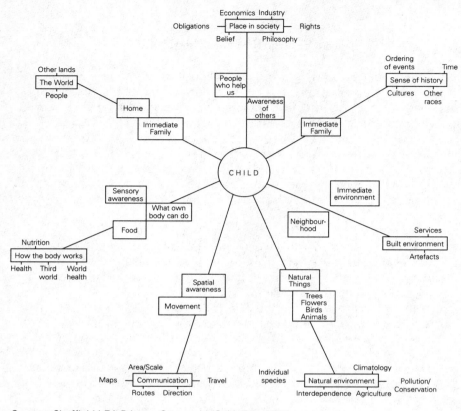

Source: Sheffield LEA Primary Geography Guidelines 1990.

Mills (1988) further suggests that to grow as geographers children need to develop and have experiences in the following ways to develop a sense of place:

1 a sense of locational awareness;
2 a sense of territory;
3 constant interaction with places;
4 association of people and places;
5 a fascination for and a curiosity about the world about them;
6 opportunity for place play;
7 feelings for places.

It can be seen that the sense of place plays an important part in children's development.

Without it people would possess no sense of home or homecoming, no sense of familiarity or novelty in a place, no awareness to recall or anticipate places, no ability to move thoughtfully around the environment or to relate other places to our own, no curiosity about our world, nor any concern for our environment. In short without a sense of place we could neither survive nor grow (Mills, 1988, p. 13).

Essentially this part of the chapter is aiming to demonstrate that the study of geography is an important part of young children's learning entitlement. The practicalities of geographical enquiry necessitate children acquiring a set of geographical skills, attitudes and concepts. These attributes will be more readily acquired through the study of photographs, maps and through active participation in fieldwork.

Geography and the Basic Curriculum

Geography can provide the context for much reinforcement of basic skills in language and numeracy. It may provide a context for structured play. For example:

In a Year 1 lesson, two pupils simulated a voyage on a sailing boat that had a rudder, and a sail that could be raised and lowered. They dressed and played their roles appropriately, and drew maps of their imaginary journey. In another class the pupils acted the role of an estate agent: locating houses on a map, drawing pictures of the houses and preparing simple descriptions for potential purchasers learned a number of valuable geographical skills (OFSTED, 1993, p. 7).

In 1993 the government commissioned Sir Ron Dearing to reduce the content in the national curriculum (SCAA, 1994) to make it more manageable for teachers in school. There were also to be recommendations for the amount of time to be spent by children on each subject. From the information in Figure 7.3 there is a clear message that some of the English and IT curriculum must be taught in the context of other subjects. Earlier responses to the national curriculum English proposals by the Geographical Association pointed out that 'for all the English attainment targets, geographical and environmental work provides a meaningful and motivating *context* for the acquisition of language skills'. This is logical when one considers that the curriculum in Key Stage 1 is often planned using a topic-based approach. As far as geography is concerned the case studies described earlier clearly illustrate the way in which geography has provided the context in which children have the opportunity to practice some basic speaking and listening, numeracy, reading and writing skills and geographical skills of observation, communication, recording of information and responding to questions about their surroundings.

Another major task will be to give your colleagues confidence that *they* have the necessary knowledge and understanding to teach geography themselves. There is some evidence that this is one of the major reasons why geography has been excluded from the primary curriculum in the past

> About half the teachers needed to be better informed about the geography order. Many of these had insufficient knowledge to plan effectively and in these cases the pupils' standard of work in geography was at a level below what was reasonable to expect (OFSTED, 1993b, p. 8).

The new orders for geography are less daunting, one attainment target for geography and no requirement for testing at the end of each Key Stage.

Last, but not least, a reminder that being a subject manager does not cease once you have your policy, resources and schemes of work in place. It will be your responsibility to monitor and evaluate the geography curriculum. Are your colleagues satisfied with the scheme and the resources? A planned meeting to discuss this is more effective than reliance on snatches of conversations picked up in the staffroom. Do you have non-contact time to support your colleagues? Can you organize this to support fieldwork particularly? Do you make time to liaise with the English subject manager to discuss the way in which the study of places can provide the context for oral and written work?

The study of our immediate locality, the work people do, the types and uses of buildings, the use of land and how people travel from home to work, from home to school and from one place to another are the fundamental firsthand experiences provided by teachers in schools to engage, motivate and interest children in their learning. These topics are also central to the study of geography. This is the message that you as subject manager need to get over to your colleagues. Good luck!

References

ALEXANDER, R., ROSE, J. and WOODHEAD, C. (1992) *Curriculum Organisation and Classroom Practice in the Primary School*, London, HMSO.

BRUCE, T. (1987) *Early Childhood Education*, Sevenoaks, Hodder and Stoughton.

DEARING, Sir R. (1994) *The National Curriculum and its Assessment: Final Report*, London SCAA.

DEPARTMENT OF EDUCATION (1967) *Children and their Primary Schools*, (The Plowden Report), A Report of the Central Advisory Council for Education (England) Volume 1, The Report, London, HMSO.

DEPARTMENT OF EDUCATION AND SCIENCE (DES) (1978) *Primary Education in England, A Survey by HM Inspectors of Schools*, London, HMSO.

DEPARTMENT OF EDUCATION AND SCIENCE (DES) (1989) *Aspects of Primary Education, The Teaching and Learning of History and Geography*, London, HMSO.

EARLY YEARS CURRICULUM GROUP (1990) *The Early Years and the National Curriculum*, Stoke, Trentham.

GANLEY, H. (1986) *Jyoti's Journey*, London, Deutsch.

HARRISON, P. and HARRISON, S. (1991) *Primary Geographer*, Autumn.

HUGHES, J., PEARSON, M., RODGER, R. and SMITH, A. (1992) *Ginn Geography Key Stage 2* Aylesbury, Ginn and Co.

HUGHES, J. and THOMAS, D. (1994) 'Geography for school children,' in MARSDEN, B. and HUGHES, J. *Primary School Geography*, London, David Fulton.

HUGHES, S. (1985) *When we went to the Park*, London, Walker.

HUMBERSIDE COUNTY COUNCIL (1992) 'Practical approaches to increasing access to geography', *Support for Learning*, **8** (2) (1993) pp. 70–76.

HURST, V. (1994) 'The implications of the National Curriculum for nursery education', in BLENKIN, G.M. and KELLY, A.V. (eds) *The National Curriculum and Early Learning*, London, Paul Chapman.

MILLS, D. (ed.) (1988) *Geographical Work in Primary and Middle Schools*, Sheffield, Geographical Association.

NATIONAL CURRICULUM COUNCIL (NCC) (1993) *Planning the National Curriculum at Key Stage 2*, York, NCC.

NUTBROWN, C. (1994) *Threads of Thinking. Young Children Learning and the Role of Early Education*, London, Paul Chapman.

OFFICE FOR STANDARDS IN EDUCATION (OFSTED) (1993a) *Geography Key Stages 1, 2 and 3, First Year 1991–92*, London, HMSO.

OFSTED (1993b) *Geography Key Stages 1, 2 and 3, Second Year 1992–93*, London, HMSO.

OFSTED (1994a) *The Handbook for the Inspection of Schools Technical Paper 11*, London, HMSO.

OFSTED (1994b) *Primary Matters. A Discussion on Teaching and Learning in Primary Schools*, London, OFSTED.

RODGER, R.S. (1994a) 'Subjects in the early years curriculum?' *European Early Childhood Education Research Journal*, **2** (2).

RODGER, R.S. (1994b) 'A quality curriculum for the early years', in ABBOTT, L. and RODGER, R.S. *Quality Education in the Early Years*, Buckingham, Open University Press.

RODGER, R.S. (forthcoming 1995) *Four Year Olds in School, An Examination of Provision and Practice in One LEA*.

SCHAFFER, H.R. (1992) Joint Involvement Episodes as a context for development in McGurk, H. (ed.) *Childhood Social Development*, Hove, LEA.

SCHOOL CURRICULUM AND ASSESSMENT AUTHORITY (SCAA) (1994) *Draft Proposals for Geography in the National Curriculum*, London, Department for Education.

SHEFFIELD LEA (1990) *Guidelines for Primary Geography*, Sheffield, Sheffield Education Department.

STORM, M. (1989) 'The five basic questions for primary geography', *Primary Geographer*, 2, Autumn.

WEIGAND, P. (1993) *Children and Primary Geography*, London, Cassell.

Useful Addresses

The Geographical Association
343 Fulwood Road
Sheffield S10 3BP
The largest subject teaching association representing the interests of geography education in the UK

Action Aid
The Old Church House
Church Steps
Frome
Somerset BA11 1PL
Good range of resources for primary schools, including photo resource packs about urban and rural life in India, Kenya and Peru

Development Education Centre
Selly Oak Colleges
Bristol Road
Birmingham B29 6LE

Learning Through Landscapes
Third Floor
Southside Offices
The Law Courts
Winchester
Hampshire
An organisation aiming to transform the quality and use of the school grounds

The Tidy Britain Group
The Pier
Wigan
WN3 4EX
A campaigning organisation working to create a litter-free and beautiful Britain

World Wide fund for Nature (WWF)
Panda House
Wayside Park
Godalmimg
Surrey GU7 1XR
Working to save endangered species and habitats

Appendix: Developing Geographical Understanding Through Stories

Books marked with an * should be useful for independent or shared reading. They are characterized by simple, bold text and colourful illustrations matched to the page text.

Going to the Seaside

ARDIZZONE, E. (1977) *Little Tim and the Brave Sea Captain*, Picture Puffin.
ARMITAGE, R. (1989) *The Lighthouse Keeper's Lunch.**
BAKER, J. (1987) *Where the Forest meets the Sea*, Julie MacRae Books.
BARBER, A. (1993) *The Mousehole Cat*, Walker Books.
FOREMAN, M. (1980) *Jack's Fantastic Voyage*, Anderson.
GARLAND, S. (1980) *The Seaside Christmas Tree*, Collins Book Bus.
HILL, P. (1985) *The Noisiest Class goes to the Beach*, Hippo.
McAFEE, A. and BROWNE, A. (1984) *The Visitors who came to Stay*, Hamilton.
McGOUGH, R. (1992) *The Lighthouse that Ran Away*, Red Fox.

Going to Other Countries

AHLBERG, J. and AHLBERG A. (1991) *The Jolly Postman*, Heinemann.
DUPASQUIER, P. (1985) *Dear Daddy*, Anderson Press*.
GANLEY, H. (1986) *Jyoti's Journey*, Andre Deutsch.
GRAY, N. (1990) *A Balloon for Grandad*, Picture Lions.
GRAY, N. and DUPASQUIER, P. (1988) *A Country Far Away*, (pbk). (This book shows very stereotyped images of life in other countries.), Puffin Books.
ISADORA, R. (1993) *At the Crossroads*, Red Fox.
MATHIESON, F. (1990) *Very Hot Samosas* (one of a series) Black.
MENNEN, I. and DALY, N. (1992) *Somewhere in Africa*, The Bodley Head. (Compare this book with *A Country Far Away* and discuss with older children how the authors represent the country.) Red Fox.
ONYEFULU, L. (1993) *A is for Africa*, Francis Lincoln (an alphabet book).
WADDELL, M. (1983) *Going West*, Andersen Press (hbk).
WILSON, B. (1991) *The Turtle and the Island*, Colour Knight.

Living in a City

BAKER, J. (1984) *Home in the Sky*, Julia MacRae Books.
BROWNE, A. (1977) *A Walk in the Park*, Macmillan (pbk).
HUGHES, S. (1985) *When We Went to the Park*, Walker*.
KEATS, E.J. (1964) *Whistle for Willy*, Bodley Head.

Rivers

ALTHEA (1977) *Desmond Goes Boating*, Dinosaur.
GINSBURG, M. (1982) *Across the Stream*, Julie MacRae Books*.
HUGHES, S. (1990) *Out and About*, Walker.

The Environment

BENNETT, D. (1990) *The Lonely Whale*, Kingfisher.
BROWN, R. (1991) *The World that Jack Built*, Anderson.

BURNINGHAM (1991) *Oi, Get Off Our Train*, Red Fox (pbk) Cape (hbk)*.
CHERRY, L. (1994) *The Great Kapok Tree*.
COWCHER, H. (1988) *Rainforest*, Deutsch.
COWCHER, H. (1990) *Antarctica*, Andre Deutsch.
FOREMAN, M. (1972) *Dinosaurs and all that Rubbish*.
FOREMAN, M. (1990) *One World*, Anderson.
JORDAN, M. and JORDAN, T. (1993) *Jungle Days, Jungle Nights*, Kingfisher.
RAY, M.L. (1993) *A Rumbly Tumbly Glittery Gritty Place*, New York, Harcourt Brace and Co.
SNAPE, J. and SNAPE, C. (1992) *Giant*, Walker.
WALLWORK, A. (1993) *No Dodos* Ragged Bears (The endangered species counting book).

The Countryside, Local Environments

HUGHES, S. (1985) *When We Went to the Park*, Walker Books*.
HUTCHINS, P. (1968) *Rosie's Walk*, The Bodley Head.
HUTCHINS, P. (1988) *Where's the Baby?* The Bodley Head.
KEATS, E.J. (1971) *Over in the Meadow*, Hamish Hamilton.
MARIS, R. (1984) *Are You There Bear?*
MARIS, R. (1987) *In My Garden*.
MURPHY, J. (1982) *On the Way Home*, Macmillan.
PFISLER, M. (1987) *Penguin Pete*, Hippo (pbk) (Antarctica and weather) (Translation by Bell, A. (1987)).
ROGERS, P. (1986) *Sheepchase*, Viking Kestrel.
TAFURI, N. (1984) *Have You Seen My Duckling?* Julia MacRae*.
WOOD, J. (1970) *Grandmother Lucy Goes for a Picnic*.

Cold Places

COWCHER, H. (1990) *Antarctica*, Deutsch.
HEDDERWICK, M. (1989) *Peedie Peebles' Summer or Winter Book*, Red Fox.
JOOSSE, M. (1992) *Mama Do You Love Me?* Little Brown.
VYNER, T. and VYNER, S. (1992) *Arctic Spring*, Gollancz.

Journeys

FLINDALL, J. (1988) *The Journey Home*, Walker.
GERAGHTY, P. (1992) *Monty's Journey*, Picture Lions.

Chapter 8

Starting Off On the Right Note

Rita Walker

It is frequently held that music is a subject best left to experts; it certainly has a 'mystique' surrounding it that is not paralleled by other subjects. In 1985 HMI noted that:

> Music is included in the curriculum of most schools for pupils up to the age of 16. At the nursery and infant stages and in classes at the younger end of the junior school, music should be an integral part of every child's daily experience. An element of specialised music teaching, often with the support of a music consultant, is introduced after the age of 8 (HMI, 1985, p. 1, para. 2).

Following an inspection of 285 primary schools in England between 1982 and 1989 and visits to schools which showed good practice in music, HMI noted that:

> All the primary schools visited included music in their curriculum, but the content of the music teaching and the quality of the musical achievements of the children varied considerably within and between the schools . . .
> Few schools had a clearly defined policy and effective schemes of work for music which also incorporated the assessment of pupils' progress and achieved a good balance of contributions from class-teachers and music specialists (HMI, 1992, p. 7).

One benefit of the inclusion of music as a national curriculum subject at Key Stage 1 might be that some of the mystique may be removed; many teachers will feel a sense of relief that general guidelines have been introduced for the subject.

This chapter will look at the coordination of music at Key Stage 1 with special regard to the achievement of continuity, progression and a whole school approach.

Why Do We Teach Music at Key Stage 1?

- Peoples from all cultures have the need to share innermost thoughts, emotions and reflections in non-verbal ways.
- Experiences can be recorded, symbolized and interpreted by systems of organized sounds in music.
- Music promotes the development of aesthetic and spiritual values.
- Music is important in assisting the development of the child's creative, expressive and imaginative skills.
- It contributes to personal development through individual satisfaction gained by singing, playing, composing and listening.
- Joy and pleasure are gained from shared experiences of music making in a social context.
- Music is accessible to children of all abilities.
- It promotes the development of communication skills.
- It can be carried over into, and can grow out of, children's music experiences outside school (from home, playgroup, church and neighbourhood), contributing to enjoyment and relaxation.

Above all, music is a unique form of expression with its own conceptual framework. The power and value of music ought to be an integral part of the life of every young child. Music experiences should be enjoyable, positive and creative.

Your Role as Music Coordinator

How do you see your role? It would be wise to read through Chapter 1 of this book, in which Mike Harrison sets out four roles.

Music coordinators have a special role in leading and supporting other members of staff who might vary from those with special music skills to those (the majority) who are hesitant in this subject area. Some basic questions for consideration will include the following. You might like to list some others.

- Would you describe yourself as a music specialist, one with a few musical skills, a facilitator or a prompter?
- How do your headteacher and governing body define your job?
- Do other members of staff have definite expectations from your role in music?
- Does your school meet the musical needs of all of its pupils?
- Does the school have a clear music scheme, familiar and available to all?
- Are the national curriculum requirements for Key Stage 1 in music being met?

Whole School Planning

It is important for all teachers to be aware of the progression of music from reception class to Year 2. A policy and scheme of work for Key Stage 1 should therefore be constructed in conjunction with all members of staff so that it is a realistic, practicable and workable document. Planning in music for Key Stage 1 is just as important as planning for Key Stage 2.

Be discreet and aware of the fact that you are at the beginning of your career, whereas other colleagues may have taught for many years, be highly experienced and skilful, and yet know little about music.

A Programme for Music at Key Stage 1

It would be wise to arrange an early meeting with the whole staff to discuss music policy and schemes of work. Several factors should assist you in this formulation, such as:

- the musical needs of your children, the circumstances and teaching situations of your school and the input that the staff can make into music;
- national curriculum attainment targets and programmes of study in music;
- published music schemes and texts such as *Springboards: Ideas in Music* (Farmer, 1984) and the *Silver Burdett* scheme. Major publishers are now producing materials to support national curriculum requirements (see section on resources);
- local authority guidelines and advisory services.

Here are some questions that you could ask your colleagues when planning for curriculum music:

- How do you provide for music education in school at present?
- Are you familiar with Key Stage 1 requirements?
- Does an overall scheme of work already exist? In a written form?
- In which areas of music do you feel confident and capable?
- Do you use any published scheme, LEA guidelines or school broadcasting to implement your plans for music?
- What are the music resources of the school? Are there any gaps? Are present materials accessible to all?
- Can you identify and plan for pupils' special musical needs?
- Do you ever attend music courses in or out of school? If so, how do you share ideas and communicate back to colleagues?

Try to get to know about philosophy, ideas and current thinking in music education in addition to national curriculum orders and guidelines. The organization of music at Key Stage 1 should be such as to promote the enjoyment, understanding and response of children through the practical activities of performing, composing and listening. This should be central to your policy and schemes, giving basic guidelines to the staff, mirroring a whole school approach to music.

Helping your colleagues to understand the national curriculum directives should form a major part of your work as coordinator. You must, of course, study them yourself, and bear in mind that colleagues are already under pressure from the demands of many other subjects.

National Curriculum Music

The Dearing Review has proposed a reduction in statutory content since the published order for national curriculum music in April 1992: 'The overall aim of the changes to the music Order is to clarify the essential skills, knowledge and understanding which should be taught, whilst safeguarding the breadth of the curriculum' (DFE 1995, p. ii).

There are now two attainment targets in England: Performing and Composing and Listening and Appraising. The attainment targets are shown by means of end of Key Stage descriptions for music pointing to the nature and span of performance that pupils should show by the end of a Key Stage.

Key Stage 1 involves the following descriptions of attainment targets:

AT1: Performing and Composing
Pupils sing a variety of songs and play simple pieces and accompaniments with confidence and awareness of pulse. They explore, select and order sounds, making compositions that have a simple structure and make expressive use of the musical elements including dynamics and timbre.

AT2: Listening and Appraising
Pupils respond to short pieces of music, recognising repetition and changes within the musical elements. They listen attentively and describe and compare sounds and pieces of music using simple terms.
(Music in the National Curriculum, 1995, p. 9)

There are now three parts to the programmes of study:

1 introductory statements taken from the general requirements in the current order;
2 general programme of study, common to all Key Stages, providing continuity of musical opportunities from the ages of 5 to 14. These opportunities are:

AT1

- *control sounds* made by the voice and a variety of tuned and untuned instruments;
- *perform with others*, and develop awareness of audience, venue and occasion;
- *compose* in response to a variety of stimuli and explore resources such as voices, instruments and sounds from the environment;
- *refine, record and communicate* musical ideas.

AT2

- *develop knowledge* of music from different times and places;
- *respond to and evaluate* live and recorded music including their own and others' compositions and performances.

3   Key Stage specific programmes of study that clarify the requirements of the present order and define essential skills, knowledge and understanding to be taught. Each Key Stage now has fewer statements; there has been a refinement of progression and direct relationships across Key Stages, together with a reduction in non-statutory examples.

There are no Standard Assessment Tasks (SATs) in music. The end of Key Stage descriptions are designed to assist teachers in judging how their pupils' attainment in performing and composing, listening and appraising meets national expectations. Assessment should be continuous and founded on the teacher's observations.

Plan Ahead

- Become familiar with Key Stage 1 in the national curriculum order for music (NCC, 1992) and the Dearing proposals (SCAA, 1994). The new orders circulated to schools in January 1995 come into effect in August, 1995.
- Attempt to locate the strengths and weaknesses of the present music provision in your school.
- Do not create a policy/statement/scheme on your own for Key Stage 1. A successful music curriculum should be a goal for all staff.
- Prior to any meetings try to write up some simple statements and criteria for broad areas of music assessment. Use the programme of study for music Key Stage 1, any LEA guidelines and existing school documentation, incorporating links between music and other subjects.
- Bear in mind that there are many ways of writing up a school music document.

A Sample Scheme for Key Stage 1

This sample should be looked upon merely as a starting-point, giving you ideas and providing a stimulus for your policy and schemes. The main aim of music teaching in school is to foster each pupil's sensitivity to, and understanding and enjoyment of, music through the activities of listening, performing and composing. More general aims include:

1 The development of skills in performing and composing music so as to be able to:

- perform rhythmic and melodic patterns by ear and from simple notation;
- sing in groups and play simple instruments;
- make up simple pieces of music;
- record compositions, store them away and play them to others.

2 The development of listening to and appraising music of various historical periods and styles:

- European classical music;
- folk and popular music;
- music from the British Isles;
- Music from varying western and non-western cultures;
- The children's own simple compositions.

Reception: 4/5 Years Old

In this year the children should be developing an understanding of basic music concepts.

1 *Rhythm* through various musical activities:

- *beat* – using body movements, clapping and patting knees, walking to familiar songs, poems or chants, using untuned percussion instruments;
- *rhythmic patterns* – speech rhythms, e.g. children's names, objects in the classroom, topic words. Combine these into short rhythmic compositions. Clap these patterns. Clap patterns of simple songs, e.g. *Lucy Locket*;
- *long and short sounds* – using instruments, e.g. claves (short sound), triangle (long sound), to explore sound and produce compositions.

2 *Melody* – high and low sounds (wide intervals):

- relate high and low to objects in the environment and to pitch levels;

- observation of sounds outside the classroom;
- pictures and charts in the classroom of high and low sounds observed by the children;
- perform songs from memory using high and low, e.g. *See Saw*;
- Percussion instruments that make high and low sounds;
- Other instruments that make high and low sounds using recorded music, e.g. *In the Hall of the Mountain King* by Grieg, *The Carnival of the Animals* by Saint-Saëns.

3 *Dynamics* – loud and soft:

- playing instruments to explore loud and soft:

  - using instruments to accompany songs;
  - choosing the best instrument to highlight the mood of songs;
  - card spinner with different instructions for sounds.

- recorded music;
- singing songs, introduce getting louder/softer.

4 *Speed/tempo* – fast and slow:

- performing songs at different tempos;
- listening to recordings that show tempo variety, e.g. movements from *Nutcracker Suite* by Tchaikovsky.

Year 1: 5/6 Years Old

This year should be a continuation and development of the reception year.

1 *Rhythm*:

- *beat* – maintaining beat using untuned percussion, drawing the beat of a piece of music;
- *rhythmic patterns* – continue speech patterns introducing more complex ones, e.g. *Li' 1 Liza Jane*. Reading patterns from simple symbols. Sound and silence – introduce a rest to patterns. Use two to four rhythmic patterns to form compositions of contrasting words/phrases;
- *long and short sounds* – further practice;
- create a sound picture using untuned percussion in response to a given stimulus – poem, picture or story etc., perhaps forming part of topic work.

2   *Melody* – high, low and in-between:

- use hand signals to show high and low (wide and narrow intervals), extend to introduce in-between sounds;
- create a sound picture as for rhythm, but including melodic instruments.

3   *Dynamics* – louder and softer:

- use hand signals to indicate if a passage of music is getting louder or softer;
- perform compositions from other areas using dynamics.

4   *Tempo* – fast and slow:
Sing or perform music (showing control of breathing, dynamics and pitch) at different tempos and discuss which is most appropriate to the music.

5   *Musical Styles*:
Introduce the children to a number of different styles and genres of music, for example:

> Negro spirituals,
> Polish and Hungarian children's songs,
> Folk music from the British Isles,
> American folk music,
> Caribbean calypsos,
> *Four Seasons* by Vivaldi.

Introduce varied characters and moods in pieces of music.

6   *Tone Colour*:
Looking at orchestral instruments and listening to the sound they produce:

> *Young Person's Guide to the Orchestra* by Britten,
> *The Little Train* by Villa Lobos,
> *Sorcerer's Apprentice* by Dukas,
> *Peter and the Wolf* by Prokofiev,
> *Lieutenant Kijé* by Kodály.

Year 2: 6/7 Years Old

The work this year should continue to build on the foundations laid in the reception class and Year 1.

1 *Rhythm*:

- explore a variety of rhythmic patterns using written symbols, e.g. Mobile Roof Game, Pass on the Message Game (Farmer, 1984);
- perform rhythm chants using dynamics;
- syncopation – using four beats, clapping for strong beats, patting knees for weak beats. Coloured cards can also be used;
- create sound pictures using rhythm in response to a given stimulus.

2 *Melody* – high, low, in-between and melodies that move up/down:

- using hand signals as for Year 1;
- teacher plays ascending/descending tunes on chime bars, xylophone, piano (or other melodic instrument) playing each note several times, children join in/compose their own tunes;
- children follow with their hands ascending/descending tunes, identifying which is which;
- create sound pictures using melodic instruments;
- representation of own compositions by graphic scores.

3 *Dynamics*:
Louder and softer should be incorporated into all composition and performance at this stage.

4 *Tempo*:
Fast and slow – further practice and continuation of Year 1.

5 *Form* – AB and ABA shapes:

- using picture cards to illustrate traditional songs;
- build AB and ABA forms using rhythmic patterns already explored;
- recognition of repeated rhythms and melodies.

6 *Tone Colour*:

- as for Year 1, but extended and developed;
- choosing and using classroom instruments to accompany songs. Use of drones and simple ostinati, both rhythmic and melodic.

7 *Texture*:
Introduce simple rounds into the repertoire of the children.

8 *Musical Styles*:
Discuss different styles of music using elements and language children

have developed whilst at school. Relate these pieces to work in history, geography, dance, drama, etc.

Making Musical Links

There are several lines of action for integrated work:

1   topic or thematic approach. Music can be woven into the topic with songs, stories with music, action games and simple creative work;
2   non-classroom activities, such as outings to the seaside, into the countryside, to an art gallery, a science museum or an urban farm, may encourage a response such as imitating environmental sounds, creating simple rhythms or melodies. Too often, on these occasions, we ask children what they *saw*, neglecting what they *heard*.
3   music can add to the understanding and appreciation of other subjects, e.g. the study of a period of history or reading a poem.

Some examples of links for integrated work in music and other subject areas:

English:	making up rhythms to words, singing songs, stimulating language development, pronunciation and vocabulary, music contributing to drama;
Mathematics:	counting and number songs, counting of notes and rests, beats and time, exploring shapes in mathematics and music;
Science:	sounds from the environment – listening, identifying and copying, sorting and controlling sounds;
Art:	responding to listening to music by creating a picture/collage/design, pictorial/symbolic depiction of music by shapes, patterns, structures and textures;
Movement/Dance/PE:	music as a stimulus for dance, rhythmic movements: fast and slow, exploring moods and feelings;
History:	the place of music in past times, different eras and countries;
Geography:	music from other countries and cultures, music helping to bring about a sense of place;
Technology:	designing and making simple musical instruments, investigating instruments, using a computer to create, edit or store sounds;
Religious Education:	hymns, songs, readings and drama in corporate acts of worship.

Figure 8.1:   *Music and other subjects*

Music can shed light on and enhance the understanding of another subject or topic (see Figure 8.1).

Musical Elements

Care in planning is essential. Ensure that the development of the children's conceptual knowledge of music is not disregarded or weakened. Some of the ideas and terms in the national curriculum documents may need to be explained to colleagues. The following musical elements which should figure in any scheme of work have explanations here using simple terms:

- Pitch: the height or depth of sounds. High/Low. Simple pictures or stretching/crouching movements can help;
- Duration: the length of sounds. Long/Short;
- Pulse: the 'heartbeat' of music. It can go slowly or quickly;
- Rhythm: the movement of music;
- Dynamics: Loud and soft;
- Speed: Fast/Slow;
- Timbre: the quality of a sound, e.g. harsh/bright/metallic;
- Texture: one sound or more at a time;
- Structure: shapes and patterns; repetition and contrast; verse and chorus.

Assessment

Assessment in music should help you to note an individual child's strengths and weaknesses and assist you in the planning of future lessons. Discuss assessment procedures with your colleagues; you will probably discover that the assessment of children's musical achievements is an area where they have limited experience.

Teachers at Key Stage 1 are required to report to parents on the children's progress. There is no statutory obligation to reach judgments against end of Key Stage descriptions. However, the assessment procedures that you eventually adopt should relate closely to the national curriculum. Some points to note:

- the scheme should be straightforward and simple, proving helpful to teachers, parents and pupils;
- it should be part of everyday classroom activities such as singing, composing and listening;
- it should take into account extracurricular or instrumental teaching;
- keep cumulative records on pupils' attainment – the end of Key Stage descriptions should assist you;
- observe children taking part in music (e.g. singing in a whole class song, making up a little composition or talking about music) and try to assess the *way* in which they work as well as the finished product;
- try to observe the children's progress over a period, noting how it is part of the child's general development and the class of which he or she is a member.

Musical Materials

As a coordinator entering into a school one of the essential things to do is to assess whether the school has the necessary resources to teach music to its full capacity. Thought needs to be given to how existing resources can best be used from a central point or in individual classrooms. This will affect the types and number of resources and instruments required and what other materials need to be obtained. Spend your limited money wisely.

Act Now

- Note the instruments that are in working order. Note their type, number, condition and location.
- Set up a repair programme for those in poor condition.
- Identify gaps in provision.
- Sketch out plans for future upkeep (e.g. maintenance and tuning of pianos, sets of spare beaters, guitar strings, etc.).

The following lists should assist you in establishing items of school music equipment:

Basic classroom percussion (untuned)
These do not give a definite pitched sound, but add rhythm, interest and colour.

Woodblocks:	including two-tone woodblocks, wooden agogo, claves, temple or tulip block;
Drums:	including tambour, snare drum (various sizes), bongos, tabla drums;
Tambourines:	headless and headed in various sizes;

Maracas:	especially tricoloured ones;
Castanets:	on a handle;
Triangles:	small and large, with holder and metal beater;
Bells:	of various size including Indian bells, sleigh bells, stick jingles, bell trees and cowbell.
Cymbals:	suspended or fitted with knobs, miniature cymbals, finger cymbals;
Guiro:	especially tricoloured fish guiro;
Gong.	

Basic classroom percussion (tuned)

These give notes of definite pitch and can be used for tunes and chords.

Chime bars:	several full sets;
Xylophone:	start with alto;
Glockenspiel:	start with alto;
Bass resonator bars.	

Other important equipment includes the following:

An assortment of beaters: felt-headed, plastic, rubber and wood; metal beaters for triangles;
Brushes;
Tuning forks (A and C);
Music stands: full-size adjustable and desk stands;
Cassette player, microphone and plenty of blank tapes;
Modified instruments for children with disabilities;
Guitars;
Piano.

An overhead projector with screen is very useful for group composing/performing activities.

Electronic keyboards and music computer programmes add greatly to the scope of musical experiences for children. The catalogues of computer software firms and educational suppliers show that there is an increasing number of packages available to support the music curriculum.

Baskets and trays are essential for storing and carrying instruments. A trolley is a great help, enabling instruments to be moved easily and safely to different rooms.

Special Needs

What action can you take as music curriculum coordinator to ensure that *all* pupils can gain from an education in music?

- You can check that, when necessary, musical instruments are adapted to help pupils with physical difficulties, e.g. special grips on beaters.
- You may need to modify musical instruments, materials and computers to assist pupils with hearing or sight problems.
- You can be aware that music is a powerful learning tool for children with speech and language problems.

Discuss with your colleagues:

- What help can be given in music to pupils with disabilities?
- How can these pupils be brought into general music activities such as performing, composing and listening?
- What opportunities can be provided by the school, LEA or local music college/children's choir/orchestra for pupils who are specially gifted in music?

Resources and References

Listed below are some key, up-to-date publications. Further information on music schemes, music, songbooks and books on music can be obtained from educational publishers, music suppliers and reviews in music and educational journals.

Official Publications

HMI (1985) *Music from 5 to 16, Curriculum Matters 4*, London, HMSO.
DES (1990) *National Curriculum Music Working Group: Interim Report*, London, DES.
DES (1991) *Music for Ages 5 to 14*, London, DES.
NCC (1992) *National Curriculum Council Consultation Report: Music*, York, NCC.
NCC (1992) *Additional Advice to the Secretary of State for Education and Science on Non-Statutory Statements of Attainment in Art, Music and Physical Education*, York, NCC.
HMI (1992) *Aspects of Primary Education: The Teaching and Learning of Music*, London, HMSO.
DFE (1995) *Music in the National Curriculum*, London, DFE, London, SCAA.

Books

ADDISON, R. (1993) *Bright Ideas: Music*, Leamington Spa, Scholastic Publications.
BEAN, J. and OLDFIELD, A. *Pied Piper: Musical Activities to Develop Basic Skills*, Cambridge, Cambridge University Press.
FARMER, B. (ed.) (1984) *Springboards: Ideas for Music*, London, Nelson.
GILBERT, J. and DAVIES, L. (1986) *Oxford Primary Music Key Stage 1*, London, Oxford University Press.
GLOVER, J. and WARD, S. (1993) *Teaching Music in the Primary School: A Guide for Primary Teachers*, London, Cassell.

KEMPTON, C. (1991) *Introducing Music at Key Stage 1: A Practical Guide for Non-Specialist Teachers*, Crediton, Southgate Publishers.
MILLS, J. (1993) *Music in the Primary School*, Cambridge, Cambridge University Press.
RICHARDS, C. (1989) *Wake up to Music*, Nottingham, NES Arnold.
STOCKS, M. and MADDOCKS, A. (1992) *Growing up with Music Stage 1*, Harlow, Longmans.
YORK, M. (1988) *Gently into Music: Possible Approaches for Non-specialist Primary Teachers*, Harlow, Longman.

The Silver Burdett Music scheme is published by Simon and Schuster Education.

The A. and C. Black songbooks, dating back to *Carol, Gaily Carol* (1973), *Appuskidu* (1975) and *Okki Tokki Unga* (1976) have been reprinted many times and attained remarkable success.

Chapter 9

Developing a Curriculum Leadership Role at Key Stage 1 – Physical Education

Sue Chedzoy

Healthy young children at play in open space love running, jumping and tumbling, skipping, hopping, chasing and expressing themselves through movement. They will make up simple games and delight in repeating their actions time and time again. These natural physical activities are encapsulated in the physical education programme at Key Stage 1.

Physical Education – Key Stage 1

In each year of the Key Stage, pupils should be taught three areas of activity: games, gymnastic activities and dance, using indoor and outdoor environments where appropriate. In addition, schools may choose to teach swimming in Key Stage 1 using the programme of study set out in Key Stage 2.

Throughout the Key Stage, pupils should be taught:

- about the changes that occur to their bodies as they exercise;
- to recognise the short-term effects of exercise on the body (DFE, 1995, p. 3).

The three areas of activity games, gymnastics activities and dance will provide pupils with a foundation of basic movements and understanding. Although athletic activities is not a discrete area of activity at Key Stage 1, running, jumping and throwing activities will naturally constitute an integral part of a balanced programme of physical education which will be further developed at Key Stage 2. Doubtless many schools with access to pools will continue to offer children a programme of swimming at Key Stage 1 although it is not a compulsory part of the physical education curriculum.

Equal opportunities is a guiding and leading principle for physical education. All children, regardless of their ability, including any impairment, sex, cultural/ethnic background are entitled to equal access and opportunities in physical education. Whole school planning in physical education requires consideration of a policy for children who have special educational needs to ensure that all children are able to participate in, and enjoy, a range of physical activities. A very helpful guide addressing many issues relating to equal opportunities is to be found in *Physical Education for Ages 5 to 16* (DES, 1991a).

Cross-curricular Matters

In formulating any curriculum policy for physical education the themes, skills and dimensions which are the responsibility of all teachers need to be considered. These are identified in the document *Curriculum Guidance 3: The Whole Curriculum* (NCC, 1990). The non-statutory guidance (NCC, 1992, Section G) provides guidance to assist teachers to plan cross-curricular provision and Wetton (1992) focuses on the opportunities available for promoting better integrated learning experiences using physical education.

Coordinating Physical Education

The responsibility for coordinating physical education is often offered to the member of staff who shows the most enthusiasm for the subject but does not

Figure 9.1: Coordinating physical education

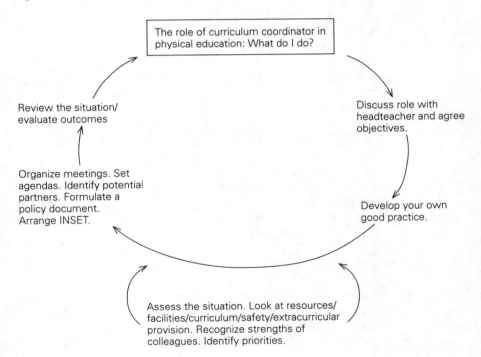

The role of curriculum coordinator in physical education: What do I do?

Discuss role with headteacher and agree objectives.

Develop your own good practice.

Assess the situation. Look at resources/facilities/curriculum/safety/extracurricular provision. Recognize strengths of colleagues. Identify priorities.

Organize meetings. Set agendas. Identify potential partners. Formulate a policy document. Arrange INSET.

Review the situation/evaluate outcomes

necessarily feel totally confident in all aspects of physical education. If this is the case it is advisable to attend courses for personal development in those aspects of the subject in which you feel less certain. It is also important that you recognize the strengths of colleagues and enlist their help in developing the curriculum if necessary.

It is often younger members of staff who are encouraged to take the responsibility for coordinating the physical education programme throughout the school, as some headteachers assume that youth and vitality are attributes which will enable a teacher to develop effectively this area of the curriculum. Certainly enthusiasm and energy are qualities required for any coordination role, but knowledge and understanding of the subject are essential in order to develop good personal practice. As a coordinator you need to be well-informed about the content of the programmes of study for the different areas of activity and the opportunities for learning the processes of planning, performing and evaluating in each area.

You need to have very clear views about the contribution of physical education to the all-round development of children. It is important that you are able to articulate your philosophy as you may find that you need to convince others of its value. You will find the document *Physical Education for Ages 5 to 16* (DES, 1991a) helpful as it clarifies terms and raises all issues that need to be addressed when formulating a rationale for a broad and balanced programme of physical education. You, the coordinator, need to emphasize these aims and encourage staff to espouse them or use them with staff to produce their own sets of aims along these lines.

The aims of physical education are very clearly set out in the non-statutory guidance for physical education (NCC, 1992):

1.1 Physical education contributes to the overall education of young people by helping them to led full and valuable lives through engaging in purposeful physical activity. It can:

- develop physical competence and help to promote physical development.
- teach pupils, through experience, to know about and value the benefits of participation in physical activity whilst at school and throughout life.
- develop appreciation of skilful and creative performances across the areas of activity.

1.2 Physical education can also contribute to:

- the development of problem solving skills.
- the establishment of self-esteem through the development of physical confidence.
- the development of interpersonal skills.

1.3 Physical activity is combined with the thinking involved in making decisions and selecting, refining, judging and adapting movements. Through these activities pupils should be encouraged to develop the personal qualities of commitment, fairness and enthusiasm (p. B1).

Attainment Target

The attainment target for physical education is the sum total of all the end of Key Stage Descriptions. In meeting the attainment target pupils should be able to demonstrate the knowledge, skills and understanding involved in areas of activity which at Key Stage 1 include games, gymnastics activities and dance (p. B1).

The DFE (1995) supplies the following general requirements for physical education:

Physical education involves pupils in the continuous process of planing, performing and evaluating. This applies to all areas of activity. The greatest emphasis should be placed on the actual performance aspect of the subject. The following requirements should apply to the teaching of physical education across all Key Stages:

1 To promote physical activity and healthy lifestyles pupils should be taught:

a to be physically active;
b to adopt good posture and the appropriate use of the body;
c to engage in activities that develop cardiovascular health, flexibility, muscular strength and endurance;
d the increasing need for personal hygiene in relation to vigorous activity.

2 To develop positive attitudes pupils should be taught:

a to observe the conventions of fair play, honest competition and good sporting behaviour as individual participants, team members and spectators;
b how to cope with success and failure;
c to try hard to consolidate their performances;
d to be mindful of others and the environment.

3 To ensure safe practice pupils should be taught:

a to respond readily to instructions;
b to recognise and follow relevant rules, laws, codes, etiquette and safety procedures for different activities or events in practice or during competition;

c   about the safety risks of wearing inappropriate clothing, footwear and jewellery, and why particular clothing, footwear and protection are worn for different activities.
d   how to lift, carry, place and use equipment safely.
e   to warm up and recover from exercise. (p. 2)

Programme of Study – Common Requirements for Physical Education Access
The programme of study for each Key Stage should be taught to the great majority of pupils in the Key Stage, in ways appropriate to their abilities.

For the small number of pupils who may need the provision, material may be selected from earlier or later Key Stages where this is necessary to enable individual pupils to progress and demonstrate achievement. Such material should be presented in contexts suitable to the pupil's age.

Appropriate provision should be made for pupils who need to use:

• means of communication other than speech, including computers, technological aids, signing, symbols or lip-reading;
• non-sighted methods of reading, such as Braille, or non-visual or non-aural ways of acquiring information;
• technological aids in practical and written work;
• aids or adapted equipment to allow access to practical activities within and beyond school.

Appropriate provision should be made for those pupils who need activities to be adapted in order to participate in Physical Education. Judgements made in relation to the end of Key Stage descriptions should allow for the provision above, where appropriate.
Use of Language
Pupils should be taught to express themselves clearly in speech.
The Curriculum Cymreig
In Wales, pupils should be given opportunities, where appropriate, in their study of Physical Education to develop and apply their knowledge and understanding of the cultural, economic, environment, historical and linguistic characteristics of Wales. (p. 1)

Neither the Department for Education nor the School Curriculum and Assessment Authority state the number of hours that physical education should be taught in schools at any Key Stage. At Key Stage 1 games, gymnastics activities and dance provide a foundation of basic movements and understanding from which pupils may progress to other recognized forms of physical education in later years. You as coordinator know that these areas of activity need to be experienced regularly and require equal amounts of time for progress to be made. You are aware that some schools manage to enable children to experience a lesson of physical education every day. Your aim will be to obtain the support of the rest of the staff in your efforts to obtain this for all pupils in your school. Certainly a lesson a week throughout the year for games, gymnastics activities and dance is something to be worked towards.

If swimming is taught there is some evidence to suggest that it is best learnt through a concentrated unit of lessons, however the recommendations in the national curriculum allow for maximum flexibility in planning this programme of study.

Lead by Example

Before attempting directly to influence the work of others, it is essential that you develop good practice in physical education with your own class. The very nature of the subject offers opportunities for you to be noticed by colleagues as you teach in the hall, on the playground or the field. You may be surprised to find that other staff will comment informally on interesting work they might see from their classroom window. For example, you may have introduced a group of children to sending skills using uni-hoc sticks which has stimulated interest from a person who had thought that they were only suitable for games with older children. This would be an opportunity to explain how they might be used by younger children to develop skills individually, and developed into simple games which they might create for themselves in pairs. Never miss an opportunity to share your expertise informally whenever possible.

Be a good role model in your personal appearance. Change into appropriate clothing to teach physical education but avoid wearing your tracksuit all day around the school. Ensure that your own class is always suitably dressed for physical education and that it adopts a code of behaviour conducive to safe practice in all situations, for example, children always demonstrating safe lifting and carrying of apparatus in the hall or the playground.

Familiarize yourself with the requirements of the national curriculum and plan accordingly. Pay particular attention to developing your own management and organizational skills. Use a range of strategies and cultivate different teaching styles and approaches, some of which you may not have dared to use on teaching practice; for example, you could experiment with a range of stimuli in dance or the use of task cards in gymnastics. Take time to refine your observational skills of children engaged in physical activity; for example you might video children's work and use it to give yourself more time to identify aspects of children's performance. It is vital that you are able to gain evidence of achievement in children planning, performing and evaluating in physical education. A useful reference is the section on 'Practical implications for the assessment of pupils in physical education' (DES, 1991a, p. 41–42) which focuses on assessment in the processes of the three strands involved, that is, planning, performing and evaluating.

Once you have gained some experience in your own teaching then you will have more confidence to influence the work of others.

Review the Facilities and Resources

Facilities

You need to assess the present situation in terms of physical education and one of the least threatening areas to start is to look at the provision of facilities and resources.

Analyse the provision; could facilities be improved with some minor changes in organization? Look at the facilities and resources that are available and take particular note of safety, provision and storage.

Inside

Look at the storage in the hall. Would the environment be safer with some adjustments to the storage of chairs, tables, piano and other musical instruments? Are the pieces of gymnastic apparatus easily accessible? Does the storage cupboard need some reorganization to enable children to move apparatus in and out?

If the small games apparatus is stored in the cupboard is there a workable system of storage? Are the baskets colour coded with a range of apparatus in each? Are there spare empty baskets to enable teachers to select one item of equipment for each child (such as skipping ropes) rather than having to take all the apparatus outside? Would it be more efficient to store the games equipment elsewhere? Is there a sufficient supply of small apparatus, for example, at least a ball that bounces for each child in the class, a bat, a skipping rope or a hoop for each child?

If dance is taught in the hall, are there any resources available there? Could an area be set aside to store tapes and stimuli such as pop-up books, poems and moveable objects which might be used as starting points for dance? Would a display area with photographs or posters of children dancing enhance the environment? If teachers want to show video material as a stimulus for dance, is a TV and video player available for use in the hall?

Outside

Check the storage hut/cupboard. Make an inventory of the equipment, note items in need of replacement.

Look at the arrangement for storage. Could access be improved? Large balls can be stored on shelves with a front lip, in sacks or large tubs. Sticks and bats can be placed in simple racks. Small balls, bean bags or skipping ropes can be kept in plastic containers or washing baskets. A colour coded system of baskets containing a selection of apparatus will also aid organization. Contents clearly marked on the outside makes checking of the equipment easier.

Look at the playground area. Would some markings on the surface of the playground or walls enhance the teaching of physical education? Would the marking of grids or lines on the field help teachers to organize their children?

Offsite Facilities

Some schools have use of the village/community hall. Consider the space in relation to teaching young children. Could you negotiate some storage space for the school's physical education equipment and resources? Is a first aid box available in that area? Could provision for physical education be improved through some shared resources with neighbouring schools? Would shared transport enhance possibilities of provision?

Enhance Provision

Having evaluated the provision of resources it will be useful to catalogue those available. These could be presented in relation to the programmes of study – games, gymnastics activities and dance – and offered to the staff for discussion.

You need to identify any gaps in resources and prioritize resource needs. This should be done in consultation with the headteacher and staff. It might be necessary to take one area of activity at a time and devise short, medium and longer term plans for purchasing new resources or improving facilities. A major consideration will be the budget, but having identified needs it might be possible to negotiate for increased funds or even to focus on physical education provision for future fund-raising events.

You need to be able to cost equipment and a list of manufacturers and suppliers of sources for Physical Education is provided in Appendix 1. Many local authorities have their own consortium from which schools may purchase equipment at competitive rates. Whatever your source of information it will be helpful if you are able to provide details of the cost of individual items to the headteacher and staff. Some items of equipment are relatively expensive and you will need to establish criteria for selection. For example, if the provision of light-weight gymnastic apparatus is poor you might need to weight up the relative value of spending all the money on a climbing frame or using the money to buy a selection of mats, benches and range of tables and consider the provision of the climbing frame in long term plans.

Always be receptive to suggestions made by other members of staff when ordering new equipment. If funds become available invite staff to state their preferences before making decisions about selection.

You might also devise a policy about use of games or climbing apparatus at break-times. Some schools encourage active play by making small apparatus (such as balls, hoops, skipping ropes) available for free play at breaktimes.

Safety

Safety is a major consideration in physical education. There needs to be a clear accident procedure which is known to all members of staff. First aid boxes should be available close to working spaces. A safety policy with regard to use of equipment must be agreed. As coordinator for physical education you need to discuss matters of health and safety with the headteacher to find out whether they are considered to be your area of responsibility.

Gymnastic apparatus needs to be maintained regularly. Discuss this matter with the headteacher and find out whether a contractor has responsibility for an annual safety check.

All staff and children should share a responsibility for general care of the equipment and report any defects or losses to the coordinator. If you consider that the storage system for apparatus or equipment needs reorganizing consult all members of staff before making any changes and make sure that all concerned are aware of any new code for use.

The Curriculum

Read the curriculum policy for physical education if it exists and any other documentation relating to the subject which might be available in the school. Try to find out what is actually being taught in physical education. This does not always relate to the documentation which may have been written by a curriculum coordinator without consultation with the rest of the staff, or it may have just become outdated. Find out if there is any extracurricular provision for children in physical education.

Involve All the Staff

Talk to staff informally and attempt to identify their knowledge and understanding of the subject area. You might start with colleagues who teach parallel classes in your year group and chat to other colleagues at break-times. These informal conversations can be quite revealing and you might find that some teachers avoid using the time allocated for physical education because they feel insecure about teaching this area of the curriculum. Worries about safety and progression are common. Some teachers resent the time spent on changing clothes with the younger classes and sometimes avoid physical education for that reason. Time allocated to the use of the hall is always precious and rehearsals for the school play, Christmas, harvest festival and assembly can sometimes cut across the physical education timetable. You need to be diplomatic in these discussions and take a positive approach. It is important to build on the strengths and interests of the staff and respect their views. It is from these informal consultations that you will begin to formulate your plan of action.

If you are able to negotiate some time away from your own class to watch colleagues teaching physical education you will find this most beneficial. Movement is transitory and unless work has been captured on video or film it is difficult to judge the quality of teaching and learning by simply talking about the processes. If you are offered an opportunity to observe, take note of content, management and organization and teaching styles. Be aware of the extent to which children are encouraged to take some responsibility in planning and evaluating their own work and work of others, as well as the general quality of performance. If a colleague feels uncomfortable about you observing a lesson you might offer to take a more active role and work alongside with a group according to the other teacher's planning.

Plan Together for Progression

Having identified what is being taught you need to consider the documentation and the breadth and balance of the physical education programme in the light of the national curriculum requirements. It will probably be most manageable to take one programme of study at a time. Begin with the area of activity in which you and most other members of staff feel most confident and try to involve all those who will be teaching in any planning meetings.

The non-statutory guidance for physical education (NCC, 1992) will be valuable in providing a framework for planning schemes of work, units of work and lesson plans (Section C). The National Curriculum Council recognized that one of the biggest problems facing teachers is making individual tasks in physical education progressive. It clarifies the process of physical education which involves the development of knowledge, skills and understanding through an interrelated process covering:

- planning;
- performing;
- evaluating.

It is acknowledged that there should be emphasis on performing but even at Key Stage 1 children may begin to take some responsibility for planning and evaluating their own work and work of others.

Within these strands, difficulty and quality are identified as elements to be considered when planning for progression. Examples of ways in which an activity can be analysed in terms of difficulty and quality and a diagram showing progression through the four sets of end of Key Stage statements is indicated (Section D). This guidance will be useful as a means of planning for progression in games, gymnastics activities and dance.

Assessment

Assessment of children's attainment is integral to all teaching and learning. It is an ongoing process which informs planning and enables teachers constantly to evaluate teaching and review objectives. Movement is transitory and teachers need to observe children's performances carefully to facilitate learning within each activity. Many teachers will have developed criteria which they use in assessing children's work in physical education. The assessment of children's work should be continuous and not solely reserved for the end of the Key Stage. The emphasis throughout Key Stage 1 will be collecting evidence of progress in performance within the areas of activity. However, children's ability to plan and describe their own work and the work of others should also be taken into account. This end of Key Stage description describes the types and range of performance that the majority of pupils should characteristically demonstrate by the end of Key Stage 1:

> Pupils plan and perform simple skills safely, and show control in linking actions together. They improve their performance through practising their skills, working alone and with a partner. They talk about what they and others have done, and are able to make simple judgements. They recognise and describe the changes that happen to their bodies during exercise (DFE, 1995, p. 11).

As a curriculum coordinator you might set aside some INSET time for the staff to discuss assessment procedures and to formulate a whole school approach for collecting and recording attainment. The record keeping at Key Stage 1 should not be too time consuming or onerous but some evidence of children's level of achievement should be available for the child, other teachers and parents. The non-statutory guidance (Section F) provides very useful information as a guide for assessment policies. The end of Key Stage description at Key Stage 1 will provide a framework for developing assessment, planning and reporting strategies.

Games: Key Stage 1

Many teachers feel confident about teaching games at Key Stage 1 and give children plenty of time to explore and experiment with a variety of equipment in order that they practise and improve performance. They keep in mind that pupils should be taught:

- simple competitive games, including how to play them as individuals and, when ready, in pairs and in small groups;
- to develop and practise a variety of ways of sending (including throwing, striking, rolling and bouncing), receiving and travelling with a ball and other similar games equipment;
- elements of games play that include running, chasing, dodging, avoiding, and awareness of space and other players. (DFE, 1995, p. 3)

You might need to persuade colleagues that simple competitive games will involve children in responding to such personal challenges as beating their own record at hitting a target, catching a ball or running against time and should not involve them in paired or group activities until they are ready.

INSET activities

If you have ordered new small games apparatus this would be an opportunity to offer new ideas to enable children to develop the skills of sending, receiving and travelling with a ball. For example, you might have ordered a variety of vinyl covered sponge balls of different weights and sizes, beach balls and vinyl rugby balls and some uni-hoc sticks, plastic bats, cricket bat shapes, and large sponge dice. It would be helpful for the staff to see the new equipment, play with it and discuss how it might be used in lessons.

Organize a workshop for teachers or children with a focus on creating simple games. Consider criteria for the assessment of the success of the games making in the light of children taking some responsibility for planning their own performance. Consider the place of competition in the games programme and share examples of appropriate activities.

Gymnastic Activities: Key Stage 1

At Key Stage 1 children should have the opportunity to take some responsibility for lifting, carrying and placing gymnastic apparatus. By the end of the Key Stage, with some guidance from the teacher, children are capable of planning their own simple arrangements of apparatus. A whole school policy is necessary to ensure progression and safe practice in the use of apparatus. Some teachers are reluctant to allow children to move and place their own apparatus; anxieties about safety and time management are common concerns. A review of the situation involving all the staff might facilitate a more coherent approach.

Pupils should be taught:

- different ways of performing the basic actions of travelling, using hands and feet, turning, rolling, jumping, balancing, swinging and climbing both on the floor and apparatus, and how to repeat them.
- to link together a series of actions both on the floor and using apparatus, and how to repeat them. (DFE, 1995, p. 3)

INSET activities

Look at the present provision of apparatus. Is it of a suitable weight and size for infant children? As a group identify any apparatus which needs to be replaced to make lifting and carrying easier for young children.

Consider the storage. Would it be practical to store the portable items around the outside of the hall? Could such a system of storage be implemented on those days of the week when the apparatus is most used? This will reduce time spent on carrying and organizing apparatus.

Make a scale drawing of the hall space and cut out a selection of diagrams to represent benches, boxes, agility tables, mats, hoops and ropes. Ask colleagues to design appropriate layouts of apparatus that are relevant to the learning focus for lessons and units of work. Try to identify clear progression and differences between Year 1 and Year 2.

A demonstration lesson is always a good starting point for INSET. In gymnastics you might ask someone to video whole or part of one of your lessons or that of a more experienced colleague. Alternatively you might invite the staff to watch a demonstration given by yourself, another member of staff or an advisory teacher. It is important to ask colleagues to consider a particular aspect of the lesson as a focus for discussion. For example:

- teaching styles – ask colleagues to identify the ways in which the teacher offers children the opportunity to plan and evaluate their own performances;
- quality – ask colleagues to identify the ways in which the teacher encourages the children to achieve quality in performance.

Dance: Key Stage 1

Many teachers rely solely on the BBC Radio Programmes *Let's Move* (designed for ages 4–6 years) and *Time to Move* (designed for ages 6–8 years) as a resource for the dance education of their pupils. Although the programmes are written by dance specialists and offer a resource that is easy to use, it would seem to be more appropriate that the scheme of work for dance reflects a systematic approach to planning that has been agreed by the staff as a whole and which links into the whole school philosophy and policy statement for physical education. The programme of study for dance will aid you in the development of a school based policy for Dance.

Pupils should be taught:

- to develop control, coordination, balance, poise and elevation in basic actions, including travelling, jumping, turning, gesture and stillness;
- to perform movements or patterns, including some from existing dance traditions;
- to explore moods and feelings and to develop their response to music through dances, by using rhythmic responses and contrasts of speed, shape, direction and level. (DFE, 1995, p. 3)

Here are some examples of ways in which you as coordinator might engage the interest and raise the knowledge base for physical education amongst your colleagues.

INSET *activities*

Discuss at a whole staff meeting the resources for teaching dance. Consider resources that individual teachers have found useful, e.g. stories, poems, chants, objects that suggest movement, paintings, photographs, pictures, music, percussion instruments and videos, and the use of educational radio programmes.

Invite teachers to explain or demonstrate how they have used the resources with their children. This might take the form of a workshop with teachers, or using children to demonstrate.

Discuss the possibilities of involving outside agencies, i.e. advisory support, dancers-in-residence, education departments of dance companies, in some INSET for the whole staff.

Arrange a practical workshop to enable teachers to feel more confident in delivering a dance idea which involves children in the three strands composing, performing and appreciating dances. This could be based on a topic and involve cross-curricular links.

A very useful resource book is *Inspirations for Dance and Movement* by Judy Evans and Hazel Powell. This will help you in your planning and will provide a sound foundation for developing a rationale for dance and is a good source for ideas and cross-curricular links.

Formulate a Policy Document

A policy document will evolve over time and should reflect the school's beliefs, intentions and practices in physical education. Schemes of work or curriculum guidelines most helpful to teachers are those developed as a result of staff discussion under the guidance of the curriculum coordinator (DES, 1991b). Most LEAs have guidelines for physical education and in conjunction with material from courses which might have been attended by teachers, these might provide a useful framework for planning and organising the subject. HMI (DES, 1991b) found that guidelines were usually most effective when:

- their production was seen as part of the in-service development of the teachers who were to make use of them;
- they identified progressive stages of development in the work;
- they offered advice on appropriate teaching methods (p. 27).

Review the Situation

You need to be realistic in self-appraisal and periodically review outcomes of short, medium or long term plans. Remember that change is a gradual process so try not to feel despondent if your initiatives are not immediately implemented. Continue to develop your own good practice and provide guidance, support and encouragement for colleagues. If necessary, enlist help from the headteacher, immediate colleagues, colleagues in other schools, advisory staff or consultants. Some addresses of other agencies that you might find helpful are listed in Appendix 2. It is important that you keep up to date with new developments in physical education and are aware of resources that will enhance teaching and learning in it. The Physical Education Association of the United Kingdom is your best source of information for details of courses, equipment and resources. Above all endeavour to develop effective communication skills to encourage all the staff to develop a safe and stimulating environment in which young children can enjoy a broad and balanced programme of physical education.

References

DEPARTMENT FOR EDUCATION (DFE) (1995) *Physical Education in the National Curriculum*, London, HMSO.

DEPARTMENT OF EDUCATION AND SCIENCE (DES) (1991a) *Physical Education for ages 5 to 16 – Proposals of the Secretary of State for Education and Science and the Secretary of State for Wales*, London, DES.

DEPARTMENT OF EDUCATION AND SCIENCE (DES) (1991b) *The Teaching and Learning of Physical Education*, London, HMSO.

DEPARTMENT OF EDUCATION AND SCIENCE (DES) (1992) *Physical Education in the National Curriculum,* London, HMSO.

EVANS, J. and POWELL, H. (1994) *Inspirations for Dance and Movement*, Leamington Spa, Scholastic Publication.

NATIONAL CURRICULUM COUNCIL (NCC) (1990) *Curriculum Guidance 3: The Whole Curriculum*, York, NCC.

NATIONAL CURRICULUM COUNCIL (NCC) (1992) *Physical Education Non-Statutory Guidance*, York, NCC.

SCHOOL CURRICULUM AND ASSESSMENT AUTHORITY (SCAA) (1994) *Physical Education – The National Curriculum Orders*, York, NCC.

WETTON, P. (1992) *Practical Guides Physical Education – Teaching within the National Curriculum*, Leamington Spa, Scholastic Publication.

Appendix 1: Firms Supplying Equipment for Physical Education

Continental Sports Products Company
Paddock
Huddersfield HD1 ASD
(01484) 539148

Davies
Ludlow Hill Road
West Bridgford
Nottingham NG2 6HD
(01602) 452203

Galt Educational
Brookfield Road
Cheadle
Cheshire SK8 2PN
(0161) 4288571

Hope Educational Ltd
ORB Mill
Huddersfield Road
Oldham OL4 2ST
(0161) 6336611

Maudesport
Unit 23
Empire Close
Empire Industrial Park
Aldridge
West Midlands WS9 8UQ
(01922) 59571

NES Annocot Ltd
Ludlow Hill Road
West Bridgford
Nottingham NG2 6HD
(01602) 452000

Newitts & Co Ltd
Claxton Hall
Malton Road
York Y06 7RE
(01904) 86551

Sutcliffe Leisure Ltd
Sandbeds Trading Estate
Dewsbury Road
Ossett
West Yorkshire WF5 9ND

Swim Shop
52/58 Albert Road
Luton
Beds LU1 3PR
(01592) 416545

Appendix 2

Amateur Swimming Association
Harold Fern House
Derby Square Loughborough
Leicestershire LE11 0AL

BBC Education Information
BBC White City
201 Wood Lane
London W12 7TS

British Sports Association for the Disabled
Solecast House
13–27 Brunswick Place
London N1 6DX

English Folk Dance and Song Society
Cecil Sharp House
2 Regents Park Road
London. NW1 7AY

Health Education Authority
Hamilton House
Mabledon Place
London WC1H 9TX

National Dance Teachers Association
NDTA Treasurer
29 Larkspur Avenue
Walsall
Staffordshire. WS7 8SR
(Publishes *Dance Matters*, £7.50 a year for three copies).

Physical Education Association of the United Kingdom
Francis House
Francis Street
London SW1P 1DE
(Publishes *Primary Focus*, £6.00 a year for four copies).

Chapter 10

Not Sunflowers Again!
Coordinating Art at Key Stage 1

Rita Ray

Aims and Issues in Art Education in Key Stage 1

At primary level much art activity takes place in the context of other curriculum areas. In infant schools paints and crayons are a familiar feature and for much of the time children are communicating through the medium of pictures. In fact, drawing is a major way of communicating at the early stages.

Prior to the national curriculum any specific art work usually depended on the interest and expertise of individual teachers. The Gulbenkian report stated:

> The most common obstacle to effective arts teaching in the primary school is a lack of confidence among teachers, combined with – or resulting from – a feeling that they themselves are not artistic (1982, para. 82).

According to an OFSTED report charting the progress of national curriculum art (1993) this is still the case. Where standards were good teachers often had specific subject knowledge, work was carefully planned, pupils were provided with a range of appropriate materials and skills were systematically developed. At the same time, opportunities were provided for children to explore their own ideas.

In the area of specialist art it has been the tradition to give credit for practical achievement such as painting and sculpture. Therefore even specialists in primary school may not be sure how to plan responses to art for children working within Key Stage 1.

The OFSTED (1993) report found that planning generally failed to discriminate between those aspects of art that were appropriately taught in a discrete way and those that could be taught through a topic-based approach. Art as an accompaniment to topic work often failed to take account of ways in which pupils might develop skills, knowledge and understanding of art. To summarize, two main issues can be identified:

- a lack of confidence among teachers;
- lack of distinction, at planning level, between art as a subject and topic-based art.

The task of tackling these issues falls upon the art coordinator whose job it is to build up and pass on expertise and practical skills. The subject specialisms assigned to teachers may not be the ones they are most familiar and confident with, but they can develop a framework for improving knowledge and expertise for all as well as contributing to the whole school planning process. Many art coordinators are not 'artistic' but are nonetheless able to tackle the role effectively.

In addressing the points raised so far I shall first look at the art attainment targets and see how they can help the subject specialist in planning whole school policy and INSET training. Secondly, I shall discuss the role of the art specialist at Key Stage 1. I believe that art is a special case in which the management component of the specialist role cannot be separated from the content. In many cases, activities must first be imparted to non-specialist art teachers before they can be made accessible to pupils.

The Programme of Study

The two main areas covered in the Programme of Study, Investigating and Making and Knowledge and Understanding, represent an attempt to fill out practical art experiences and to introduce and develop a knowledge of artworks and enable children to respond to them by talking about them and linking them to their own work. There should be a balance between looking at artworks and learning to use materials. Progressively children will be able to engage with surface features such as colour and form and deeper features such as symbol and meaning, as well as studying the contexts in which the artworks were produced.

Although the Programmes of Study have been set out in relation to Investigating and Making and Knowledge and Understanding, this does not mean that teaching activities and learning opportunities should be designed to address them separately.

Key Stage 1 Programme of Study and End of Key Stage Descriptions
Investigating and Making
Pupils should be taught to:
- record what has been experienced, observed and imagined;
- recognize images, objects and artefacts as sources of ideas for their work;
- select and sort images and artefacts, and use this source material as a basis for their work;
- experiment with tools and techniques for drawing, painting, print-

making, collage and sculpture, exploring a range of materials, including textiles;

- experiment with visual elements, e.g. pattern, texture, colour, line, tone, shape, form, space to make images and artefacts, using the range of media listed above;
- review what they have done and describe what they might change or develop in future work.

End of Key Stage description:
Pupils record their ideas and feelings confidently and show a developing ability to represent what they see and touch. They choose resources and materials for their visual and tactile qualities to stimulate and develop ideas for their work. They work practically and imaginatively with materials, tools and techniques, and present their work in two and three dimensions.

Knowledge and Understanding
- identify in the school and the locality the work of artists, craftspeople and designers;
- recognize visual elements, e.g. pattern, texture, colour, line, tone, shape, form, space, in images and artefacts;
- recognize differences and similarities in art, craft and design from different times and places;
- respond to the ideas, methods or approaches used in different styles and traditions;
- describe works of art, craft and design in simple terms, and explain what they think and feel about these.

End of Key Stage description:
Pupils describe and compare images and artefacts in simple terms. They recognize differences in methods and approaches and make links with their own art, craft and design work.

What to Teach at Key Stage 1 – Issues for INSET

Helping Teachers to Gain Confidence

What kind of activities can teachers present to ensure that the aims and objectives of the Key Stage 1 art curriculum are fulfilled? The specialist must first help teachers themselves to become confident with art activities. Often they are afraid to do the wrong thing. A rule of thumb to follow is to teach skills and techniques which will empower children to express their *own* view of the world. Teachers appreciate INSET training which gives hands on experience of techniques such as printmaking and suggestions which will help them and their pupils to engage with and respond to artworks.

Figure 10.1: Art in the curriculum

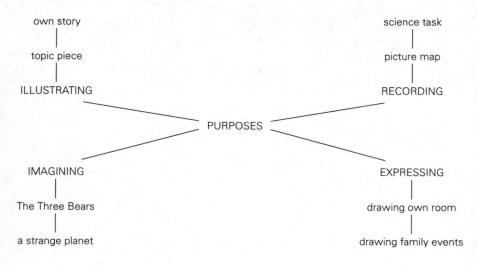

Topic-based Art

As already pointed out, at Key Stage 1 art is very much part of daily routine and is a means of expression across the curriculum. Figure 10.1 shows some ways in which art may be highlighted in other areas of the curriculum which also exemplify different purposes of art – illustrating, recording, imagining and expressing.

When different purposes of art are identified and categorized it is easier to see where they fit into the topic plan. Figure 10.2 is a modified version of a framework for planning from the non-statutory guidance which gives scope for links with other areas of the curriculum.

Responding to Artworks

In a Year 2 classroom I saw a 6-year-old boy take up a thick hog's hair brush to make a copy of a Turner sky. He mixed the pale yellow and faded the edges of the sun gradually into the vaporous bluish white. He looked at it for a few seconds, frowned, then declared, '*That's* not a sun.' Dipping his brush into the pure bright yellow, he made a bold disc with spikes all around it and smiled broadly. Although he had mastered colour-mixing skills he felt compelled to paint what *he* knew about the sun, not what Turner knew. In considering the art document and its interpretation at Key Stage 1 we must take child development into account and not only provide meaningful activities but also match them to the child's understanding.

Figure 10.2: A framework for planning

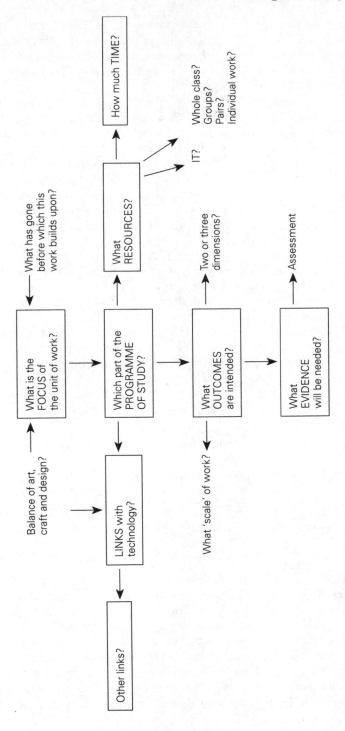

(*Source: Adapted from D2, NCC, 1992*)

The example suggestion in the art document (DFE, 1995) that 'pupils could: compare the way they use colour in their own drawings and paintings of flowers with the work of other artists, e.g. William Morris and Vincent van Gogh' seems to have spawned a plethora of powder paint forgeries in school entrance halls across the land.

Nor does teaching children to respond to art mean giving them fancy élitist terms to describe paintings. They *do* need technical terms like 'lighter shade', 'thin brush', 'wax resist', to describe tools and processes, but at infant level response to artworks should be direct, fresh and personal.

In expressing their enjoyment, their likes and dislikes, the foundations are being laid for the appreciation of art. The philosopher Wittgenstein said that there is a difference between *enjoyment* and *appreciation* of art. Enjoyment is a more immediate response. To appreciate art you need more background knowledge. It is even possible to appreciate a piece of art, to know it is 'good', yet not enjoy it.

Aspects of both Investigating and Making and Knowledge and Understanding combine in most cases of response to art. Children may respond by commenting and by practical follow-up, using similar techniques, processes or subject matter. They can use the skills and techniques to enhance their own view and vision rather than to copy someone else's.

The non-statutory guidance (NNC, 1992) offers examples of how to go about planning responses to the work of different artists. Published schemes, such as those produced by Ginn (Peppin et al, 1992) and Oliver and Boyd (NCC, 1990), offer good colour reproductions with suggestions for discussion and follow-up work. A training session could be spent looking at these materials and planning how they might be used progressively throughout Key Stage 1.

Making Art Accessible to Young Children

The following are examples of art forms that are particularly accessible to younger children and which could form a basis for discussion on a training day.

1 Using galleries and exhibitions
   Example: Picasso Exhibition at the Tate Gallery (Many of the works in this exhibition are reproduced in Williams (S.), 1994).

   This exhibition seemed particularly interesting for teachers of young children because of its use of a wide range of materials and simple techniques in collage, cut and fold, card sculpture and junk modelling. Children visiting the exhibition responded to the variety and especially enjoyed the representations of animals. One child stood before a metal sculpture called *Woman in a Garden* and cried, 'I love it. It's like a dinosaur on fire!' – a truly direct, fresh and personal response. I like to take a tape recorder to record children's remarks to transcribe selectively later. They soon learn to take the tape recorder for granted. Amongst other things, we have made group poems and display captions from their remarks.

2   Art that has a direct appeal to children

An art magazine (*The Artist's and Illustrator's Magazine* or *AIM*) has published interviews with well-known children's illustrators, such as Raymond Briggs and Quentin Blake, and with the Oscar-winning animator, Nick Park, who made the animated film, *The Wrong Trousers*.

Raymond Briggs explains how he plans and draws the illustrations for books such as *The Snowman* and *Father Christmas* (*AIM*, 87, December 1993) and Nick Park tells how he makes the Plasticine characters and shows the story boards on which the plots are planned in pictures (*AIM*, 94, July 1994). Although written for an adult audience, the articles are copiously illustrated and are informative for teachers, who could easily present the content to children. These are examples that children could identify with and go on to produce work using the same kind of media. There are many accomplished children's illustrators whose work children enjoy and can relate to.

3   Relating an artwork to the child's own experience

The painting of Van Gogh's bedroom may be used as a starting point for children to discuss and paint parts of their home or school which have significance for them. Several artworks may be used in this way as starting points.

4   Developing descriptive language

When children's observational drawings and paintings are displayed, the language used to describe the objects can be displayed too. For example, on a board of snowdrop pictures on black paper painted by a Year 1 class the teacher put up strips of paper with sentences, phrases and words quoted from the children's comments: 'They look like drops of ice', 'wet and cold', 'silky', and so on.

Planning for Progression

There are several ways in which the national curriculum documents may be used in planning. The non-statutory guidance offers useful advice. Items from the programme of study may be grouped together and activities matched to them and the end of Key Stage statements used to check on children's attainment. Although the non-statutory guidance was conceived in relation to the first art document, the ideas it contains are still relevant and can be modified to suit the new orders.

The General Principles of Progression in Art

Progression is manifested through greater depth of knowledge and applying skills more expertly in increasingly challenging contexts. Pupils should develop the ability to select for themselves the methods and materials most appropriate to the task.

It is important that the art specialist coordinates the experiences presented in each year group ensuring that there are continuing opportunities to consolidate and improve skills and techniques already introduced.

A Practical Framework for the Subject Specialist

Updating Personal Expertise

There has always been an emphasis on the practical aspects of art. School examinations are biased towards practical products and specialism is seen as producing artworks rather than knowing about theory or art history. There are many interesting aspects of art, now acknowledged in the programmes of study, and those who feel they cannot paint need not feel excluded.

Knowledge can be updated through reading and attending courses but constraints of time make it necessary to seek material that will organize the knowledge for you as well as providing inspiration and enthusiasm that can be passed on to colleagues. Schemes for children, aimed at covering national curriculum requirements, e.g. *Approaches to Art* (Peppin et al, 1992), can provide the necessary background material for teachers too. A basic start in practical skills and materials may be gained from a book such as *Guiding Young Artists* by Gaelene Rowe, which not only explains techniques clearly but also sets out progressive lesson plans in the use of skills and materials. Resources such as these give confidence to the non-specialist and can also aid planning and delivery of the national curriculum for teachers who already have expertise in art.

Staff Development

The coordinator has to fight for course feedback and INSET time and the demands of the core subjects push art to the back of the line. Try to negotiate specified time for art training with the headteacher. Teachers spending their time at courses and meetings, especially after school, need inspiration as much as they need information. Non-specialists appreciate clear, practical input, non-threatening and relevant practical activities and the opportunity to look at and discuss schemes and resources. The materials and skills to be introduced to the children can be tried out by teachers first. The emphasis should be on the practical with a result guaranteed, for example simple printing, rather than an activity that relies heavily on personal expression. Many teachers were educated in classrooms where artistic talent was lauded and those judged to be without this mystery ingredient were left to their own devices, so they do not feel confident about their efforts. Part of the coordinator's role is to act as an enabler and facilitator. As confidence grows, the discussion can move to aspects of expression and response. Some teachers may be happy to start with these aspects. Each school staff is different and, as with children – for our cognitive processes do not change much as we grow older – it is best to start with what we know and feel comfortable with. Teachers could use their own favourite artworks as a starting point.

Organizing Resources and Information

After making an audit of existing resources the coordinator has to make practical decisions, in consultation with colleagues, about the gaps to be filled in the school's art supplies. Some materials will be needed in large quantities by every class. In the case of other materials, one or two sets per class, or in a central place, will be sufficient. These judgments can be made with reference to past experience and in relation to the requirements of national curriculum. Some basic items are:

- a variety of pencils, charcoal, sketching sticks and other 'mark making' implements;
- felt tipped markers;
- crayons – various qualities and thicknesses; include 'skin colours' such as the Early Learning Centre's 'People Crayons';
- oil pastels;
- variety of paint, including watercolour boxes;
- sketch pads (cheap variety or stapled paper);
- brushes, long and short handled, size 0–11;
- trays for printing;
- rollers;
- variety of paper – large white, sugar paper, craft paper, some good watercolour paper;
- coloured card.

Care should be taken concerning the use of dusty pastels and fixative, especially with young children and children who may have asthma or allergies. If paint is donated for use in the classroom, check the labels since many real pigments are toxic. Safety rules should be observed with other materials too, such as glue and felt-tipped markers.

Other resources include books and schemes for teacher reference, collections of items for sorting, observational drawing, etc., paper, magazines and 'junk' for collage and craft. The latter needs orderly management and maintenance so that it remains tidy and accessible. Junk can soon become rubbish. Examples of practical books and resources are listed in the references.

Formal and Informal Consultancy

The art coordinator cannot be expected to be the fount of all knowledge. Knowing where to look for the answers to main queries is as much as can be expected. A major way of effecting change is to let people see examples of good ideas in action. As well as being a role model, the art coordinator can arrange visits to suitable places where evidence of good practice can be seen, taking care that comparisons are not made and that the visits have positive aims. The art department of a linked high school could be a good, non-threatening starting point. The object is defeated if teachers feel they are being given an impossible goal or that there is implied criticism of their own art teaching.

A simple example of informal consultancy is when colleagues raise some point or question about art education in the staffroom at break-time or as they pass in the corridor.

Informing Governors

Curriculum plans and documents will be scrutinized by the governors. The coordinator may be called upon to present and expand on the art policy document.

Forming Working Groups

The size of a working group will depend on the size of the school staff, but usually consists of about three people. Involving others in curriculum planning and the devising of a curriculum document gives scope for discussion and for the presentation of different points of view. Other members of staff feel a sense of ownership in the process of policy making while the curriculum specialist has a forum for ideas and a mechanism for effecting change.

Working group meetings must be well planned if members are to feel that their time and expertise are being used efficiently. A framework for discussion should be handed out prior to the meeting (possibly an aspect of the planned document as suggested below) and an action plan arrived at by the end of the meeting.

Compiling a Curriculum Document and Information Resource Bank

The OFSTED (1993) report said that art policies and guidelines did not take enough account of programmes of study, balance of Investigating and

Making and Knowledge and Understanding or the need to build on previous experience.

The term 'curriculum document' rather than 'policy statement' will be used in this chapter. The document should not be so long and unwieldy that teachers do not use it. It can be set out in short, concise sections so that the relevant information can be found quickly. One way to do this is to use a ring binder with plastic page covers so that information can be added, changed or modified.

Strictly speaking, a policy is simply a statement of the school's beliefs about teaching art. This can be contained in a short 'statement of rationale'. Since the introduction of the national curriculum, much of the policy is already outlined in the programmes of study. The non-statutory guidance gives advice on issues to be addressed in a school policy (NNC, 1992). How this programme will be put into practice is the concern of the rest of the document.

A framework for a curriculum document might be:

Statement of rationale

This will be largely derived from the programmes of study and will be a statement of the thinking behind the art programme to be offered in the school. It sets out beliefs about what ought to be taught in the area of art for the particular age group concerned. For example:

Children should be given opportunities to develop their creativity, imagination and practical skills and to explore the properties of materials and processes of expression in a free and relaxed atmosphere. As they develop they should be taught skills which will increase their capacity to express themselves and to use art for a variety of purposes.

There should be a balance between theory and practice, between topic-based and subject-focused art, according to the age and maturity of the pupils.

Art activities should be appropriate for the child's stage of development. Through art activities children can learn to work together, collaborating on class projects, as well as working on individual pieces. Art provides settings in which aspects of multicultural awareness and equal opportunities can be introduced and explored. The traditions of diverse cultures and religions can be introduced naturally through art. Children should be able to respond to art in various ways and to use appropriate language to describe artworks and their feelings and ideas about artworks.

The school's approach to the arts is holistic. We believe in the importance of an aesthetic environment to promote the well-being of the children. This should be manifested not only in display and other obvious artistic areas but also in the school surroundings, the choice of furniture, classroom materials, care of books and resources and presentation of work, by both staff and pupils. Such standards will be maintained by a consistency of approach and attention to detail on the part of the staff.

At Key Stage 1 the following ongoing threads will be kept in mind when planning schemes of work in art:

> stages of child development;
> cross-curricular themes;
> progression;
> balance between Investigating and Making and Knowledge and
>   Understanding;
> assessment and recording.

There should be opportunities for the children to work with a wide range of art materials and to learn a variety of practical and theoretical skills. Art resource areas should be maintained in a way that makes teaching manageable and learning accessible.

A set amount of time in the school's timetable of INSET will be allocated for the sole purpose of attending to issues in the art curriculum.

Assessment/recording

Satisfactory methods of recording progress are still on trial in many schools. Figure 10.3 has been adapted from those suggested in the non-statutory guidance and can be modified to suit the school context.

Indicators of pupil progress/development – examples of assessed work

A set of samples of work showing progress through maturation and development through a taught programme of skills and knowledge will help as a basis for discussion. It will be sufficient to study the work of four or five children, chosen to represernt the range at Key Stage 1. Indicators of progress can be derived from these samples.

List of resources

The contents of the school's central stock of art and craft materials will be listed here so that the teachers are aware of the range of items. Simple instructions on how to use some of the materials can be placed in the appendix. There will be a list of display materials, collected objects, materials for use in the teaching of colour and texture. Any 'schemes', or resources such as prints and postcards can be listed here.

Figure 10.3: *Record sheet*

Unit no.	Title of unit:	Main focus of the unit: AT1 Work practically and imaginatively	Pos 8 a b d f
Class/year: 2	Ourselves and Others	AT2 Recognise different kinds of art	9 a b c d
Duration: 3wks		General requirements: Balance of art, craft and design	
Term: Spring			
Record responses, including observations of natural and made environment	Observing and recording own expressions Drawing round our body shapes to show different movements, postures Designing costumes for special occasions		AT1
Gather resources and materials, using them to stimulate and develop ideas	Collecting photographs and pictures of clothing – people in other countries to show different costumes, headdresses, masks		*
Explore and use 2- and 3D media, working on a variety of scales	Using different scrap and 'found' materials to create a mask, headdress or costume for a special occasion; play; event		*
Review and modify work as it progresses	Explaining our ideas and the materials used and listening to others. Adapting ideas as needed		
Develop understanding of work of artists, craftspeople, designers – apply knowledge to own work	Talking about the design of our clothes esp. clothes for different occasions		AT2
	Looking at paintings, prints and designs by well known artists which show costumes from different times in history: and from different cultures.		*
Respond to and evaluate art, craft and design, including own and others' work	Comparing the way they have used different materials in their work with the work of other artists, designers		
Outcomes – tasks: drawings, designs, costumes	Criteria for success: – willingness to explore ideas and materials and adapt – looking closely at the work of other artists		Resources: *

(Source: Adapted from D9, NCC, 1992)

References and booklist

Many art books are expensive and it is more realistic to borrow them from the library, but existing art books in the school and class libraries can be identified and listed. The school may subscribe to art or craft periodicals.

Appendix

The appendix is the place to put instructions for using and maintaining materials, as well as other extra bits of information, such as how to organize an artist-in-school visit, that are useful and necessary. Each page should have its own plastic cover (rather than stuffing several pages in one cover), the first page being a list of appendix contents. Teachers need to find this kind of information quickly and easily.

In attempting to meet the requirements of the national curriculum let us not lose sight of the joy, charm, delight and surprise that make young children's art an infinite source of pleasure and interest for us all.

References and Resources

PEPPIN, A., SMITH, R. and TURNER, A. (1992) *Approaches to Art* Aylesbury, Ginn Scheme.
Artists' and Illustrators' Magazine
The Fitzpatrick Building
188–194 York Way
London N7 9QR
BARNES, R. (1987) *Teaching Art to Young Children 4–9*, London, Routledge.
CLEMENT, R. and PAGE, S. (1990) *The Arts 5–16: A Workpack for Teachers*, Harlow, Oliver and Boyd.
DEPARTMENT FOR EDUCATION (DFE) (1995) *Art in the National Curriculum*, London, HMSO.
FOLENS PRIMARY ART PACKS (1992) Key Stage 1: 1 *Influential Artists*, 2 *Modern Artists*, 3 *Art of Different Cultures*, Dunstable, Folens.
GULBENKIAN FOUNDATION (1982) *The Arts in School*, London, Calouste Gulbenkian Foundation.
NATIONAL CURRICULUM COUNCIL (NCC) (1992) *Art Non-Statutory Guidance*, York, NCC.
OFFICE FOR STANDARDS IN EDUCATION (OFSTED) (1993) *Art – Key Stages 1, 2 and 3*, London, HMSO.
WILLIAMS, S. *Picasso: Sculptor/Painter A Brief Guide* (1994) Tate Gallery, London.
ROWE, G. (1987) *Guiding Young Artists*, Melbourne, Oxford University Press.
BUGG, S. (1993) *Understanding Art*, Leamington Spa, Scholastic.

Chapter 11

Developing the Role of the Key Stage 1 IT Coordinator: A Case of the Hare or the Tortoise?

Tony Birch

The coordinator's role was crucial in influencing colleagues and in developing work with computers across the age range (HMI, 1991, p. 31).

Introduction

In 1980 there were very few computers in English primary schools but the Department of Trade and Industry's 'Micros in Schools' initiative was instrumental in every primary school being supplied with a machine. Today many primary schools have one per class (or more) and some schools even have one per child! The arrival of cheap, portable machines suggests a further burgeoning and there is little doubt that the information technology (IT) coordinator's role is going to grow and grow into the twenty-first century.

With this technological downpour it is important that IT coordinators have a clear notion of the educational outcomes they wish to achieve and of how to enhance staff capabilities. As a new IT coordinator taking on this fast-changing area it may be worth remembering that computers are not an educational panacea but are a means of enriching and extending children's education.

IT in the National Curriculum

Translating the ideas recorded in the national curriculum into the policies and practice of the school is an essential part of the coordinator's role. The original statutory orders lacked coherence for the non-specialist and there seemed to be many dimensions and some inevitable jargon. It remains to be seen how accessible Dearing's SCAA (1994) new orders will prove but as coordinator your understanding and your ability to transmit the key messages will be significant. You should help staff to understand that the documentation which forms the current orders represents the distillation of the many ideas and approaches to using IT which have been tried and tested over more than a decade. Many of the ideas for using word processors, databases and so on remain just as relevant as before the review, as does the need for IT to grow out of the best in Key Stage 1 practice. Your key task will be to communicate, in a meaningful and practicable way, the idea that children must use a variety of applications and a variety of equipment in increasingly challenging tasks with a developing sense of audience.

National Curriculum: What Is It All About?

The programme of study for Key Stage 1 argues that children should have opportunities to:

- use a variety of IT equipment and software, including micro-computers and various keyboards, to carry out a variety of functions in a range of contexts;
- explore the use of computer systems and control technology in everyday life;
- examine and discuss their experiences of IT, and look at the use of IT in the outside world.

In practice this means that pupils at Key Stage 1 need to be introduced to the range of ITs available in the school. This will include computers but also the stop-watches, tape recorders and such like around the building. At other times children might spend time doing IT with the secretary or caretaker. Young children have a natural curiosity for things like burglar alarms. Visits out might include learning about how the supermarket cash tills work or the mini-bank at the local bank. There are many opportunities for IT within and beyond the school. By visiting IT in various contexts and using various software in their classrooms young children grow aware of the information society in which they live. So-called content-free software such as word processors and databases are particularly useful because they link with any curriculum area. For example, young children can use a word processor for numerous tasks including weather reports, poems, family trees; the limit is the imagination of teacher and child.

The orders for Key Stage 1 also state that children should receive teaching in two key areas.

Communicating and Handling Information

The so-called 'level descriptors' stress the use of IT as a means of communicating *ideas*. IT allows us to communicate through 'text, tables, pictures and sound'. Word processing, databases, drawing and music programs all have a role in Key Stage 1, as do the use of multimedia packages. How far children progress in their skills with these packages will determine their ultimate end of Key Stage level. Children should be encouraged to develop skills in loading, saving, retrieving and amending information in different software environments.

Your role as coordinator is to stress first of all the range of software available and then the importance of communicating through these media. Children will have greatest understanding when the tasks they are asked to do link with their other classroom work and are based in real situations. For example, Year 1 children in one primary school had visited a local art gallery and had liked some modern paintings based on geometric shapes. Resultant work led them to use a drawing package to emulate the work of these artists. Similarly effective database work using SortGame was closely linked to Year 2 children's work in sorting and classifying in the maths curriculum.

Children should be taught to:

- generate and communicate their ideas in different forms, using text, tables, pictures and sound;
- enter and store information;
- retrieve, process and display information that has been stored.

Controlling and Modelling

Word processors and databases are among the more common and recognizable aspects of IT. There are other ways of using IT which involve children in the control of the computer and provide them with opportunities to explore new situations.

Controlling the computer should not simply be equated with programming; other opportunities exist for Key Stage 1 children to be involved in real control in exciting and motivating situations. Reception children enjoy using programmable toys. A maze was constructed in a shared area outside one classroom and the children, with the help of an NNEB (nursery nurse), were encouraged to get Ronnie (the Roamer) out the other side. In this way the children learned about signals and commands. Another teacher taught children about how a smoke alarm worked in class work on 'the home'. Children's control work might then involve them in using a Turtle Graphics-like program such as Tiny Logo.

Children are also encouraged to learn through IT-based models or simulations. 'Granny's Garden' or 'Scenarios' allow children to investigate situations and make decisions. 'Viewpoints' is another way of using IT; in this software children are put in a new situation such as exploring wildlife as part of an environmental project. The children are thus able to explore different habitats and take photographs of the animals they meet for use later.

Children should be taught to:

- recognize that control is integral to many everyday devices;
- give direct signals or commands that produce a variety of outcomes, and describe the effects of their actions;
- use IT-based models or simulations to explore aspects of real or imaginary situations.

Getting Started as an IT Coordinator

Meeting the challenge of the national curriculum is daunting. If you are new to teaching and new to the school then that challenge may seem even more intimidating.

In most schools your first responsibility will lie with your class. This, in itself, presents your first opportunity. As coordinator you must get IT up and running in your classroom; motivated and skilled children help to raise the profile of IT.

Start exploring the school's current position. Find out, for example, how many computers are currently in the school. Sometimes this can provide surprising answers. A friend once found a machine languishing in the cupboard, supposedly out of order. It was quickly mended with the purchase of a new lead – a much cheaper solution than buying a new computer. Some IT coordinators keep the oldest equipment running reliably well beyond their supposed obsolescence. There is software for the ageing BBC series of computers which can be highly interesting to children and meet many of the aims for IT presented earlier. You might produce an inventory of hardware and software and distribute this to colleagues.

Take opportunities to find out about what people are doing in their classrooms and start to form mental pictures about IT in your school. Speak to the headteacher early on and ascertain his or her view. Start reading relevant literature; does the school have Anita Straker's *Children Using Computers* or the National Council for Educational Technology's *Focus on IT*? If not it may be worth ordering them. Gather together any LEA documentation. Another valuable step is to introduce yourself to the local IT adviser or advisory teacher. Find out from them whether any training is available and if possible enrol on a course. It is worth stressing to the headteacher how important this is; there is a technical level of knowledge, a need to be *au fait* with software and considerable curricular and organizational elements that have to be acquired one way or another.

Building a Sphere of Influence: A Foot in the Door!

For the new coordinator there may be many laudable aims. None is more important than establishing your own credibility. To have, in the eyes of your colleagues, the general classroom capabilities is vital in the first instance. It makes one part of the staff team and is the basis for securing respect. The classroom is also the launching pad for demonstrating the potential of IT. Using a program like 'Pictogram' to produce attractive displays of children's survey work could be effective, for example. Your classroom can provide a vehicle for demonstrating the variety of opportunities, links across the curriculum and also the quality of work possible by young children. Interested others might then ask, 'Could I do that with my class?' This is the basis for productive working relationships with colleagues and, having used a variety of software, colleagues come to know that you are a useful source of information and advice. Remember that some of the most critical reviewers can be children and you may wish to give them opportunities to write reviews and make these available to colleagues. An important task may be to create a school software directory giving useful information.

A challenge for you will be to wean staff away from thinking of you as a technical problem solver. You may be asked to do things like change printer ribbons or put a new roll of paper in a printer. On such occasions try to show your colleague how to do this so that in the future they can sort it out themselves. Other times it may be an actual fault with some aspect of the machinery. Dealing with such problems is one reason why your own training is so important.

Sometimes messages for help will arrive at your classroom. There is a dilemma here and many coordinators do not like having their class interrupted. The argument that your class is most important during teaching hours is a valid one, but if a simple answer can be given which will get a teacher in need operational again then this may well be appropriate. Otherwise offer to help at the earliest convenient moment. My own experience suggests that it is important to keep computers functioning as smoothly as possible in the classroom. Momentum is quickly lost, especially when there is only one machine in that particular room.

This reactive part of being an IT coordinator is unavoidable, sometimes irritating, but certainly important. Complaints that 'computers always go wrong' are best dealt with by prompt, efficient action. Offer advice carefully, however, as you will soon learn that people's attitudes to IT vary greatly. Encourage and reassure when technical difficulties occur but try to equip people with skills. Take steps to help teachers by having 'help' cards available that explain some of the more common difficulties that teachers might run into (your LEA IT centre may well have some prepared).

You will have to resolve how much of a technician you are prepared to be. One day in the future primary schools may have their own technicians but they are virtually non-existent at the moment. There are some pitfalls worth avoiding if you are expected to fulfil any technical difficulties. Basically some forms of technical support are feasible and others are not. Most coordinators will attempt to solve software problems. The worst that can happen is that you ruin the program and either have to buy another one or make another copy. However, beware anything that involves electrical components or opening the main casing of a machine. Beyond the usual temperamental leads and printer ribbons leave the rest to specialist companies or the LEA. If necessary negotiate with the headteacher for a contract with one of these. Look at costs when doing so but also value promptness of response as machines left out of order for long periods reduce the amount of time pupils spend doing IT. You might talk to your local secondary school and find out if they have a technician or IT expert who can help with any difficulties.

From the first stages of using the computer effectively in your classroom this need to react to technical problems can be frustrating but it is important in winning confidence and keeping computers up and running in classrooms; the relationship this builds with allow you to move towards a more pro-active approach.

Developing the Role: Making It Yours

There will usually be some expectations of a coordinator generally and the IT coordinator specifically when you arrive at a school. Aspects of *technical* activity have already been discussed. Usually your role will involve some *organizational* work; rotas will need preparing, hard disks will need organizing and software may need copying and distributing, *development* work will involve improvements to existing practices and may be achieved by presenting INSET, developing policy and schemes of work and the introduction of new and different equipment (e.g. CD-ROM, portables) would come under this umbrella. A *monitoring* role is a fourth dimension of your role that should be addressed; this is an ongoing process centred on making practices as efficient and effective as possible. For example, you might want to investigate how often particular equipment is used or whether your word processing packages are meeting the children's needs.

Getting Organized

Organizational work is a vital part of what IT coordinators do. You will almost certainly be involved in preparing some sort of rota system; a clear system which is not overly rigid will be the target here: 'In general, flexible arrangements maximised the amount of hands-on time available to different groups of pupils and ensured that computers were in classes when they were most needed' (HMI, 1991, p. 33).

A further aim of such a rota is to get computers into classrooms with the minimum of disruption to teachers. Older pupils in one primary school wheeled out the infant department's computers each morning and away again at the end of the school day. In one infant school it was the responsibility of the NNEB, at another the caretaker kindly obliged in fulfilling the task.

Be aware! There may be times when a class will want more than one computer at a time (or none at all). Data handling, for example, may take a long time with just one computer in the classroom, especially if the planning requires pupils to have several hands-on sessions during a short-lived project. Arrangements can be made. Several years ago during end of Key Stage assessments several computers were made available in one classroom to make this more manageable. You may decide that having three computers in a classroom with six pupils doing IT is a more viable use of teaching time and that this will become a regular approach. The more computers you have, the more flexible arrangements can be made. As numbers increase your ability to allocate them creatively is likely to become crucial.

One danger when organizing IT is that we tend only to include computers on the rota system. It may be worth producing a list of other ITs available in the school and disseminating this at the beginning of the school year. Much IT work can be done using stop-watches, tape recorders and programmeable toys. Toys such as Roamer and Pip can be excellent introductions to ideas of measuring and controlling in Key Stage 1. Children enjoy taping themselves and others and such work is at the heart of children learning to communicate.

Getting hardware into classrooms is an essential organizational task. Related to this is the distribution of software. Many coordinators choose to have a set of master disks. These may well be hidden away in a cupboard and for use only by the coordinator with the purpose of keeping one copy of each piece of software safe and protected from being copied over. The coordinator then gives copies to the teachers who will be using that piece of software to keep in their classrooms or increasingly copies the software onto the hard disk of the machine they are using. Until hard disks become the norm in your school and as disks are relatively cheap, it is worth having a considerable supply with plenty of back-ups of popular software available to teachers. Some even advocate every child having their own individual disk on which to save their work.

Keeping the existing base of equipment well organized and running smoothly is important to teachers; it allows them to get on with the very important job of using IT in their classroom. A word of warning: beware any software that arrives in school of which you do not know the origins. There are two dangers; one is breaking the copyright laws and the second is introducing a computer virus into your machines. You may decide that your school will have a virus killer; used only once such software probably recoups its value.

Moving Forwards: Developmental Activities

Development in IT should be considered as an ongoing process; 'whilst a school policy was found to be important, this was not sufficient in itself as it was found that the use of IT was dependent upon the interest of individual teachers', (Watson, 1993, p. 3). For our purposes here a policy is seen as a statement of what is happening now. It should not be an idealistic statement bearing no resemblance to practice in the school. It should be a working document which reflects where the school is now. When seen in this light it seems logical that current practice will have its limitations and that some form of action plan will be required. You may be asked for an action plan by the person responsible in your school for curriculum coordination or for the school development plan. An action plan will document the steps you have to take to improve quality of provision and set realistic targets for achievement.

In drawing together either a policy or an action plan you will need to ask the staff what they do in their classrooms. You may glean a considerable amount of information and it may be that there are obvious gaps. For example, the Year 2 teacher may not do any word processing or in reception there is no use of a programmable toy. An informal chat may allow you to suggest that FullPhase, for example, would be an appropriate next step for the Year 2 teacher. Always offer to support any requests that you make. By saying 'I could show you if you like', it gives the opportunity for the responsibility to be shared and steps taken together.

As well as a policy, some identifying of 'who does what' needs to be recorded possibly as a scheme of work. Some schools have adopted a 'tool box' approach. In this way of working, each year group is allocated a set of software with which they will be asked to work. This might not be completely comprehensive but would offer coverage of different aspects of IT. For example, a Year 1 teacher was asked to ensure her pupils had worked with MyWorld, Easel, Pictogram, Phases and the Roamer. This same teacher was able to use some favourite software alongside the basic toolbox. The example given in Figure 11.1 shows how a Key Stage 1 department attempted to come to terms with allocating their software for the 'communicating' aspect of IT, making use of both BBC and Acorn machines. It was not intended to be a perfect system but to make effective use of existing resources.

Figure 11.1: Communicating

	Reception	Year 1	Year 2
General	My World Word and Picture Matching	My World Scenarios	
Text	Folio with Concept Keyboard Phases with Concept Keyboard	Folio with Concept Keyboard Phases with Concept Keyboard	Folio/Pen Down Phases/Pen Down
Pictures	Easel	Easel	First Paint
Music		Compose	Compose

Large amounts of hardware and software are no guarantee of effective IT. Having a range of skills that reflect pupil capability is another means of developing the IT curriculum. These skills would range in complexity from nursery to Year 2 and may be based on a series of 'I can . . .' statements. Figure 11.2 was produced by Alan Cross of Manchester University as a possible checklist during a project exploring portable computers and could easily be developed.

Figure 11.2: IT checklist

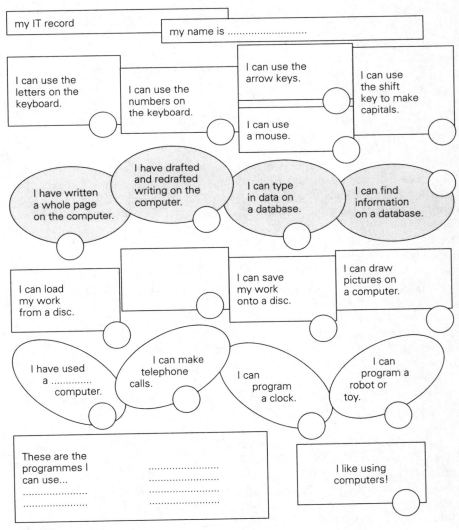

AC 1993

Please colour in each rectangle or oval to show you have achieved this goal and put the date into the circle. Let me know what you think of this record.

Figure 11.3: Development of IT

Theme: .... (e.g. communicating/data handling)

Year	Programme of Study	Focus Skills	Classroom Activities	Suggested Software
Reception				
Year 1				
Year 2				

In another school a pro forma was used as the basis of a staff meeting (Figure 11.3). This pro forma listed national curriculum levels and there were columns for statutory criteria, software and the kinds of activity children might undertake.

The use of this pro forma identified, as most exercises of this type do, some areas of weakness. At any point as coordinator you may discover that a particular area of IT is underdeveloped. There may be little use of data handling software in your school and you may decide that this will form the focus for an INSET session. Any neglected area should be fully explored. The reason for underdevelopment may be lack of resources in a particular area. In my own school there was a conscious decision taken to look at communicating and data handling first and then to look at measurement and control at a later date. This was recorded in the school policy however.

You will certainly want to record aspects of classroom organization in your policy. In one policy statement a school included a sentence to the effect that computers would always be used inside classrooms rather than outside. The staff had agreed that this meant computers were more readily part of the everyday activities of the classroom rather than something special.

Some aspects of policy can be drawn up on a one-to-one basis while others need discussing as a whole staff. If you are not confident with leading a staff meeting call in the help of the headteacher or the deputy to help in its management.

Once your policy is drafted and ready for publication try to develop plans for action. You may be asked to talk to governors and certainly you will need to discuss it with the headteacher. Ask the staff what help they need and prepare to give it to them. There may be a tension between the staff's perceived needs and your perception as coordinator. They may ask for time to look at software and you may want to focus the school on a new dimension of IT, for example data handing. If this is the case look for the possibility to put them together so that everyone goes away feeling a sense of satisfaction and achievement. Motivating teachers is, after all, your foremost target as IT coordinator.

Getting into INSET

Coordinators should realize that most teachers will get most of their information about IT from the school and most probably from you. This key role of the coordinator is two-fold: first to present clear, up-to-date, relevant information and second to equip teachers with confidence and competence in IT.

To keep up-to-date you may decide to join a professional organization like Micros and Primary Education (MAPE) whose journal, *Microscope*, is full of up-to-the-minute information. Additionally, they produce occasional software and some specials which focus upon a particular area of IT (such as Logo or multimedia). There is an annual conference and regional support groups to give local support. The *Times Educational Supplement* also produces regular 'computer updates' with reviews and information. Make use of any drop-in facilities organized by your LEA and talk to colleagues who are IT coordinators in other schools when possible.

When planning an INSET be clear about your aims and how you will accomplish them. You must decide if you will present the session yourself or invite an outsider. Advisory teachers are an invaluable source and representatives of local higher education departments can be involved. However, there is every likelihood that there will be a cost involved when using visiting presenters. There are advantages in presenting INSET yourself; the most important of these is your working knowledge of the school. If you decide to go it alone you will need to find activities to help you. There is a growing range of resources. The National Council for Educational Technology (NCET) in particular, have produced a range of materials which would be an asset to any coordinator. *Focus on IT* (NCET, 1991) enables the coordinator to go beyond the technology and deal with issues such as progression and continuity. Your LEA may have some further resources and activities.

The most common way of disseminating information and developing confidence and competence is through an INSET session. Such an event can make you anxious. To offset this, it is best to be well prepared and consider all the eventualities. Spare disks are essential and do not rely on all the computers in the school being available. One might break the day before or, even worse, on the morning of the session itself. Another useful tip can be to involve others. In one session a coordinator enlisted the help of two confident and motivated members of staff to run inputs on software they had used extensively in their classrooms. It may not be just you who is feeling nervous. Some of your colleagues may be feeling insecure. Sometimes people gain confidence when working with a partner – especially if that person is sensitive to their needs. Creating the right atmosphere is vital. Allow those who want privacy to have it, but supportiveness should feature with you as coordinator setting the lead. It helps greatly to find activities that are interesting to do. One teacher educator showed students how to use the program 'Draw' and asked them to produce a card that introduced them. If, through skilled teaching, you can ensure that everybody achieves something in your session then it will make it worthwhile. Another idea is to present open-ended activities in which children might also participate. First Paint, for example, was used open-endedly to engage teachers in a first-hand observation session alongside other art materials in an joint session with the art coordinator.

One of the dangers with an INSET session is that it can appear to be a one-off. Any session needs to be related back to practice. One method is the trial and feedback approach. This might start with an INSET morning given over to exploring two or three pieces of software on a theme with the agreement that each teacher will try out at least one of them and report back at an agreed meeting. Even better is the opportunity to follow up work alongside teachers in their classrooms. While this may be expensive in terms of supply cover it does enable a further dimension to be added to the coordinator–teacher relationship.

Finally look for additional opportunities; IT is nothing if not cross-curricular. If the maths coordinator is doing an investigation session then there is a role for IT, possibly through Logo or a programmable toy. In addition you could try out your new software in the staffroom so that everyone gets to see what is new. It is perhaps wise to remember that it is the cumulative effect of a number of INSETs over a period of time that builds lasting change. Maintain the freshness of your INSETs by switching between formal and informal approaches. Use sessions concerned with the technology alone but balance this with others which start with a practical context and use IT to investigate through first-hand experience. Blease and Cohen found in a longitudinal study that 'probably the most important lesson about training that arises from our work at Broadwood School is that you cannot afford to rush people into things' (1990, p. 135).

Resources

> If the IT coordinator doesn't communicate and liaise and ask the staff and then let the headteacher know what is needed then things can't be updated (primary school headteacher).

When the original DTI initiative was announced, Pam Linn (1987) contrasted this huge investment with the fact that no similar initiative has ever been undertaken for reading. For the coordinator there will always be a tension between spending money on hardware and buying peripherals such as printers, hard disks and of course software. You will probably never have enough money! You may well be allocated your own budget for IT and will have to decide how to spend it. The answer will always lie in your unique school circumstances. Some of the following questions might be useful in identifying your needs:

- How many computers are there in the school? Have I got one per class? How old are they? What is my target for acquiring machines over the next three years?
- Is there suitable software for progression from nursery to Year 2?
- Would any peripherals add to existing provision? A touch screen for nursery reception use perhaps?
- Is there sufficient breadth in the software currently available?
- Are there enough consumables (disks, printer paper etc.) to last the year?
- Have I left enough money for maintenance and mending damaged equipment?
- Should any money be spent on sending people on courses or buying in a visiting speaker?

Once you have decided on your priorities, get the equipment you intend to buy ordered. Check catalogues for prices and consult with your LEA centre to see if they have arranged special deals with any of the suppliers. Look at the catalogues produced by organizations such as Northwest SEMERC, Longman Logotron and Resource who have a range of software at affordable prices. The newest technology might be the most expensive so have a look for details on models which may only just be outdated and ask whether it can do the job for you. The saving may be used to fund another purchase elsewhere. The quality of the hardware and software is important. Key Stage 1 is not in the business of using software simply because it is available or cheap. It should be chosen to meet the needs of children and their learning. Children will need to experience the same piece of software on several occasions if they are to gain a thorough understanding and they will need to contrast similar software. During INSET sessions encourage teachers to use different kinds of database, for example, and then reflect upon their different purposes. Ask them to do the same with their children.

Aim for quality in your purchases and stress the depth of learning as well as variety of experience. One Key Stage 1 coordinator spent an entire year's IT budget on purchasing a hard disk, touch screen, concept keyboard and software so that the nursery and reception classes had a machine that met their needs fully and in the hope that a much fuller use could be made of the machine.

With many schools having limited money to spend, the ways in which resources are purchased is very important. Look out for any special evaluation projects going on. My own school was involved in the national evaluation of portable computers and equipment was supplied to the value of £2000. If you take over as coordinator and resources for IT are inadequate, then you might consider a bid to the governing body for additional funding or press for IT to have a high profile on the next year's school development plan. Sometimes you may have to press hard to get the resources you need.

Under Review: Some Themes for Consideration

All the areas mentioned so far will need to be monitored carefully to check that quality is as high as possible. You may want to invest in a document like NCET's *Reviewing IT* (1994) to help you. You may also decide to keep a number of other issues under review too. The themes presented forthwith are important ones which should be integrated into all your activities as IT coordinator.

Equal Opportunities

> The issues that are important to equality of opportunity are the very same issues that are important to good primary practice (Ellis, 1986, p. 3).

Equal opportunities, issues particularly with regard to gender, do have significance in the primary years. If you are a male IT coordinator then it is important that children are not presented solely with a male image of IT expertise. Efforts may have to be made to challenge any stereotypes of this kind. In this case you may wish to invite a female computer expert from industry to talk or work with children or call in a female advisory teacher.

Similar issues can present themselves with children. One teacher said, 'It's who you put next to each other – there is a need to look at some groups carefully'. It is not sufficient just to have mixed groups; any group or set of groups needs to be observed carefully. While it may not always be boys who dominate the computer, it is important to see who performs which tasks. Are there children who dominate the thinking aspects of the work? Are there children who always type the instructions or text? Are there children who do nothing or just observe? Is observing an acceptable strategy? There may be some children in your class who are very confident and skilled because they have access to computers at home; others may be timid simply due to lack of exposure to IT. These things should make a difference in your grouping and as coordinator you will need to raise awareness and encourage a reflective approach among your colleagues. You may wish to suggest that while small groups at the computer is the norm there may be some children who need access alone.

Finally, with equal opportunities in mind, ask whether the software you are using has any biases for gender, disability, class or race. Much software is 'content-free', as has been explained earlier, but even then the choice of task could lead to culture bias. Everyone needs to be aware of this issue.

Special Needs

Inevitably within the school there will be children with differing abilities and capabilities. This raises a number of questions. Should all children have access to the same software? Some children may be given access to a word processor through the use of a special keyboard whereas others may be accessing IT through the qwerty keyboard with little difficulty. Do all your staff know how to configure the mouse to slow it down? This can have a considerable effect on some children's success. You need to stress as coordinator that children's uptake is mediated by both the match of hardware and software to their needs and also by the task that they are asked to do. One teacher used a database called 'Ourfacts' with all her children and was able to differentiate the levels of search they were introduced to. Another teacher let her Year 2 children work on Phases but also felt that a group of three able children had reached a point where they needed further extension in terms of their IT capability. She introduced them to a second word processor as a means of contrasting experiences and asked them which they preferred.

Sometimes teachers might find that a particular concept is causing a difficulty for a child. In such circumstances a specific program to support learning in that area can be appropriate. One child was allowed to use a spelling program during registration as part of a more general programme. Principally IT has the potential to help many children; it is the ways in which it is applied that will be most significant. As coordinator the idea of 'matching' IT work may well be one that you have to stress.

Parents

If you are lucky enough to have large numbers of portable computers you may be able to send them home with the children, but if you do not have enough equipment there are other ways of making links with home. One way is to produce a booklet suggesting helpful ways of using home computers in children's education. Some schools have given parents practical 'hands on' sessions with the computers the children use. On some occasions parents who have attended these courses have gone on to work with children and computers in classrooms.

Assessment and Record Keeping

The demands on the assessment of IT may have diminished recently with the focus of attention reverting to the core subjects. This does not mean that systems of recording progress should be ignored. As coordinator you should first insist that IT is included in every teacher's planning; the details of this will undoubtedly depend upon your school's chosen approach. The level descriptors are a useful basis for evaluating pupil capability. An agreement trial can be a challenging way of looking at the detail of IT capability and this might feed into your school portfolio. Encouraging children to record their own progress is important too. Giving them a checklist of 'I can . . .'

Figure 11.4: Self-evaluation for IT

Name of child: ....
Year: ....

Date	Communicating and Handling Information	Controlling and Modelling	Date
	I used		
	I did.....		
	I used		
	I did		
	I used ...		
	I did		
	I used		
	I did		
	I used		
	I did		
	I used		
	I did		
	I used		
	I did		

statements is one way. Another is to get them to record the software they have used and any comments on it they choose (Figure 11.4). When children get to Year 2 they can then look back at their own progress easily and see the range of skills they have achieved.

It is important to keep assessment and record keeping closely tuned to the classroom; no system should be onerous or time consuming. Encourage teachers to base assessments on contexts where the child is familiar so as to look at their achieved level of capability.

Keeping IT Moving: A Balanced Approach

As a new coordinator there are many things to be done and the task, depending on your point of view, can either be exciting or daunting. Often small steps achieve much. That half hour with Mrs Smith showing the potential of a colour printer or sorting out Mr Brown's recurring disk fault can achieve almost as much as an elaborately planned and skilfully executed training day. Aim for balance in your presentation styles. Aim to maintain your current practices, to develop others and to keep the whole scenario under review. My advice would be to stress the applications of IT constantly (e.g. word processing, databases, multimedia); they link with other aspects of the curriculum so readily and can be used by the children to meet their own needs as they mature as IT users.

Be aware also of the tendency to concentrate on the technical aspects of IT. The Key Stage 1 curriculum is about quality classroom organization and management and a lively and engaging curriculum; IT should mirror this and build upon it. The title of this chapter referred to the hare and the tortoise; there is certainly something to be said for intensive bursts of action with regard to IT but a steady approach is also vitally important. Only when the use of IT has become engrained in the practice of your institution can you say that it has taken root. It can be a slow process but the satisfaction of seeing teachers growing in confidence, becoming more skilled and children enjoying and learning from their work is ultimately a great reward.

References

BLEASE, D. and COHEN, L. (1990) *Coping with Computers: An Ethnographic Study in Primary Classroom*, London, Paul Chapman.

ELLIS, J. (1986) *Equal Opportunities and Computer Education in the Primary School*, Manchester, Equal Opportunities Commission/Sheffield LEA.

HMI (1991) *Aspects of Primary Education: The Teaching and Learning of Information Technology*, London, HMSO.

LINN, P. (1987) 'Microcomputers in education: Living and dead labour', in SCANLON, E. and O'SHEA, T. (eds) *Educational Computing: A Reader*, Chichester, John Wiley.

NATIONAL COUNCIL FOR EDUCATIONAL TECHNOLOGY (NCET) (1991) *Focus on IT: School Focussed Development Materials for Key Stages 1, 2 and 3*, Coventry, NCET.

NCET (1994) *Reviewing IT*, Coventry, NCET.

SCHOOL CURRICULUM and ASSESSMENT AUTHORITY (SCAA) (1994) *Information Technology in the National Curriculum*, London, DFE.

STRAKER, A. (1989) *Children Using Computers*, Oxford, Blackwell.

WATSON, D. (ed.) (1993) *The Impact Report: An Evaluation of the Impact of Information Technology on Children's Achievements in Primary and Secondary Schools*, London, King's College.

Some Other Useful Literature

ADVISORY CENTRE FOR COMPUTERS IN EDUCATION (1992) *Planning for Assessment: Teacher Assessment of IT IT Capability at Key Stages 1, 2 and 3*, Cardiff, ACCE.

BRITISH COMPUTER SOCIETY (1992) *IT Ideas*, Swindon, BCS.

CROMPTON R. (ed.) (1989) *Computers and the Primary Curriculum 3–13*, London, Falmer Press.

MANCHESTER UNIVERSITY PORTABLES PROJECT (1994) *Portable Computers, Portable Learning: An Evaluation of the Use of Portable Computers in the Primary Years*, Manchester, Manchester University.

NCET (1992) *Assessing IT: Curriculum Materials to Support Teacher Assessment of IT at Key Stages 1, 2 and 3*, Coventry, NCET.

NCET (1994) *IT Works: Stimulate to Educate*, Coventry, NCET.

SCHOLASTIC PUBLICATIONS (1992) *Bright Ideas: Computer Activities*, Leamington Spa, Scholastic.

Useful Organizations and Publications

Your LEA computer centre, if they still operate one, is a useful first port of call.

NCET produces a range of publications of interest to IT coordinators. Your school should receive some information automatically. The address is:

NCET
Milburn Hill Road
Science Park
Coventry CV4 7JJ

MAPE, as already mentioned, produces a magazine and also produces software annually. Its regional support groups can be a useful contact point. Application forms from:

Mrs G. Jones
The Old Vicarage
Skegy Road
Normanton on Trent
Notts NG23 6RR

Northwest SEMERC undertakes a range of activities and also produces and sells a range of quality software. Your LEA may well be a SEMERC centre.

Northwest SEMERC (Oldham)
1 Broadbent Road
Watersheddings
Oldham OL1 4LB

The journal *Educational Computing and Technology* includes software reviews and articles on the application of the technology.

Educational Computing and Technology
Jubilee House
The Oaks
Ruislip
Middlesex HA4 7LF

Child Education and *Junior Education* both include reviews of software and short articles on doing IT in the classroom. Contact Scholastic Publications, CV1034, Westfield Road, Southam, Leamington Spa, Warwickshire, CV33 0BR.

Finally the *Times Educational Supplement* has a regular page devoted to IT and computers. Additional 'updates' provide a supplement full of the latest information and are a useful way of keeping up-to-date with what is happening in IT.

Suppliers

There are a wide range of both hardware and software producers. NCET, SEMERC and MAPE are all worth contacting about software but the following list (by no means exhaustive) could be worth following up. The focus here is on software. There is a lot to be said for the 'try before you buy' philosophy and your local IT centre will probably have some of the software contained in these brochures. Your local IT centre is probably the best place to enquire about local hardware suppliers and dealers; also try IT coordinators in other local schools. Educational requirements should be first on your list of criteria for evaluating software.

Advisory Unit: Computers in Education
126 Great North Road
Hatfield
Herts AL9 5JZ

Brilliant Computing
P.O. Box 142
Bradford BD9 4BR

Clares
98 Middlewich Road
Rudheath
Northwich
Cheshire CW9 7DA

Colton Software
2 Signet Court
Swanns Road
Cambridge CB5 8LA

Computer Concepts
Gaddesden Place
Hemel Hempstead
Herts HP2 6EX

Educational Electronics
Leighton Buzzard
Beds LU7 7NR

ESM
Abbeygate House
East Road
Cambridge, CB1 1DB

ESP
Holly Tree Cottage
Main Street
Strelley Village
Nottingham NG8 6PD

4Mation
14 Castle Park Road
Barnstaple,
Devon EX32 8PA

Hampshire Microtechnology Centre
Connaught Lane
Portsmouth PO6 4SJ

Keyboard Technology
51 High Street
Kegworth
Derby DE74 2DA

Longman Logotron
124 Science Park
Milton Road
Cambridge CB4 4ZS

Northern Micromedia
NORICC
Coach Lane Campus
Newcastle-upon-Tyne NE7 7XA

Research Machines
New Mill House
183 Milton Park

Abingdon
Oxon OX14 4BR

Resource
Exeter Road
Wheatley
Doncaster DN2 4PY

Risc Developments
117 Hatfield Road
St Albans
Herts AL1 4JS

Sherston Software
Swan Barton
Sherston
Malmesbury
Wiltshire SN16 0LH

SPA
P.O. Box 59
Tewkesbury GL20 6AB

Tedimen Software
P.O. Box 23
Southampton SO9 7BD

Topologika
P.O. Box 39
Stilton
Peterborough PE7 3RL

Widgit Software
102 Radford Road
Leamington Spa
Warwickshire CV3 1LF

Chapter 12

Tackling Technology in the Early Years

Deborah Boekestein

Background

Design technology in the primary school has grown out of a strong tradition of craft lessons. Teachers were confident delivering craft in a form with which they felt comfortable. For some pupils these were the days of 'This is what we're going to make; this is how you do it.' And 'Here's one I made earlier'. Although these types of lessons could, at worst, culminate in thirty-six pencil tidies made out of three toilet roll holders, some glue, paint and a spot of fabric, with little or no individuality in the designs created and few skills taught, they could also provide pupils with the potential to make simple design decisions and a range of finely honed practical skills to be used in later life. The technology order (DES/WO, 1990) picked up on all the strands of good practice in operation in classrooms, combined them with the requisites of a society, deemed by the late 1980s to be at the forefront of many scientific and technological advances, and changed the emphasis of craft lesson to design technology lessons. The 1990 national curriculum stated that:

Pupils should be able to identify and state clearly needs and opportunities for design and technological activities through investigation of the contexts of home, school, recreation, community, business and industry. [AT 1]

Pupils should be able to generate a design specification, explore ideas to produce a design proposal and develop it into a realistic, appropriate and achievable design. [AT 2]

Pupils should be able to make artefacts, systems and environments, preparing and working to a plan and identifying, managing and using appropriate resources, including knowledge and processes. [AT 3]

Pupils should be able to develop, communicate and act upon an evaluation of the processes, products and effects of their design and technological activities and those of others, including those from other times and cultures. [AT 4] (DES/WO, 1990)

Overnight a new terminology was introduced into schools. Alongside this there were new demands and a new way of thinking about craft and technology. No longer were nearly identical objects to be the goal of a craft lesson, rather each child was expected to experiment both with self-generated ideas and with skills and techniques. Also specified in the 1990 attainment targets and programmes of study were a wider range of flexible and rigid materials than most teachers had been used to. Teachers also had to contend with planning lessons that would encourage unfamiliar objects to be made in a wider range of contexts than most were used to. Both Key Stage 1 and Key Stage 2 coordinators were faced with the problem of where to begin. It was generally agreed that the technology documentation was difficult to understand and that non-specialists were worried by the demands set. It is fair to say that specialist teachers at all levels found it difficult to marry the demands of the attainment targets and the programmes of study into coherent schemes of work.

During this period countless books were published, suggesting instant technology exercises; particular construction techniques waxed and waned in fashion. Local authorities provided different kinds of training ranging from practical skill building for teachers who had never used wood, plastic or metal before to theoretical justification for the use of a business context within school. While it was threatening for teachers, it was also frustrating for a child whose design had to be first generated, then planned, maybe modelled and only then made. Teaching technology was seen as difficult and very unwieldy. Like Jack's beanstalk it grew and grew and grew and teachers met many hazards on their way to creating the golden design technology lesson.

By May 1992 the technology curriculum was being revised by the National Curriculum Council. Their September 1993 recommendations formed the basis for those made by the School Curriculum and Assessment Authority (SCAA) in March 1994. These in turn formed the basis for the draft proposals for design and technology published in December 1994.

The result of all these revisions is that the design and technology curriculum is described in terms that can be understood by all. Design technology has been refocused. This focus is now upon a range of activities that combine the acquisition of particular skills and knowledge with the investigation and evaluation of existing products, ultimately leading to a pupil designing and making a new object. The SCAA has determined 'level descriptions' for all national curriculum subjects. Level descriptions

describe the types and range of performance that pupils working at a particular level should characteristically demonstrate. In deciding on a pupil's level of attainment at the end of a Key Stage, teachers should judge which description best fits the pupil's performance. Each description should be considered in conjunction with the description for the adjacent levels. By the end of Key Stage 1, the performance of the great majority of pupils should be within the range of levels 1 to 3 (DFE, 1995).

Design technology now has two attainment targets instead of four. The level descriptions for them are:

Attainment target 1: Designing
Level 1
When designing and making, pupils generate ideas through shaping, assembling and rearranging materials and components. They recognise the simple features of familiar products and, when prompted, relate them to their own ideas. They use pictures and words to convey what they want to do.

Level 2
When designing and making, pupils use their experiences of using materials, techniques and products to help generate ideas. They use models and pictures to develop and communicate their designs. They reflect on their ideas and suggest improvements.

Level 3
When designing and making, pupils generate ideas, recognising that their designs will have to satisfy conflicting requirements. They make realistic suggestions about how they can achieve their intentions and suggest more ideas when asked. They draw on their knowledge and understanding of the appropriate programme of study to help them generate ideas. Labelled sketches are used to show the details of their designs.

Attainment target 2: Making
Level 1
When designing and making, pupils explain what they are making and which materials they are using. They select from a narrow range of materials and use given techniques and tools to shape, assemble and join them.

Level 2
When designing and making, pupils select from a range of materials, tools and techniques, explaining their choices. They manipulate tools safely and assemble and join materials in a variety of ways. They can make judgements about the outcomes of their work.

Level 3
When designing and making, pupils think ahead about the order of their work, choosing tools, materials and techniques more purposefully. They use tools with some accuracy and use simple finishing techniques to improve their products. They cut and shape materials

and components, with some precision, to help assembly. Their products are similar to their original intentions and, where changes have been made, they are identified (DFE, 1995).

It must be remembered that these level descriptions are meant to be used at the end of Key Stage assessments only and not as a tick-list to be used all the time. However, parents have a legal right to be informed of their child's progress at the end of each academic year and these level descriptions are useful reminders of what teachers should be looking for during ongoing assessment throughout Key Stage 1.

You, as the newly qualified and appointed design technology coordinator, have a much more manageable task than would have been the case earlier. You have a terminology in place that you can convey to others and you need to set an agenda for your school that will result in quality experiences in design technology for your children.

Where Do I Begin?

Mike Harrison's Chapter 2, which deals with how to write a school policy, will provide a template for you to use with your staff. However, all design technology coordinators are now faced with the task of revitalizing design technology in school. It will be useful for you to discuss the rationale behind design technology with the staff and to make them enthusiastic about its relevance to life both inside and outside school. One starting point for this might be to consider how all-pervasive design technology is. Wherever you are sitting right now, somebody nearby will be indulging in a technological activity – either making an aeroplane out of a bus ticket or creating the evening meal out of whatever is left in the kitchen cupboard, choosing a music system, maybe customizing a DIY flatpack kit, or merely building castles in the air! As adults we design and make all kinds of things without really thinking about it. As children we did the same – from the earliest drum made with saucepan and spoon, through making a bus on the stairs, to using a selection of building bricks to design a car or a house, we improvised and created things for both our own and for others' entertainment and use. Basically that's what design technology is all about – using the resources we have around us to fulfil, match or suit our needs. As a preschool child the desire to do this was a spontaneous one. As a school age child this desire can be indulged, expanded and refined so that by adulthood there is both a knowledge of the skills necessary for and an appreciation of good design. As a Key Stage 1 teacher it falls upon us first to channel the enthusiasm for design brought from home and to begin to introduce the skills and knowledge necessary for adult life.

A Key Stage 1 coordinator has the task of ensuring that design technology is well-integrated into the early years curriculum. If it is well planned, it will enhance all other curriculum areas. The new orders are not a return to the 'TV method' of making things nor are they solely a 'discover for yourself' scenario. Rather, the new order has picked up on all that has been positive over the last few years. The order specifies a wide range of materials; skills are given a high priority; prior knowledge is valued and the designing and making of new products is crucial to the whole. There is a real chance here for a coordinator to establish design technology as a subject in which useful knowledge is applied to positive effect. As well as having fewer attainment targets, the new orders have a programme of study for each Key Stage during which

> pupils should be taught to develop their design and technology capability through combining their Designing and Making skills with Knowledge and Understanding in order to design and make products (NCC, 1995).

The new Key Stage 1 programmes of study list areas of knowledge to be addressed. These are:

Designing skills:
- generating ideas;
- discussing ideas;
- assembling, rearranging materials;
- drawing and modelling*;
- suggest ways forward;
- consider design ideas.

Making skills
- selecting materials, tools, techniques;
- measuring, shaping materials;
- assembling, combining components;
- apply finishes;
- suggest ways forward;
- evaluate product.

Areas of knowledge and understanding
- mechanisms, e.g. wheels, axles;
- structures and their stability;
- products and their applications;
- notion of quality;
- health and safety;
- technical vocabulary.

The development of these skills throughout Key Stage 1 will enable a child to develop a design and technology capability. You will need to discuss with the rest of the Key Stage 1 staff which of these skills is appropriate to introduce when. This will form part of the design and technology scheme of work. This is discussed in the next section.

Note* Modelling in technology means making a mock-up of a design before making the real thing.

Implementation

How Should I Plan for Design Technology for My Class?

Close your eyes and think of your planning sheet. I would be very surprised if it wasn't full of separate items to be taught in maths and language. Then there will either be a number of individual subject topics or a general topic web with subject areas making up parts of the topic. Either way there will be lots of different aims and objectives listed. There may also be a story, range of stories or a thematic approach to the story listed. There might also be a planned structured play area centred around either a different or a complementary topic. Sounds really complicated doesn't it? It is what good planning is all about!

As the technology coordinator you need to make sure that technology has an especially high profile in your classroom because otherwise people will only say 'Well, *you* don't do it like that'. The thing to do is not to panic if colleagues are critical of the apparent lack of technology in your classroom. Emphasize to them that design technology is a very chameleon-like subject. It can be all things to all subject areas. It can be the focus for a whole topic (machines, wheels, packaging, housing, clothing) or it can be used in a completely cross-curricular way supporting and complementing other curriculum areas. The key idea here is *where appropriate*. Don't make the links tenuous. Make them something that the children will appreciate, find useful and enthuse over. Technology will soon have a high profile in your classroom. Build the technology activities into your planning. For example there is design technology in:

- *Science:* Use knowledge about materials to aid the design of a cover for the sand-tray.
- *History:* Use knowledge about old toys to design a game for a Roman child.
- *Geography:* Use knowledge about the local area to design a park.
- *Maths:* Use knowledge of measure to design a box that is two straws long and has square faces.
- *PE:* Use knowledge of movement to design a game using two balls.
- *Story:* Read the story of *The Blue Balloon* and as a follow-up ask if something can be made to keep the blue balloon in.

Activities such as these do not form forced links. They will soon become a natural part of your planning. They easily fulfil the Key Stage 1 programme of study assignments that state that the design and making of products should draw upon knowledge from the programmes of study of other subjects. One more thing to remember when you are starting out is that, like the other national curriculum subjects, you do not have to be addressing all the design technology attainment targets or sections of the programme of study at the same time. Teachers do not often teach 'Light' and 'Living Processes' together in science. They are very far apart. However they may link handwriting and spelling together in English. These subjects are not so far apart. So pick the parts of the programme of study that fit your purpose. Don't feel pressurized to do them all. In the reception class, for example, you may spend three times as long making a Playdough plate of food for Little Red Riding Hood to give to Granny (making skills: measuring, shaping, cutting and applying finishing techniques) as you do talking about the types of food that may travel well in a basket (knowledge and understanding: relate the way things work to their intended purpose, people's needs). However a word of caution – you do at some time have to cover all the attainment targets and address all of the programme of study, so don't think that you can miss out on the bits you don't feel confident with. You can't! This way though you'll soon see easy ways to integrate structures and mechanisms into the other national curriculum subjects.

Once you have decided upon the form technology is going to take in your room, cross-curricular or not, decide on the balance of activities you wish to have for a half term. Which parts of the programme of study are you going to try to teach? The thing to remember is that just as we don't expect children to learn cursive writing without showing them letter formation, we cannot expect children to cut and shape a piece of card without showing them how to use scissors. Once staff see that this is a manageable way into technology and is working for you, you can encourage them to ensure that the activities planned for each year group are part of a programme designed to encourage progression of both the designing and making skills.

How Should I Encourage Design Technology in Key Stage 1?

As a Key Stage 1 coordinator encourage the cross-curricular approach to technology. Link particular areas of the programme of study to topics which suit them. Use individual teachers' own strengths and interests to help design activities that will allow for quality teaching of a small area of the design technology curriculum.

As you work around the school with the staff in their classrooms, enthuse about all the design technology opportunities there are and encourage them towards the good practice you identify as a team. In any Key Stage 1 classroom, design technology can be in operation most of the time. Kits can be used as a table-top or a carpet activity. Initially encourage free play and then begin to introduce design elements, e.g. build a car with only red bricks; build a car with six wheels; make a bed for teddy, etc. Encourage staff to ask the children to leave their design complete until there is a chance to discuss it with them. This can be as simple as counting the wheels to see if they have fulfilled the criteria or discussing how to improve the model's stability.

Remind staff that design technology can be in operation in the structured play area, perhaps by creating the artefacts to go in the area if you have an airport or a shop. Once the play area is established, a design technology activity could be introduced daily, by careful placing of materials and stimuli. We encourage children to write by placing writing materials around play areas, so bricks, card, Playdough and material will encourage them to generate and make designs. Remember, just like writing, children like to rehearse and practise their responses so let them do the same in design technology. Encourage staff to repeat popular activities and to alter and/or support activities that were spectacular failures. Both teacher and pupils gain much from sessions where there is joint exploration. Remind staff that it is natural to teach a cutting technique in a structured play situation, as a child will immediately see both a practical purpose and an application for that skill.

Encourage and enable staff to model technology themselves and to show children techniques in action. We all model writing for our children and create books, so why not model a design technology process for the children? Using shared carpet time to make something from scratch, either linked to a story or a topic, or picking up on ideas spontaneously generated by the children and talking about what is being done is an amazing stimulus for them. Remember it doesn't matter how 'good' the finished product is, it is the doing that is important!

Remind teachers that the profile of technology can be lifted in a room through display. Displays may show the whole process or just the finished product. Interactive displays such as those throwing out a challenge may elicit responses from parents or other children. Provide materials and encourage makers to display their results. Establish a practice of going on visits wherever practical or necessary. They don't always have to be expensive trips to museums. Trips to a bus-stop to look at waterproof shelters, to a newsagent's to look at card racks, to a bridge to look at its structure, to a supermarket to look at wheels on a trolley are all trips where you see real technology in action. Teachers should gauge the needs of their children and build on the out-of-school experiences they have had and complement or extend them.

An important issue for both your own classroom and for you to encourage staff to think about is the grouping of children. Gender grouping is the major issue here. Single-sex groupings will encourage girls to experiment with materials and construction kits, often alien to them in out-of-school situations. Obviously the reverse can be true and boys may be less familiar with the traditionally female spheres of textile and food technology. Again, encourage staff to allow for differentiated exploratory sessions in the early years. As the children mature, mixed gender groupings may encourage skill sharing. However it may help certain children if the design technology policy and scheme of work does not preclude staff from introducing new techniques and skills to single gender groupings, if it is considered necessary or appropriate. Running alongside this issue is that of choice of design tasks. Remind staff that when they are designing tasks to ensure that the choice of topics is potentially stimulating for both boys and girls. Again, this is made easier by encouraging staff to adopt a cross-curricular approach to design technology as more than one option can be given for any particular topic. Figure 12.1 suggests a progression of technology activities and skills which can be developed from general class topics.

Figure 12.1: A technology programme of study using class topics across Key Stage 1

Reception	Year 1	Year 2
Main topic: Houses and homes *Designing Skills* 1 Generate/discuss ideas: Talk about variety of own homes; homes of animals; needs of animals and people; Story: *Three Little Pigs* – discuss needs of pigs and what each pig did. Which house did its job?	Main topic: People who help us *Designing Skills* 1 Generate/discuss ideas: Talk about/draw different types of machines, used by those who help us, e.g. postal worker's bag, trolley, van, fire-fighting equipment; what kind of a bag would a teacher/doctor/parent need?	Main topic: Light *Designing Skills* 1 Generate/discuss ideas: Draw/write different kinds of lights around school, home; Why are they appropriate for where they are? What kind of light would you take on a night walk?
2 Assembling skills: Cardboard net of house; Lego bricks to make a stable wall; textured fabrics to make a house-shaped picture.	2 Assembling skills: Graphic (picture) collage of objects useful to people who work at night/in the cold; follow a kit design to make a wheelbarrow/trolley model.	2 Assembling skills: Components to make a circuit; choose materials which could be used to make a waterproof cover for a battery.
3a Drawing skills: Draw a house using templates; draw the inside of a house built for a child/mouse/pig (teacher can annotate this).	3a Drawing skills: Freehand drawing of caretaker's trolley.	3a Drawing skills: Accurate drawing of components used in a torch.
	3b Modelling skills: Design a container for Fireman Sam's helmet in plasticine before making it with reclaimed materials.	3b Modelling skills: Design a portable light with kit materials before making it with rigid materials.
4 Suggest ways forward: How could stick pig make his house stronger?	4 Suggest ways forward: How might the headteacher's desk be reorganized?	4 Suggest ways forward: After looking at torches how could you make them more appealing to children?
5 Consider design ideas: Does your wall stand up? Can you make it less wobbly?	5 Consider design ideas: Check designs with head; would they really be useful?	5 Consider design ideas: How sturdy is your child's torch? Check materials used.
Making Skills 1 Selecting materials: Choose from artstraws, lolly stick or Lego to make a house tall enough for a small toy.	*Making Skills* 1 Selecting materials and tools: Choose materials for a container a farmer might use to transport a bag of carrots.	*Making Skills* 1 Selecting materials tools and techniques: Choose all of above to aid design of an illuminated toy for a baby.
2 Measuring materials: Find the roofs which fit a variety of house shapes; make a roof to fit a base.	2 Measuring materials: Use standard or regular measures to aid design of a holder, to be used by lunch-time supervisor to carry six items of cutlery.	2 Measuring materials: Use standard, accurate measure to improve quality of design; design a torch no longer than 25cm long. Battery must be inside torch.

Figure 12.1: (cont'd)

3 Assembling materials: Assemble solid shapes, kits to make houses with doorways, opening doors.	3 Assembling materials: Assemble wheels, pulleys and simple gears to make a factory conveyor belt.	3 Assembling materials: Begin to join and combine components from a wide range of materials in design of a van/room/greetings card with at least two lights.
4. Finishing techniques: Paint houses to look bright/ to be camouflaged.	4 Finishing techniques: Varnish (PVA dries clear) Choose a finish that is waterproof.	4 Finishing techniques: Apply a covering of thin fabric to a reclaimed model of a lighthouse/child's torch.
5 Suggesting ways forward: Make suggestions to a teacher obviously combining components incorrectly, how to proceed.	5 Suggesting ways forward: Does conveyor belt carry its load? If no, how can it be made to? If yes, how could it carry a wider/heavier load?	5 Suggesting ways forward: Encourage children to look for poorly finished products and to reassemble parts that are not working correctly.

6 Evaluating product: *Evaluating is very difficult for Key Stage 1 children. Encourage staff to set criteria before children begin, so that they all have something to compare their work against, e.g. object must be blue/two straws long/wheels must turn/battery must be hidden, etc.*

Does it do what it should?	Does it do what it should? Is it well finished?	Does it do what it should? Is it well made?
Knowledge and Understanding from 'Houses' Mechanisms Structures and stability	*Knowledge and Understanding* form People who help us Mechanisms	*Knowledge and Understanding* from Bulbs and batteries Mechanisms Structures and stability
	Products and applications Quality	Products and applications Quality
Health and safety Technical vocabulary	Health and safety Technical vocabulary	Health and safety Technical vocabulary

Whole School Planning for Design Technology or Schemes of Work

As the Key Stage 1 coordinator discuss with the staff which tools, materials and techniques are appropriate for each year group. A non-specialist teacher will feel happier if faced with a small number of skills to teach and refine, rather than being presented with a huge mass.

A chart could be drawn up (through staff discussion and practical workshop sessions) listing tools, techniques methods of joining and finishing. A scheme of work should be drawn up matching skills to age range. This would not preclude other teachers from developing skills they wanted or were highly skilled in, but would provide a baseline from which a less confident teacher could begin. An example of such a scheme of work is shown in Figure 12.2.

Figure 12.2: Example of a scheme of work: Skills

Skill	Tool	Introduced in Year
Measuring	Templates (to be drawn round accurately)	Reception
	Standard measures (e.g. 1cm cubes)	Year 1
	Safety metal rulers	Year 2
	Fabric tape measure	Year 2
Marking out	Pencil, chalk	Reception
	Felt pens	Year 1
	Chinagraph, tailor's chalk	Year 2
Cutting and Shaping	Dough cutters	Reception
	Dough spatulas	Reception
	Dough knives	Reception
	Rolling pins	Reception
	Scissors snipping	Reception
	cutting line	Reception
	cutting curve	Reception
	cutting freehand	Year 1
	cutting a window	Year 2
	Circular cutter	Year 2
	Hole punch	Year 1
	Hacksaw (pistol grip type to protect fingers) and bench hook	Year 2 c/s*
	Hand drill (pistol grip) and drill stand	Year 2 c/s*
Joining	Tape	Reception
	(Joining invisibly)	Year 2
	Paste (joining)	Reception
	(using sparingly)	Year 1
	(using invisibly)	Year 2
	PVA (joining)	Reception
	(using sparingly)	Year 1
	(using invisibly)	Year 2
	Gluesticks	Reception
	Paperclips	Reception
	Split pins	Year 1 c/s*
	Staples and stapler	Year 2 c/s*
	Gluegun	Year 2 c/s*
	Light hammer and nails	Reception c/s*
	Small screwdriver and screws	Year 1
Finishing	Sandpaper	Year 2
	Files	Year 2

Each skill can be revisited and refined during Key Stage 1 using a variety of materials.

*Note: * close supervision necessary*

The recording of technology also needs to be decided upon as a staff. Teachers will want a simple framework to record both class and individual records. Children will want a record of their own work, as well as taking the project home! Decide what is appropriate to keep in a profile and/or record of achievement. A design technology portfolio could be developed for each child or each class. Examples of what could be kept include: video diary, audio cassette diary, montage of photographs or photograph of completed product, child dictated and adult written description, annotated drawing from one or more stages of design process. Whatever is kept, remind the staff that it should have relevance for the child, should be presented in an appropriate way and should be manageable for all staff to administer. Grand schemes will fall by the wayside if they are too cumbersome to be carried out during a 'normal' day's teaching.

Resources

Design technology by its nature needs a wide range of resources. Basically you need:

'Reclaimed Materials' or Junk

These are a cheap and user-friendly introduction to many design techniques. The storage of these materials is a major headache. Sorting them into bottles, cartons, plastics, etc. helps. Extra storage is made by flattening packets and boxes. This has two advantages; first the children get the practice of putting a net together and second you can encourage them to put nets together with the pattern side inside so that there is a plain surface to paint on. Be ruthless with junk – do not store too much. Encourage children to only bring it at certain times in the term and use it pretty soon afterwards, keeping some spare stock for spontaneous activities.

Textiles

This category includes fabric, felt, Vivelle, ribbon, thread, wool, etc. Store expensive felts and suchlike separately. A useful way to store fabrics for day-to-day use is to store them by colour. (There are plenty of plastic washing baskets in different colours to help maintain order) Try to encourage a collection of useful sized remnants. Also have a collection of random patchwork sized pieces in a separate bin. Keep ribbons, wools and threads separate. This takes a bit of time to establish but will soon run itself. Encourage staff to throw useless scraps away. You don't have to keep everything!

Sheet materials

These materials include balsa, Corriflute, PVC, plastic, acrylic, etc. They can be stored in paper storage cupboards clearly marked. Decide which material is suitable for which year group and order enough for each child. This can be expensive so ensure that staff are familiar with the best way of using these materials. Get in touch with your adviser or supplier for a demonstration or even visit another school yourself with a video camera and film an 'expert' or even children using the material.

Construction Kits

There are various commercially produced construction kits on the market. You must decide what you want from a kit and what its technological functions are going to be The children might follow a plan to make an object; the kit might be used to introduce components such as gears, pulleys, etc. The amount of kit you can buy will depend on your budget, so store in (lidded!) plastic bins for easy portability if necessary. Establish a rota for use of kits in each room if necessary.

Foodstuffs

They are either stored as you would at home or purchased when needed. Health and safety and hygiene regulations must be followed when using food in schools.

Tools

Children will need access to a range of tools including scissors, rulers, clay knives and spatulas, hammer, nails, hand-drill, saw, bench hooks (for sawing safely on), safety cutters, safety compasses, staplers, wire and wire cutters, pins and needles, screws and screwdrivers, and glueguns.

Some of these tools will be in general classroom stock. Others will be needed from time to time. Store in conditions suitable for your school. It is useful to place tools on a shadow board so that children can replace them easily. Again, establish a rota so that teachers can plan to use equipment at a given time in the week or term.

A major implication for the resourcing of design technology is the cost of the consumable materials and the construction kits. Be realistic in what you buy. Buy small amounts of a new sheet material and try it out before committing the school to an unused pile of Contiboard. Remember you can use a history textbook for several years but you can only use a roll of sticky tape once. Encourage staff to tell you when things are running out and try to have spares of the most used items, e.g. batteries for control mechanisms, gluesticks for glueguns etc.

The storage space you have and the accessibility to it will determine who has access to the equipment. If it is to be the children, it needs to be clearly labelled so that it can be returned correctly. If the staff collect equipment themselves, encourage them to offer children a range within the classroom. The most important thing to remember is that other staff won't use it if it is difficult to get. Ensure that there is access to all.

How Can I Help Other Staff?

Encourage the staff and support them. What design technology needs most of all is a period of consolidation. Teachers worked hard to make the 1992 orders understandable. There was a great deal of thought put into helping children to achieve their technological entitlement. The 1994 orders will give teachers confidence that there is now a workable document from which to create a practical, useful and challenging scheme of work. However look at the school management plan. This will help you to gauge how much time the staff will have to spend on design technology during the year. However, whatever the management plan says, it is not unreasonable to have a staff meeting about an aspect of design technology at least once a year. During these sessions you can make small changes to schemes of work or the policy document.

Encourage staff to plan for technology in a cross-curricular way. When other subjects are being reviewed, suggest technological links and try to provide resources for these areas. This will help staff to integrate technology into their own planning. Ensure that staff are kept up to date with INSET opportunities within the authority or elsewhere, and with LEA health and safety documentation.

Provide in-house training. Encourage workshops where staff share their skills – clay, needlework, Jinksframe building, etc.

Do not demoralize staff by giving them too much information or too many new practices too quickly. Rather keep on top of technology in your own room first and offer support or advice where required.

How Can I Keep Myself Motivated?

Have a plan of action. Decide what you want to achieve over one academic year for yourself; for the policy; for the staff; for the schemes of work; for the resources. Break this down into short term goals and review them. Identify the strengths in your plan and feel good about the goals you have achieved. Consider the weaknesses in your plan and decide why other goals have not been achieved. Add to your review goals you achieved which you had not planned. You'll soon realize how much you are actually achieving!

References

DEPARTMENT FOR EDUCATION (1995). *The National Curriculum*, London, HMSO.

DEPARTMENT OF EDUCATION AND SCIENCE AND THE WELSH OFFICE (1990) *Technology in the National Curriculum*, London, HMSO.

INKPEN, M. (1989) *The Blue Balloon*, London, Hodder Headline plc.

SCHOOL CURRICULUM AND ASSESSMENT AUTHORITY (SCAA) (1994) *National Curriculum Orders*, London, HMSO.

Chapter 13

The History Coordinator at Key Stage 1

Julie Davies

Introduction

As a relatively inexperienced professional taking over the role of history co-ordinator it will be useful to reflect on the change in the quality and quantity of history teaching your colleagues will have experienced in primary schools over the last five years. The national curriculum made history teaching mandatory on a profession which had little experience of teaching it and with meagre resources at its disposal. HMI surveys of 1978 and 1989 found little evidence of history being taught and where it was being taught they judged it to be less than adequate in 80 per cent of infant classes and 66 per cent of junior classes seen. This probably means that you, as the history coordinator, will be working with many people who may, until several years ago, never have considered history to be an essential ingredient in their curriculum provision, except as a bolted-on fragment to a topic whose central thrust was some other area. An OFSTED report (1993), however, notes that history in primary schools now has a 'significant and accepted place'. In 1992–3 standards in history were satisfactory or better in 80 per cent of Key Stage 1 lessons and 70 per cent of Key Stage 2 lessons seen. The inspectors praised the teaching of the skills of sequencing and chronological understanding and the confidence of children in handling sources. Your job, then, would appear to be significantly easier now than if you had taken it over five years ago. History seems to have won an accepted place in the primary curriculum and its teaching appears to be steadily improving. To continue this upward momentum requires a clear picture of where your school is, in history curriculum development terms, so that realistic goals can be set for the future benefit of children's historical knowledge and understanding. This chapter aims to help you define the key tasks of the curriculum coordinator for history and offer you a range of practical activities that will assist you in your new role.

Before discussing in more detail where you might begin as history coordinator it is important to remember that though nursery and reception aged children (that is, those not yet 5 years old) are not subject to the national curriculum statutory requirements, they are likely to be included in the whole school curriculum. While the nursery children will be catered for, in curriculum terms, through their teachers' use of the human and social area of learning to plan activities to develop early historical understanding, it is probable that the reception children will be introduced early to the national curriculum. This is because planning separately for children under 5 and those already 5 is an extra burden hard-pressed reception teachers can do without. We are not talking here about match of work but about specific content.

Where to Begin

You will need to develop in teachers both an understanding of the nature of history and a pedagogy to sustain quality history teaching and learning in the early years. This means spending time with staff discussing two fundamental questions:

• Why should history be taught?
• How should it be taught?

Why Should History Be Taught?

A strong sense of *why* history is being taught should pervade all curriculum planning, influencing the selection of content and methods of teaching. (NCC, 1991)

The simple answer to the above question is because it is a statutory requirement. However, you will only get vigorous worthwhile teaching from teachers who believe that what they are doing is right for their children's all-round development. Getting teachers to acknowledge that history has an important place in the primary curriculum will make your job of enhancing their skills and confidence to do it considerably easier.

Philosophy has had a bad press lately with its place in teacher education derided as of no practical value. I would argue that sitting down to think about such fundamentals as 'Why teach history?' is a most useful exercise if it clarifies ideas and opinions and will affect practice radically. As history coordinator you need to make some of the INSET time you have available for history to discuss the purposes of school history with your colleagues. You could use those listed in the non-statutory guidance as a start. It is always helpful to begin with the teachers' own views, however, before producing the 'official line'. The purposes of school history are listed as follows in the non-statutory guidance (NCC, 1991):

1.2   There are two main aims of school history:

- to help pupils develop a sense of identity through learning about the development of Britain, Europe and the world;
- to introduce pupils to what is involved in understanding and interpreting the past.

1.3   Other purposes follow:

- to arouse interest in the past;
- to contribute to pupils' knowledge and understanding of other countries and cultures;
- to understand the present in the light of the past;
- to enrich other areas of the curriculum;
- to train the mind by disciplined study;
- to prepare pupils for adult life.

Each purpose is worthy of discussion with your staff. If this is done, the purposes will not remain theoretical statements of good intent, but become translated into achievable objectives with classes of children specifically in mind. Think about the first aim as an example.

How can you, as coordinator, help children develop a sense of identity through learning about Britain, Europe and the world? Does it feed your children's sense of identity to be told about the Romans or the Greeks? Of course not. This can only be achieved by finding effective links between the child's experience now with that of people in the past. In this way we will nurture their sense of identity. It is by engaging in these sorts of discussions that teachers will be able to see that simple transmission of historical facts is not what the early years history teacher is about.

Key Stage 1 Programme of Study

The history that Key Stage 1 children are entitled to is easily spelled out. The difficulty is how to teach it effectively. Pupils should be given opportunities to develop an awareness of the past and of the ways in which it was different from the present. They should be helped to set their study of the past in a chronological framework and to understand some of the ways in which we find out about the past.

The areas of study and the key elements, outlined below, should be taught together.

Areas of Study

1   Pupils should be taught about the everyday life, work, leisure and culture of men, women and children in the past, e.g. clothes, diet,

everyday objects, houses, shops and other buildings, jobs, transport, entertainment. In progressing from familiar situations to those more distant in time and place, pupils should be given opportunities to investigate:

- changes in their own lives and those of their family or adults around them;
- aspects of the way of life of people in Britain in the past beyond living memory.

2 Pupils should be taught about the lives of different kinds of famous men and women, including personalities drawn from British history, e.g. rulers, saints, artists, engineers, explorers, inventors, pioneers.
3 Pupils should be taught about past events of different types, including events from the history of Britain, e.g. notable local and national events, events in other countries, events that have been remembered and commemorated by succeeding generations, such as centenaries, religious festivals, anniversaries, the Gunpowder Plot, the Olympic Games.

Key elements which are closely related to and should be developed through the study units are itemized as follows:

- chronology;
- range and depth of historical knowledge and understanding;
- interpretation of history;
- historical enquiry;
- organization and communication.

The outline of history content for early years teachers appears to be compatible with what they would see as appropriate for young children: going from the known in time – themselves, families, communities and neighbourhood – to the unknown – their families, communities and neighbourhood in the more distant past. In addition, they are to be made aware of several aspects of British history which are, by their nature, more impersonal and distant in time. The history programme of study will be in the national curriculum orders but it is essential it is also embedded in the school history policy and scheme of work so that its 'fit' with what is planned is always at the forefront of teachers' minds in the planning and assessment stages. What has to be covered in Key Stage 1 is easily read but needs very careful thought for its realization in practice.

There is a great deal of work for you to do with the staff if history is going to be taught in a holistic way rather than in a fragmentary fashion where the areas of study are taught discretely and the key elements are taught and practised without any historical context. Staff development meetings concentrating on the programme of study will give you a platform for developing history as a study of the evidence that has survived about the past. The emphasis in one key element of the ability of pupils to make links and connections between events and developments needs to be used by you to encourage the staff to see the areas of study within the programme of study not as isolated elements but as interconnected, through time, in all sorts of ways. By working through each of the key elements in relation to these areas you should help staff give children the chance of seeing history as the seamless robe of the past that it is.

INSET Activities

To alert teachers to the central importance of continued debate about 'what' history, it will be useful to carry out a couple of short INSET activities. The first activity will help in the development of the area of study that expects pupils to be taught about the lives of different kinds of famous men and women, including personalities drawn from British history, e.g. rulers, saints, artists, engineers, explorers, inventors, pioneers.

Who is important in history?

Put up a piece of string across the room the ask the teachers to write on slips of paper two or three names of people who lived in the past to whom they would like to talk and question. Then given them paper clips to attach these papers onto the string 'time-line' in chronological sequence. You should identify which end of string is the present and which one the distant past.

First this exercise nearly always illustrates the glaring omissions in the history teaching experienced by the participants when they were children. History is portrayed, when viewed from these lines, as the story of rich, powerful men in Britain or Europe. It is useful when this exercise has been completed to look again at the purposes of school history, one of which is to help pupils develop a sense of identity. Discuss with teachers whether their feelings of identity are heightened or marginalized by looking at the lines. Second, through mapping the people recalled by the staff onto the areas of study, it will be shown which groups have insufficient, or even non-existent, female examples to be used with children. You can make a significant contribution to the quality, breadth and balance of Key Stage 1 children's history experience by leading the staff in a search for a wide-ranging databank of men and women from the past which is multicultural and diverse in historial periods.

The statements game

Teachers will have many ideas about the nature of history. These may be explored by the use of statements like the following which may be used to provoke debate.

- History is a series of events to be learned in chronological order.
- History tells us how modern humans are superior to prehistoric humans.
- History is concerned with understanding, seeing the past from the inside, from another's position, empathetically.
- History is argument without end.
- History is concerned not with the conveying of accepted facts but with the making of informed judgments, and to the displaying of the evidence on which those judgments are made.

How Should History Be Taught?

The School Curriculum and Assessment Authority (SCAA) has emphasized that teachers are free to teach how they wish as long as they teach the content prescribed. For history, of course, the *how* is more complicated. It is not simply about what proportion of time to give to whole class, group or individual teaching. It is also about the quandary of whether to teach history as content or process. Of course, both content and process are indispensable features of history; it is getting the balance right that is so important. As coordinator you will want to have worked through your own understandings. It is important for the staff also to come to grips with their view of what history is as this will affect their practice. What follows is a short discussion of this important feature.

This question can only be answered when you, as history coordinator, are clear in your mind as to what history is. History is two things: the past, and the study of the past. If you believe the former is an agreed, unchangeable body of knowledge then the way you study it will be different from the way you will study it if you consider history to be constantly in need of reinterpretation. History as 'process' involves us in an examination of sources and in making interpretations in a critical appraising way in order to generate theories about their validity and reliability. In other words history methodology is characterized by scrupulous respect for evidence *and* disciplined use of the imagination. Encouraging teachers to view children as budding historians will certainly help channel their energies towards providing first-hand sources on which the children can practise these skills. As I have mentioned earlier, teaching history in an appropriate way which takes cognizance of young children's intellectual stages of development is also a critically important aspect to be taken on board by Key Stage 1 staff.

Planning the History Curriculum

While the history curriculum is set out in the areas of study there are still choices to be made about depth, content and emphasis and these need to be carefully considered. There is also the need to ensure continuity and progression, with minimum repetition across reception, Year 1 and Year 2. You may need to convince your staff that whole school planning is, therefore, essential to ensure:

- continuity within Key Stage 1 and between Key Stage 1 and Key Stage 2;
- progression in content, concepts, skills and attitudes from Year 1 to Year 6;
- balance between the various types of history: social, political, cultural and aesthetic, religious, economic, technological and scientific;
- balance between local, national and world history;
- balance between ancient and modern history;
- balance between the history of men, women and children, rich and poor, powerful and powerless.
- cross-curricular themes are addressed: economic and industrial understanding, health education, education for citizenship, environmental education, careers education guidance.

In addition, you must:

- prioritize the collection of resources to support these decisions;
- target some aspects of INSET provision as essential if the school is to move forward in its history provision.

Agreement about all these aspects is vital so that the child moving through the primary school has the opportunity of sampling the richness and variety of history. In addition, the organizational framework for the teaching of history needs to be agreed on. It is a case of assessing the value of single subject teaching against the subject biased topic approach. At Key Stage 1 it seems appropriate to use the latter.

The History Biased Topic

While there seems to be a move towards subject specific teaching at Key Stage 2, at Key Stage 1 it is unlikely to be the answer to how to fit the content of the nine subject areas into the time available. The way forward seems to be for focused and carefully planned subject biased topic work. Here your job will be to give history the highest possible profile when its turn comes for special attention. What follows are some key points for you and your staff to discuss with governors and parents should they need convincing of the strait-jacketing effect single subject teaching can have on an area as broad as history.

The integrated approach, at its best, is fundamental to good primary practice and the requirements of the national curriculum. Children need to learn how:

- to seek information from many sources and to judge its validity;
- to organize facts and form generalizations based on facts;
- to carry on a discussion based on facts and to make generalizations or conclusions;
- to plan, to carry out plans and to evaluate the work and the planning;
- to accept responsibility as part of living;
- to develop a set of values for judging right and wrong actions.

The Teacher's Role

History can be an exciting activity-based subject that involves children in a process. If our main aim is to get children excited and interested in finding out about the past then they will need to spend time considering how historical investigations might proceed. Teachers may find it useful to discuss the modes of investigation and draw up a list as an *aide-mémoire* to their planning which might include investigating by: problem solving, going out, measuring, raising questions, making connections, thinking, talking, reading, interrogating, observing, listening, hypothesizing, thinking, interpreting. Communicating what they have found out is an equally important part of the historical investigation equation. Teachers know that there are many ways through which to communicate such as dance, drama, music, writing, charts and tables, graphs, IT, maps and plans, model-making, artwork, debate, discussion. They should be encouraged by you to use all these avenues, where relevant, when planning history outcomes.

There is a need for you to work with staff so that they use their discussion and questioning time effectively with the children. The aim, in history, is to enable children to understand, explain and make intelligible what they have learned. Teachers are supremely able at developing oral language through discussion but they need to be aware of the need to encourage children's historical skills and concepts and to develop a critical approach to historical evidence when history is the focus of the session. For example, children may be looking at a town hall or a terraced house and noting such things as the number and type of windows, the materials used in its construction and in making a count of the people using it. This is fine as an information gathering exercise. To get the children thinking historically, however, the teacher has to get them to ask such questions as:

- How old is it? (time)
- Has it changed in any way since it was built? (continuity/change)
- Why have the changes occurred? (cause/consequence)
- Can you put the changes in chronological order? (sequence)
- Is the building like the others near it? (similarity/difference)
- Why has it survived?

- What evidence have you to support your conclusions?
- Is the evidence sufficient?

The historical process can be summarized as pupils comprehending a historical issue, posing questions and ideas about it, locating sources of evidence, using, interpreting and evaluating the material, recalling, analysing and synthesizing the findings and communicating the information and explanation in an economical, relevant and lucid way. This is a tall order when thinking of Key Stage 1 but the foundations must be laid when the children are young and eager.

If teachers have gone through some of the processes outlined above, with you as the enabler and catalyst, the job of developing a whole school approach to the history curriculum will be much easier. They will be more sure about what they perceive to be the particular contribution history has to make to children's cognitive and affective development. In addition, their views of what history is to them will clarify other aims and objectives for teaching primary history. In all probability, there will already be a scheme of work for history. Your first job will be to see whether it is translated into reality in the classroom. Using it as a starting point for further development is necessary. That it cannot remain unaltered is clear from the radical review history has undergone since Dearing (SCAA, 1993). It is always useful when leading staff meetings to provide basic information from which your colleagues can easily and quickly work to produce, for example, aspects of a scheme of work. The Key Stage 1 programme of study and key elements is one essential for such a meeting. Following on from Figure 13.1 – or something like it – might be helpful. It encapsulates the sources and the content for Key Stage 1 in a visual way. By working towards filling in the boxes, staff will gain a growing understanding of the interconnectedness of process and content in history as well as the need to search for materials for empty boxes. This emphasizes that there might be opportunity for children to behave like historians: to handle evidence, draw tentative conclusions about it and understand how there may be different interpretations of what they are studying. The exercise will also help staff to ensure continuity and progression across Key Stage 1 as they plan cooperatively to cover the programmes of study.

Assessment

History is a non-core foundation subject which means it is not subject to nationally administered standardized summative tests at the end of each Key Stage. However, there is a statutory duty for schools to report to parents annually on their children's progress in all areas of the curriculum. It is of course also good practice for records of children's development to be passed on to the next teacher so that continuity and progression can be built in the following year.

Figure 13.1: The Key Stage 1 Programme of Study

History from:	Family history	Famous men and women	Events in the past	Period beyond living memory
Stories (variety of cultures and periods)				
Photographs/ pictures				
Objects real/ reproductions				
Written accounts – diary, newspaper, books etc.				
Film/TV				
Museum				
Living history				
Music (voice/ instrument)				
Oral				
Built environment				
Archaelogy				

Level Descriptions of Assessment

Teachers must read carefully the introduction to the proposals (History Draft Proposal, 1994) where it is made clear that

> it is the POS [programmes of study] which should guide the planning, teaching and day-to-day assessment of pupils' work. The essential function of the level descriptions is to assist in the making of summary judgements about pupils' achievement as a basis for reporting at the end of a Key Stage. (p. i)

Essentially, the level descriptions serve a summative purpose. The whole purpose of the new descriptions is to look at pupil performance as a whole and consider which level provides the best fit. The introduction to the new proposals is clear on this issue.

> Teachers will be able to balance one element against another using professional judgement rather than counting numbers of statements of attainment mastered and using a mechanical rule. The introduction of level descriptions will reinforce earlier messages that there is no need for elaborate tick lists as a basis for assessment.

National curriculum assessment is a whole school issue. Teachers of Years 2 and 6 must carry out their end of Key Stage teacher assessments and will rely on the records that have been built up through the Key Stage in a format which is consistent and manageable. It is not essential to keep vast quantities of work as evidence; only a few selected samples of pupils' work need be retained; 'what is needed above all is a sense of proportion and a combination of professional judgement and common sense, in the use of available time' (SEAC, 1991/92).

Because the programmes of study describe the content and the level descriptions describe the cognitive skills the children should have acquired through its study, there is no way they can remain divorced at the planning stage. You may need to remind your colleagues of this so that while they are planning they will also be looking at how the outcomes can be assessed. While this may be difficult for staff to grasp initially, some joint planning sessions with you, either at the whole staff, or individual teacher level should set them on the right path. One of the key ways to develop staff assessment abilities is to discuss, at length, if necessary, what the level descriptions actually mean. Clarifying this area is essential, because the staff will then have a common definition in mind when they make their assessments of children's progress. Once they have got into the habit of looking for the assessment opportunities at the planning stage they will realize the need for good quality resources that will help them in their teaching and assessment of children.

This brings us on to the next big area of preoccupation for the history coordinator: what resources are needed to help implement the national curriculum?

Resources

Given that history was rarely taught in infant schools until four years ago, it is not surprising that resources for it were meagre and consisted of an overreliance on textbooks or TV programmes. The targeting of resources on history is therefore necessary. The OFSTED 1992/93 report provides a figure of £2.50 per pupil – a small increase over the previous year. You can use data such as this to compare your school's spending on history resources with the national or local average. It will add bite to your claims for more resources if your school spends little on history. However, OFSTED has praised the use by schools of history resources outside the classroom. Teachers have used their locality, living history sites and local communities imaginatively.

The national curriculum has emphasized the process side of history and demands that children be allowed to learn about the past from a wide range of historical sources, including:

artefacts,
pictures and photographs,
music,
adults talking about their past,
documents and printed sources,
buildings and sites, and
computer based material.

Two problems immediately spring to mind: where do you get these sources from, and what do you do with the resources when you have collected them? If you remember that one of your main purposes in teaching history to children is to give them a sense of personal identity then you will look for sources within the community that the school serves. Artefacts – the correct term for objects looked at historically – are plentiful in every house and garden. Think of the change there has been in irons over the last fifteen years (even if you cannot get any older than that). Children will bring in pieces of clothing, books and various household utensils that can be handled in a historical way to discuss change and continuity, causation and time. Similarly, pictures and photographs are readily available to be used. A letter requesting artefacts from home for a particular topic will result in pupils bringing in a bewildering array of objects. Some schools still have access to loan collections which can be utilized when appropriate. The older members of the community are treasure troves of memories and opinions and welcome being interviewed about many of their experiences. The use of local experts such as archaeologists, local archivists and museum curators broadens children's historical diet. Local craftspeople and musicians, retired police officers, teachers, carpenters etc., add to the variety of historical sources that can be effectively tapped within communities. The local built environment is near at hand, familiar yet interesting to budding historians. Written sources do not have to be marriage or birth certificates. They can be local newspaper accounts of famous local events or sporting stories, they can be postcards and letters from different periods, or the school log, old advertisements, recipe books or catalogues. As coordinator, you have a role in the collection of resources. However, it is not up to you to do all the running around to gather them up. Rather it is to help support and direct your colleagues' energies towards fruitful areas of artefacts and suchlike. Their enthusiasm and confidence in teaching history as process will grow as they begin to make personal contributions to the resource centre.

In a sense, of course, you will have had specific aims in mind to focus your collections so you and the staff will be committed to teaching and assessing history already, through first-hand experiences using primary or secondary sources wherever possible. Having said that, there is still a good deal of INSET to be done to ensure that teachers use the resources in a historically accurate way to develop children's historical understanding. Too often, the activity can end up as a useful oral language session or an inspiring art and design experience rather than a session that extends children's historical concepts. To keep a check on how resources are used and the effectiveness of this, it helps to have clarified, through staff meetings, the purpose of any materials introduced into the classroom for the teaching and learning of history. Below I have listed the key types of materials with references for you to follow up on their uses in the classroom. It is essential that the process of coming to one's own understandings about the merits or demerits of particular resources is gone through with the staff rather than they be given a list and told to get on with it.

What follows is a very brief section on resources with what I consider to be key publications where appropriate. Each section can be expanded into a section in your school history resource file of course. A great deal of help can be obtained from the Historical Association on many aspects of history at Key Stage 1.

The Historical Association
59A Kennington Park Road
London SE11 4JH

Artefacts, Portraits and Pictures

DURBIN, G., MORRIS, S., WILKINSON, S. (1990) *A Teacher's Guide to Learning from Objects*, London, English Heritage.
MORRIS, S. (1990) *A Teacher's Guide to Using Portraits*, London, English Heritage.

In addition, and useful for INSET purposes, English Heritage produce a slide pack *Using Portraits* which takes you through twelve slides with careful notes so that your observation skills are enhanced.

Stories and Narrative

COX, K. and HUGHES, P. (1990) *Early Years History: An Approach Through Story* (available from Liverpool Institute of Higher Education, Stand Park Road, Liverpool, L16 9JD).
FARMER, A. (1990) 'Story-telling in history', *Teaching History*, January.
HMI (1985) *History in the Primary and Secondary Years*, London, DES.
HMI (1989) *Aspects of Primary Education. The Teaching and Learning of History and Geography*, London, DES.

LITTLE, V. and JOHN, T. (1988) 'Historical fiction in the classroom', *Teaching of History*, Series No. 59, London, The Historical Association.

Sets of books are also available from:

Madeline Lindley
Early Years History: An Approach through Story
79 Acorn Centre
Barry Street
Oldham OL1 3NE

Stories for Time book box from Badger Publishing Limited
Unit One, Parsons Green Estate
Boulton Road
Stevenage
Herts SG1 4QG

Oral History

PURKIS, S. (1987) *Thanks for the Memory*, London, Collins Educational.

Buildings

For further information on this primary source see the English Heritage series of videos and accompanying booklets for various historic sites. In addition they produce a series of videos which show how a historian needs to be like a detective in looking for clues and evidence in order to reach conclusions about buildings and objects. These can be fruitfully discussed in staff development time. Information for these and all English Heritage material can be obtained from:

English Heritage Education Service
Key Sign House
429 Oxford Street
London W1R 2HD
Telephone: 0171 973 3442/3

Written Sources

There is a rich variety of documentary material available such as school log books, census returns, parish records, letters, inventories and government reports, marriage and birth certificates and wills. In addition, newspapers, directories, advertisements, posters and other printed matter provide useful material on which to work.

Original documentation will probably be precious and available only to look at carefully and not to work from. Photocopies of documents are a good substitute for they provide children with a chance to study the layout, language and writing of the original without fear of damage. You should collect as wide a variety of these materials as possible but it is essential to catalogue them and to ensure that staff know their whereabouts and that they have decided how best they may be used. One aspect of documentary evidence needs exploring with the staff. A piece of writing from Victorian times will be difficult for children to decipher. Should this be translated into present day script? The answer depends on what you want the children to get from it. Essentially, the medium is as important as the message so should not be tampered with lightly. The very act of carefully looking at and deciphering text is an important and necessary skill for all historians and one children should be inducted into as soon as possible.

One pack of documents which makes the past accessible to children has been produced by Charlotte Mason College and Cumbria Archive Service and is called *Could Do Better. Children at School 1870–1925.*

Living History

This involves children in a dramatic reconstruction of an event in the past. It is useful to inform staff of what is available within reasonable travelling distance in terms of 'in role' days so that these can be planned within a topic rather than become a bolt-on afterthought. The costs involved make it essential that there is maximum follow-up, so that the children get the most out of the experience and the governors and parents feel the money has been well spent.

Information Technology

Its first and most significant contribution to the history curriculum lies in the databases that can be created to deal with the material generated from studies involving the local community such as census returns or school rolls. The second area where IT can enhance the history curriculum is through the series of computer-aided learning programs becoming readily available from publishers, but you must be discriminating in the choice of programs which will fully support good teaching.

TV and Published History Schemes

One important piece of information that you need to disseminate to staff regularly until they have absorbed it is that HMI found that where there was poor primary history practice there was also overreliance on TV programmes and published schemes. Teachers must come to an understanding that schemes can be useful if used selectively but are not the complete answer to history teaching. There is good material on the market, of course, but there is also a lot that is not suitable for teaching history as effectively as a resource bank built specifically to meet the needs of a particular set of children tackling a particular study unit.

Equal Opportunities and Multicultural Education

National curriculum history requires that children be taught about the cultural and ethnic diversity of past societies and the experiences of men and women. Therefore each time a study unit is planned these two requirements should be carefully catered for. We have all been exposed to history teaching supported by textbooks that largely ignore the part played by women and minority ethnic groups in the development of British society. We must be aware of this bias in our own knowledge so that we do not pass it on by default to our children. Your school will no doubt have an equal opportunities and multicultural education set of guidelines. It would seem sensible to use the principles involved in setting them up as a basis for planning your history units. Below are two references I have found useful as a starting point for staff discussion.

COLLICOTT, S. (1986) *Connections*, London, Haringey Local-National-World Links (published by Haringey Community Information Service in association with the Multicultural Curriculum Support Group, Central Library, Wood Green, High Road, London, N22).
COLLICOTT, S. (1991) 'A woman's place', *Junior Education*, May.

Concluding Remarks

Your commitment to history teaching and quality of learning is vital. Hopefully you will not be the unwilling conscript who has drawn the short straw of history; you will be the enthusiastic volunteer who will stimulate his or her colleagues through love of the subject. There seems no better way of developing staff confidence in teaching history than for you to pilot various methods and materials and to share your findings with them before encouraging them to share their own successes with the rest of the staff. Staff development exercises which involve looking not just at how to use a resource but also how to plan for progression in its use is another way in which you can ensure children get a broadly balanced history curriculum. Ultimately, though, as I have said, your personal enthusiasm for history will be a crucial factor in the staff's commitment to its place in the early years curriculum.

References

DEPARTMENT of EDUCATION and SCIENCE (DES) (1978) *Primary Education in England: A Survey by HMI*, London, HMSO.

DEPARTMENT of EDUCATION and SCIENCE (DES) (1989) *Aspects of Primary Education: The Teaching and Learning of History and Geography*, London, HMSO.

OFSTED (1993) *History Key Stages 1, 2 and 3 Second Year 1993–94*, London, HMSO.

NATIONAL CURRICULUM COUNCIL (NCC) (1991) *History Non-Statutory Guidance for History*, York, NCC.

SCHOOL EXAMINATION and ASSESSMENT COUNCIL (SEAC) (1991) *Moderator's Handbook, 1991/92*, London, SEAC.

SCHOOL CURRICULUM and ASSESSMENT AUTHORITY (SCAA) (1993) *The National Curriculum and its Assessment*, London, SCAA.

Chapter 14

The Religious Education Coordinator in the Early Years

Gwen Mattock and Geoff Preston

Introduction

Religious education (or RE) is an entitlement in law for all registered pupils in schools. Under the requirements of the 1988 Education Reform Act it is required that all county, controlled and voluntary aided schools provide religious education and collective worship. The legislation placed religious education in the basic curriculum of the school and left the content of the teaching to be determined locally, rather than nationally.

This means that there are no national curriculum documents for RE – no nationally determined programmes of study or level descriptors. This might be thought to imply that RE is less important than the other subjects in the primary curriculum, but this was certainly not the intention of the Department for Education. Indeed one of the earliest sections of the 1988 Education Reform Act states that the primary curriculum must be broad and balanced and promote 'the spiritual, moral, mental and physical development of pupils' (Section 1). There appear to be two major reasons why RE is locally determined. One is that there have been local syllabuses, agreed by representatives of several different groups of persons, since the early years of the century. This arrangement was first made to ensure that religious teaching in state schools was not biased in favour of any religious group. The second reason, particularly appropriate now that we live in a multiethnic, multifaith society is that the balance of persons belonging to different faith groups is not constant across the country and so it is more appropriate to arrange work to meet local need.

In practice this means that in county schools religious education is taught by reference to the LEA's agreed syllabus, although additional denominational teaching can be given at the request of parents. In voluntary aided schools religious education is in the control of the foundation governors who may choose to use their own syllabus or that of the diocesan authority, where appropriate. It should be noted that parents have the right in law to withdraw their children from the teaching of religious education (as is the case, also, with collective worship).

There were other significant provisions of the 1988 Act. One was to require each local authority to set up a Standing Advisory Council for Religious Education (SACRE) which must include representation from four groups of persons. These are

- such Christian and other religious groups as will represent the local community;
- the Church of England;
- the LEA;
- teachers' associations.

The SACRE's purpose is to advise the LEA on matters to do with collective worship and RE. It has powers to hear requests from schools wishing to opt out from the Act's requirements regarding collective worship and to decide whether or not to grant a 'determination'. It also has the power to require an LEA to review and amend its agreed syllabus.

The 1993 Education Act adds further weight to the statement quoted above indicating the importance of the role of RE in the spiritual, moral and cultural development of children and makes reference to the National Curriculum Council (1993) document, Spiritual and Moral Development: A Discussion Paper. Additionally, the Act provides some more detail concerning agreed syllabuses including the requirement that any LEA which has not produced a new RE syllabus since 1988 must set up a writing conference by 1 April 1995. Syllabus conferences must have representation from the same four groups of persons as the SACRE.

DfE Circular 1/94, *Religious Education and Collective Worship*, although not an authoritative legal document, provides much useful guidance. A copy was sent to each school and the coordinator should find it a valuable point of reference. One of the issues with which it deals is the kind of content which should be found in LEA syllabuses. The Introduction (para. 7) declares that the legislation is designed 'in RE to ensure that pupils gain both a thorough knowledge of Christianity, reflecting the Christian heritage of this country, and knowledge of the other principal religions represented in Great Britain.' Once an LEA has secured approval for its syllabus it becomes the basis for all RE in its maintained schools, via a school policy and scheme of work. Paragraphs 31–39 of Circular 1/94 indicate that agreed syllabuses must and school schemes of work should:

- ensure that in total content and at each Key Stage, teaching on Christianity should receive the largest proportion of the time available;
- identify which of the religions other than Christianity should be taught at each Key Stage. Not all need to be taught at each Key Stage or in equal depth. The balance is often decided by the proportion of different faiths found within the area covered by the syllabus;
- provide sufficient detail of what is to be taught to fulfil the points

above. This detail must form part of the syllabus and not simply be provided in an accompanying non-mandatory handbook.

- provide sufficient detail of what is to be taught to fulfil the points above.

Clearly it is important for the coordinator to be aware of these rulings when thinking about the preparation of a school policy and scheme of work since they should guide the choice of appropriate material for early years children.

Policy and scheme of work preparation will be a significant element of your work as the coordinator. Others will include:

- drafting the school's scheme of work;
- outlining approaches to the teaching of religious education;
- resourcing the subject;
- promoting the subject.

We will look at each of these elements in turn.

Drafting the School's Policy and Scheme of Work

A key document for the subject area will be the policy document for religious education. Do recognize that this subject is a sensitive one in many schools with a wide range of teacher responses, ranging from total commitment to a refusal to teach it. It is essential that you draw your colleagues into consultation about the scheme of work. It is good for you and for them that ownership of the document can be as broadly based as possible. You will then be able to utilize their expertise and share with them evolving issues such as the introduction of a new agreed syllabus.

It is important to be realistic about the amount of time that you expect teachers to spend planning the RE work. However it is also important to allow the sensitivities and the uncertainties to surface and be discussed. Some teachers have concerns about the idea of 'teaching a faith' and, in the early years especially, about indoctrination. Everyone needs to be clear that, in county schools you are *not* teaching a faith but teaching *about faiths*. It is an educational, not an evangelistic exercise.

It is also worthwhile taking time to plan on a macro level. This should have the twin virtues of avoiding straight repetition while allowing for reinforcement of knowledge and development of concepts by returning to central points from a different focus – the kind of thing that Bruner calls a 'spiral curriculum'. It will also, of course enable maximum benefit to be obtained from identifying and developing an appropriate RE strand in the broad themes often used as a basis for teaching in early years classes and using cross-curricular links.

Summarizing, your scheme of work is likely to cover the following areas:

- aim(s);
- objectives/attainment targets;
- approaches to teaching, e.g. cross-curricular or direct RE;
- methods/skills and process, e.g. investigation, story, role play, interpretation, reflection, exploring, visits, artefacts;
- attitudes, e.g. commitment, respect, enquiry, self-understanding;
- assessment and record keeping;
- resources, including local community resources.

Aims

These are likely to be included in the agreed syllabus of your LEA. In recent times they tend to be two or three in number. Examples might include the following:

- RE will enable all children to explore some religious beliefs and practices of faith communities within the area in which the school is located.
- Pupils will be encouraged to respect the differences found within belief systems and help in the promotion of a harmonious society.
- Pupils will be encouraged to explore the fundamental questions of life raised by human experiences.

It is, of course, essential for the implementation of the aims that they are discussed and worked on by the staff until they feel comfortable both with their content and the language used to express them. This section must never be rushed because the goodwill and enthusiasm of the staff for the rest of the scheme of work depends on it.

The aims of the school's religious education should be in tune with the overall statement of school ethos since the 1993 Education Act requires school brochures to include information about;

- the ethos of the school which underpins pupils' spiritual, moral, cultural and social development;
- RE and collective worship provided at the school (DfE, 1994, para. 123).

Objectives/Attainment Targets

Your local agreed syllabus will provide you with appropriate outlines to work on with your colleagues. Although, as indicated above, there is no national requirement for programmes of study, level descriptors or assessment arrangements, clearly each agreed syllabus has to provide adequate guidance on content and as new syllabuses are produced the majority also appear to be indicating appropriate markers in other areas. As the coordinator it will be your task to work out with colleagues how suggested level descriptors might fit in with what is being identified in other areas and how assessment and recording could be arranged. More will be said below concerning assessment.

Approaches to Teaching

In the early years it is likely that religious education will be taught within the context of a topic based approach to learning. This may be achieved in three ways:

Explicitly Religious Topics:
religious festivals,
religious stories,
religious artefacts,
religious customs.

Topics where RE has a substantial place:
festivals and celebrations,
books,
signs and symbols,
remembrance.

General Topics with an RE element:
myself,
people around me,
the family,
time,
clothes,
journeys.

The realization of the objectives for religious education will only be attained by careful planning as outlined in the school's scheme of work for religious education. In the scheme of work the topics should be identified and the type of topic (i.e. explicit, general) should be indicated. The topics should be selected so that a balance and relevance is achieved in each year's programme for religious education.

However, the balance will be uneven, with less time allocated to the specifically religious group of topics than to the other two. Across the curriculum it is generally agreed that teachers need to build on children's existing experiences as a way of presenting new material and enabling sound concept development to take place. Religious education is certainly no exception to this, indeed since many religious concepts are abstract it is absolutely essential that children build a sound base in concrete understanding in order to be able to make the move from concrete to abstract. Consequently much religious education in the early years is laying foundations on which later structures will be built and some of this work may not appear to be *overtly* very religious. It is often referred to in RE textbooks as the 'implicit approach', and depends very much on helping children to explore their thoughts, feelings and emotions about themselves and the situations and people who most concern them at a given point in their development. This provides a base for later teaching of many of the doctrines of the major world faiths, particularly those that revolve around an interpretation of the nature of humanity, relationship between individuals and between individuals and deity. Some of the more recent writings on RE and some of the agreed syllabuses suggest that teachers ought, in their planning, to be thinking about knowledge, conceptual development, experience, skills and attitudes and these concerns should guide the choice of content.

As an example, a theme about 'myself' rarely fails to interest young children, it provides a huge cross-curricular potential and the RE element might include exploration of emotions such as anger, fear, jealousy, hurt, as well as the more obvious ones of loving, sharing, caring. Children need to be enabled to recognize that everyone has a darker side to their personality and to be helped to deal with it without great feelings of guilt. Such a theme could also branch out into 'things I like to do', which could include going to worship or celebrating festivals or family happenings such as birthdays, new babies or weddings. In this way some more specifically religious teaching could be included. All of the areas identified above could readily be brought into such a theme.

Do indicate in your scheme the importance of children's questions and their direct experiences. For instance, the death of someone close to a child involves questions about life and death. Likewise, the breakup of a friendship or physical aggression are events that raise issues about reconciliation and forgiveness. These experiences should be used to explore further the religious aspects of the events. Issues of right and wrong arise within the classroom and home situation – understanding of which school property may be used in school but must be left at school, borrowing and keeping each other's possessions, responding to aggression, racist remarks, bullying. None of these may sound specifically religious, although they are certainly appropriate moral and social education, but in fact they are also incorporated in more adult guise in the ethical teaching of the major faiths. Some of these areas may be planned into the curriculum at various points in the early years pattern while others may arise in response to situations. In the latter case it is important to use the opportunity presented; young children are not able to put such issues 'on hold' because it does not figure in your school plan until the following term! There will almost certainly be occasions for any class teacher when a child comes to school distressed because something serious has happened in the family – a major relationship broken, serious illness, death. It may indeed take time for what *has* happened to emerge, unless a member of the family comes in to explain. It is very important for children to be given the opportunity to talk about it, when they are ready, and to share their thoughts with the class – and that teachers try to ensure that there is no conflict at such a time between what the family might be saying and anyone else's views. The teacher may have to assure the child that people do have different ideas about various events and that this is acceptable.

Unless a school has a large proportion of children who are actively involved in one of the major faiths, when it might be possible to launch straight into a specifically religious theme on, for example, Divali or 'Stories about Jesus' (depending on the faith background of the children) religious education is likely to be more meaningful to children when approached through their current interests and experiences.

Methods and Skills

Teachers should be encouraged to use a wide variety of methods in the teaching of religious education. These might include RE through story, the use of artefacts, video, role play, active learning, written work, visits and visitors. There are a number of general skills and processes that should be used in the teaching of religious education. These will include investigation, reflection, evaluation, analysis and interpretation. For instance, a visit to a worship centre will allow pupils to ask relevant questions about furnishings, the use of the building and to reflect on the experience and information given to them.

If the need for a conceptual framework for any scheme of work in RE (as opposed to the collection of a ragbag of information) has been recognized and implemented, there still remains the task of deciding how to present the concepts in ways most likely to be assimilated. In other words, what strategies should be used?

Artefacts

Capturing and keeping the interest of children is a vital stage in ensuring that learning will take place. One of the most attractive ways of doing this in RE is by use of artefacts, but it is essential to emphasize that whatever is being used must be treated with respect and handled carefully. It is an article of importance to members of that faith group. It is also essential to ensure that the objects chosen are acceptable for this purpose in the view of that faith group. For example, you would not choose to use a copy of the Qur'an because there are particular requirements about how it is handled and where it is kept, but it would be acceptable to use a string of prayer beads or a prayer carpet. Wherever possible this kind of work is best done in groups rather than the whole class. There is opportunity to examine the artefact more closely and more likelihood of participation by the majority of children.

Children could be asked to:

- see what they could tell you about the object;
- decide what they think it is used for and why;
- make a list of things they want to know about; this could be done as a group with the teacher scribing if necessary.

Depending on the age and ability of the children and the resources available the object could be identified and knowledge expanded by teacher input, input from a member, adult or child, from the faith group, use of reference books/information sheets, or use of video material. This could then be further extended:

- by some kind of factual written and/or illustrated account;
- by imagining that the object belonged to you and writing a story about it;
- by creating a dramatic scene around it.

The nature of the artefact would determine which of these could be appropriate.

Picture/poster work

This is also best suited to work in groups. Posters produced by Pictorial Charts Educational Trust could be used or pictures and posters without any text, such as some of those produced by Christian Education Movement (CEM) could be used to stimulate open-ended enquiry, asking questions such as, what do you think is going on here and why do you think that? A more imaginative approach might be: imagine that you are x in the picture and describe how you feel.

Another good use for pictures is to provide background information about, for instance, life in the biblical period, as a preparation or back-up to stories. It is important that the detail is accurate. Alternatively, pictures provide some idea of what a synagogue or temple might look like inside.

Year 2 children could begin to look, for instance, at as many pictures of Jesus as possible – prints of old masters as well as modern illustrations. Consider the varieties of physique, dress, expressions portrayed and consider possible reasons.

Story/drama/music

These are all ways of actively involving children in RE. Few children fail to respond to a good story well told or read and story is an important element in most world faiths, either as a vehicle for recounting its history or presenting its teaching.

It is important to be sure that the stories used are from sources that have been approved by the faith concerned, so that the details and emphases are a true reflection of the teaching or happening. Addresses of faith groups are often included in the supporting materials linked to an agreed syllabus or may be obtained from faith groups themselves, from the local SACRE or advisory teachers.

For Key Stage 1 children the story will usually be presented simply as a story from the appropriate faith. It is also appropriate to use stories that are not from the faith traditions but which embody significant truths – stories about love, sharing, overcoming difficulties, jealousy and other social and moral realities of the world of the young child.

Children retelling stories is another way for them to feel their way into situations and characters and this is closely linked with drama which could be a further development. Drama is particularly valuable in helping children to express their own feelings and empathize with those of others. Both of these are important skills for RE.

Music is an important part of the worship of some religions and might be linked with the kind of music used in the school for collective worship. A different way of the use of music is as a stimulus for role play or a background to short periods of quiet. Some schools use the latter as part of collective worship and preparation in the classroom would be valuable. In addition to listening, children should be encouraged to create their own music for these kinds of situations.

Audio and visual materials

These are invaluable in RE because they are another way of helping children to enter into situations and experiences without imposing any demands for personal commitment or involvement. Materials are now available from various sources including the BBC, Independent Television and CEM. As with this kind of material in any subject area, there needs to be preparation and follow-up.

Visitors and visits

Visits to places of worship provide an opportunity which few children would otherwise have and from which they may gain in gathering information but will possibly gain much more by experiencing the 'feel' of the place. As with any other visit it needs to be arranged carefully, with teachers making preliminary visits (this might be a valuable in-service session for everyone) and discussing with the person concerned what the children will hear about and be able to see and do – will they be able to move around independently or will they remain together in one place? Checking up on any requirements for appropriate dress, for example removal of shoes or bringing a head covering, should be part of these discussions so that children know what is expected of them. It will be necessary to give careful thought to any recording of information which might be done during the visit. Whatever approach is used it is important to give children a little time to absorb the atmosphere. It may be possible for the person who will talk to the children to visit them in the classroom first, which would help to indicate at what level the children are working. Such mutual hospitality creates the beginning of a positive relationship as well as being a useful bridge for the children to the visiting of a new place and giving the teacher a further opportunity to talk about the practicalities of the visit – what degree of detail the children will understand and how long they will be able to listen.

Inviting members of different faith groups into school to demonstrate or talk about various aspects of their faith or practice is a way of enabling children to hear first-hand things that they might otherwise only read in books or hear from their teacher. Again, it needs preparation. It very often works best if done in a class setting rather than with a much larger age phase group and if the session is kept fairly brief. It is easier for most people to make themselves heard in a classroom than in a much larger space like a school hall and if things are being shown to the children there is a more informal atmosphere in the classroom. If a school has limited contacts with members of faith groups, the local SACRE may be able to suggest possible speakers. Patterns of visits and visitors could be built into the school RE syllabus so that they are evenly distributed throughout the Key Stage or even spread over both Key Stages.

Celebrations

Taking the celebration of a festival as a school or class theme is another way of helping children to enter, in a limited way, into the experience of what it means to be a member of a particular faith. For this to have real value a considerable amount of attention needs to be given to planning and clear decisions made about which subject areas will be incorporated into the celebration and the amount of time that will be devoted to it. A number of the approaches to RE outlined above will probably contribute either to preparation or celebration. Particular resources may be obtainable through parents or advisory teachers, or the local SACRE may be able to suggest suitable contacts within the faith community. Many LEAs produce booklets for use in multicultural education which contain ideas and activities for festivals and, increasingly, publishers' lists include such materials.

SHAP (registered charity) produces an annual calendar of religious festivals which would be a useful addition to a staff library or RE resource area. Since, as indicated above quite a lot of time will be needed, it would be appropriate to consider which festival(s) would be celebrated in major ways each year, possibly changing the emphasis over a period of time. This does not mean that all others would be ignored but that mention would be more low key. Choices will usually be determined by the ethnic and cultural backgrounds of children in the school.

Attitudes

There are some attitudes which, hopefully, will permeate all areas of school life. These include respect, care and concern for people and property. In addition there are other attitudes that are necessary for anyone who studies religions. These include in the early years the following: curiosity and interest, a sense of wonder and awe, a willingness to develop a positive attitude to others and life, understanding the importance of commitment.

Assessment and Record Keeping

In recent times emphasis has been placed on assessment and evaluation of religious education. It may be that your school has a general policy relating to both these issues. Do check, and, where such a policy exists, draw up appropriate guidelines for the subject. Where such a policy does not exist it would be helpful to check what support is available from the local agreed syllabus in terms of general guidance and what information is available in respect of attainment targets.

If you do decide to produce an independent assessment pattern, when you plan your scheme of work for RE set out the programmes of study based on the principles of concepts and knowledge, experience, attitudes and skills. Then ways of assessing progress in each area can be built into the programme of study. For the most part this will be a continuing formative process based on observation of children's responses and developing awareness and sensitivity – a more holistic approach then simply a catalogue of 'facts known about . . .' Ways of asking children to record their work will vary according to the nature of the study and the age and ability of the children.

It should be possible to identify lines of continuity from the agreed syllabus to the children's work via the school syllabus and teachers' records of work done. As well as providing information for official visitors this is a way of checking on continuity and progression. There are very useful detailed considerations of these areas in *Attainment in RE – A Handbook for Teachers* (1989) and *Assessing, Recording and Reporting RE* (1991) both from the Midlands Regional RE Centre.

Resources

It is important that your colleagues know what resources are available to support their teaching of religious education. What is your current stock in terms of pupils' and teachers' books? What artefacts are available? Do you have a range of boxes covering several faiths? What videos are kept in school? Do note any general education programmes that include a religious element, for example *Watch* (BBC) programme includes a religious slot most terms. If you have developed good contact with local faith groups do indicate what is available in terms of human resources and worship centre. Finally, your SACRE should be a useful source of information.

Clearly if you are to be able to function effectively as a coordinator you will need to negotiate a budget for building up the resources stock but you may also find that individuals will offer you artefacts as long as you are able to assure them that they will be looked after properly. Travel agents are sometimes willing to donate posters when their emphasis on particular areas changes and friends or family travelling abroad can often buy small articles much more cheaply than you can do so in Britain, if they know what you need. Alongside the collection of materials you will need to arrange storage space for them and a clear understanding of what the borrowing requirements are. Otherwise things will gradually vanish into classrooms not to be found until the end of year clearance.

More Challenges for the Religious Education Coordinator

You Must Be Prepared to Listen – and to Ask for Help

As has been previously mentioned, colleagues may have difficulty with the teaching of RE. Some find it difficult to identify a religious strand for a topic. You will need to reassure them that not all topics have an RE element and help them to develop skills in finding a relevant religious strand in certain topics. However, you may also find that, as you show yourself receptive to offers of help and support that some colleagues are able to bring in resources from a personal background. They may have family or community connections with several faiths that they can capitalize on in their own teaching and share with the rest of the school. It is a particularly good situation where colleagues come from a variety of faith backgrounds.

You Must Be Prepared to Extend Your Knowledge of New Initiatives in Religious Education

One way in which this may be done is to attend courses run by the LEA for RE teachers. These may also be offered by the local SACRE and it is always useful to keep in touch with their activities. Another possibility is to join a professional RE association (see the end of this chapter for details). You may feel that it is a valuable development to establish a group for RE coordinators from neighbouring schools to meet termly and review issues. A way of keeping yourself and your colleagues in touch with national developments and at the same time contribution to the stock of RE resources is to persuade your school to take the CEM primary mailing.

You Must Be Prepared to Initiate Change in Your School

Colleagues need time to appreciate new ideas and resources for class use. Curriculum initiatives should be shared at appropriate times and new resources displayed for staff information before being transferred to the RE resources bank.

Colleagues will value input into training days in which new schemes, resources and initiatives may be outlined. This may be a showing of a new TV programme or something far more significant such as a new agreed syllabus.

See if there is room on a staffroom notice board to display relevant information including requests and ideas for in-service.

Do an audit of your school's RE practice against what an OFSTED inspection would be looking for. Use this as a basis for an in-service programme.

Be Prepared to Promote the Subject

A regular RE display in a prominent position in the school such as the entry or hall can help to raise awareness and interest. Likewise a regular report to the governing body will help to promote interest. You may be initiating partnership work in the community which would be deemed newsworthy by the local press. A tea party for the aged, paying the cost of drilling a well for water in a developing country, distribution of harvest gifts, the development of a link with a retirement home are all initiatives for local newspapers.

Needless to say, it is essential that such projects should be supported across the school. It may be that one or two projects a year could be planned into the whole school programme – another good example of the cross-curricular approach to RE.

Taking up even some of these challenges will demand a great deal of time and careful planning. If they are to be accomplished alongside the effective management of a class it will be absolutely essential for a co-ordinator to be able to negotiate some time in which to work – alongside and on behalf of colleagues.

Resources

Publication for policy documents/staff handbook:
The Agreed Syllabus (GM/LEA/VC Schools), the Diocesan Syllabus (VA

Schools), DfE circular 1/94 on RE and collective worship, Ofsted report on RE and collective worship, Inspections 92/93 (1994), SACRE advice or guidelines from the LEA.

Teacher reference (general):
CEM School Mailing Service, includes *RE Today*, *Exploring a Theme*, *School Worship File*. Three mailings a year from CEM Royal Buildings, Victoria St., Derby DE1 1GW – about £22.

Shap Calendar of Religious Festivals, Alan Brown, National Society's RE Centre, 36 Causten St., London SW1P 4AU.

LYNCH, M. *Tell Me a Story, Story and RE*, from B.F.S.S. National R.E. Centre, West London Institute, Isleworth, Middlesex – £4 + p.p. 75p.

Teacher Reference (Pupil Related):
Laying Foundations for Religious Education, *Autumn* (1990), *Spring* (1991), *Summer* (1991) and *Open the Door* (1994) – Taylor, D.S. from BFSS National RE Centre, West London Institute, Borough Road, Isleworth, Middlesex, TW7 5DU.

Understanding Religions: Birth Customs (Rushton, L., 1992), *Death Customs* (Rushton, IL., 1992), *Food and Fasting* (Prior, K., 1992), *Initiation Customs* (Prior, K., 1992), *Marriage Customs* (Compton, A., 1992) and *Pilgrimages and Journeys* (Prior, K., 1992) – from Wayland Publications, Western Road, Hove, Sussex.

Blueprints: Religious Education Key Stage 1 (Palmiter, R. and Price, M., 1993), *Religious Education Key Stage 2* (Palmiter, R. and Price, M., 1992), *Christmas Key Stage 1* (Fitzsemmons, J. and Whiteford, R., 1992) and *Christmas Key Stage 2* (Palmer, J.A., 1993) – from Stanley Thorne Limited, Wellington Street, Cheltenham, GLSO 1YD.

Exploring a Theme a wide range of themes including, Myself, Food, Water, Symbol, Spring Festivals, Festivals of Light – from CEM Royal Building, Victoria Street, Derby DE1 1GW.

Brain Waves: RE First Topics (Ages 5–7), (Cato, P. and Washford M.R., 1991), Exploring Themes (Ages 7–11), (Cato, P. and Washford, M.R., 1991), *RE Celebrations*, (Kurtis, J. and Curtis, P., 1991) – from Folens Publishers, Boscombe Road, Dunstable LU5 4RL.

Artefacts:
Articles of Faith, Bury Business Centre, Kay St., Bury BL9 6BU.
Religious Artefacts in the Classroom, Hodder and Stoughton.

Pictures and Posters:
Westhill Project – pupils' and teachers' posters and photo packs on four religions – RE Centre, Westhill College, Selly Oak, Birmingham, B29 6LL.

My Religion – colour photographs showing children in the five major religions in Britain – Pictorial Education Trust, 27 Kirchen Road, London W13 OUD.

References

BRUNER, J. (1974) *Beyond the Information Given*, London, Allen and Unwin.

DFE (1994) *Circular 1/94: Religious Education and Collective Worship*, London, DfE Publications Centre, P.O. Box2193, London, E15 2EU.

MIDLANDS REGIONAL RE CENTRE (1989) *Attainment in RE*, Birmingham, Westhill College.

MIDLANDS REGIONAL RE CENTRE (1991) *Assessing, Recording and Reporting RE*, Birmingham, Westhill College.

NATIONAL CURRICULUM COUNCIL (NCC) (1993) *Spiritual and Moral Development: A Discussion Paper*, York, NCC.

SHAP publications may be obtained from: Alan Brown, The National Society's RE Centre, 36 Causten St., London SW1P 4AU.

The National Society RE Centre also has a wide selection of books and materials for religious education.

Notes on Contributors

Jane Birch is deputy headteacher at Harpur Mount Primary School in Harpurhey, Manchester. Her curriculum responsibilities include coordinating English and equal opportunities. She was involved in the preparation of the Manchester English in the National Curriculum Resource Pack (Key Stage 1). Currently she is studying part time for a modular Master's Degree in English Language and Literature at the University of Salford.

Tony Birch is deputy headteacher and IT coordinator at Castle Hill Primary School, Bolton. Previously he spent four years as an IT coordinator in a Manchester primary school and was part of the LEA INSET presentation team. Recently he co-directed the Manchester University Portables Project and is now involved in a related project 'New Developments in IT'. He has written a number of articles on IT in the primary school.

Deborah Boekestein is currently a Special Educational Needs coordinator in a large village school. After reading for a degree in Politics and German at Lancaster University and a career in retail management, she studied for a PGCE. She entered teaching in 1988 when the National Curriculum was introduced and for five years taught across the primary age range in Greater Manchester.

Kathryn Bowe is a primary teacher in Tameside. At present she is head of infants in a large primary school and science coordinator for Key Stage 1 and Key Stage 2. Kathryn does not claim to be a scientist; she gained her degree in English Literature at Bangor University and became involved in science when teaching and attending various courses at Manchester University. Kathryn enjoys the practical side of teaching science and strives to promote and develop science throughout her school.

Sue Chedzoy is currently a lecturer in Education at the University of Exeter where she has responsibility for coordinating and teaching Physical Education to undergraduate and postgraduate students training to teach the early years, junior and middle years age range. An experienced teacher, advisory teacher and researcher, she is a regular contributor to the *British Journal of Physical Education* and has written numerous articles for teachers to support their teaching of physical education in primary schools. Sue Chedzoy is a member of the Executive Committee and Chair of the External Relations Commission of the Physical Education Association of the United Kingdom. She edits the research supplement of the *British Journal of Physical Education* and is author of *Fitness. Fun – Promoting Health in Physical Education.*

Julie Davies, formerly an infant headteacher, is a lecturer in primary education at Manchester Victoria University. She teaches English and History Curriculum and Methods Courses. Her research interests include children's attitudes to school and the curriculum, their self-esteem, their attainments in maths and reading and the uses of standard assessment tasks. She has published extensively in these areas.

Mike Harrison, was a primary teacher and headteacher for sixteen years. A scientist, he is currently the Director of the Centre for Primary Education in the School of Education at the University of Manchester, where he has been responsible for science and mathematics in initial training and higher degree courses. He currently acts as leader for the Primary PGCE course and has run a variety of senior and middle-management training courses for the university and many LEAs. He is an OFSTED registered inspector specializing in mathematics, IT and school management. Since managing a project on the training of curriculum coordinators in the foundation subjects in the primary school he edited *Beyond the Core Curriculum*, published by Northcote House, aimed at helping primary teachers to coordinate the non-core foundation areas in the national curriculum. He is a joint author of *Primary School Management*, published by Heinemann Educational in January 1992 and has been appointed series editor for the three books in this series. He is editor of the second volume in this series.

Ian Hocking is currently a local education authority inspector consultant and INSET provider and a registered inspector (OFSTED). Previously he worked as a teacher in all phases of education and was a primary headteacher.

Gwen Mattock taught in primary schools in the south of England for eleven years. Currently the leader of the Primary Postgraduate Certificate in Education Course at the Manchester Metropolitan University, she was involved with in-service education for a number of years including a variety of RE courses for LEAs. She has published a pair of teachers' books in the Lutterworth Topic Book series, contributed to an IBRA series of bible reading notes for young people and to *Beyond the Core Curriculum* edited by Mike Harrison and published by Northcote House in 1994.

Geoff Preston is a graduate of the Open University. He has experience of teaching in primary and secondary schools in the northwest of England. Following lecturing at Mather College and City of Manchester College he became SACRE Secretary and RE adviser for the Rochdale LEA. He is a visiting lecturer at Manchester University.

Rita Ray, B.Ed. (Hons.), MA, Ph.D.
Poet and Writer-in-School, working in Primary and Special schools. Writer of educational materials. Lecturer in Education, Primary Centre, University of Manchester. Previous experience: Research Associate working on the development of National Curriculum assessment materials for English in England and Wales and Northern Ireland. Reading Advisory Teacher, Salford LEA. Teacher in primary and special (MLD) schools.

Rosemary Rodger is a senior lecturer in early years education at the Manchester Metropolitan University. She is deputy course leader of the primary postgraduate course and a registered inspector. Her research interests involved her in coordinating a two year collaborative research project with Salford local authority which aimed to identify those factors contributing to a quality learning experience for children under 5. Her own research focused on provision and practice for 4-year-old children in four reception classes. She has recently embarked on a research project with Manchester and Salford LEAs which is aiming to identify factors contributing to effective schools and school improvement with an emphasis, in her case, on the way in which base-line assessments are used to calculate the 'value added' by the education of children by the time they are assessed at the end of Key Stage 1. She is co-editor of *Quality Education in the Early Years* (Oxford University Press 1994) co-author of *Ginn Geography Key Stage 2* and a geography consultant to BBC *Watch*. She provides in-service courses for several LEAS in the northwest of England.

Barbara Stewart is presently working with students in primary teacher training in the School of Education, at the Manchester Victoria University and with teachers on in-service courses. She was formerly a headteacher and a member of the steering group for the national Calculator-Aware Number (CAN) Curriculum Continuation project of the Primary Initiatives in Mathematics Education (PrIME) project 1985–92.

Rita Walker trained at Liverpool Institute of Higher Education where she was awarded the Susan Willis Memorial Prize. She is based in Stockport, having taught at Cheadle Catholic Infants School from 1991 to 1994 and has recently joined the staff of St Mary's R.C. Primary School, Marple Bridge. She contributes to courses on music as a primary curriculum specialism in the initial training of teachers at the University of Manchester.

Index

access:
   to art 146–7, 152
   to education 14–15
   to geography 100
   to IT 168–9
   to music 110, 122
   to PE 124
   to play 89
   to reading 25
   to resources 64
   to technology 187–8
accuracy 20
Action Aid 99
action plan 10, 26–7, 35, 150, 162, 164,
   188
activity:
   INSET and history 194–5
   staff development and geography
     90–100
   see also cross curricular activity; extra
     curricular activity
aesthetics 110, 151
aims:
   art 141–3, 145, 150–1
   English 34–6, 39
   geography 81–3, 85, 99
   history 190–2, 197, 201–2
   IT 155, 158, 165
   mathematics 52–3, 55–8, 63
   music 114–18
   PE 126, 129, 134
   reading 21, 23, 32
   religious education 210
   role of coordinator 5, 13–14
   science 79
   technology 180, 188–9
Alexander, R. *et al* 82
Arnold, H. 28
art:
   coordinating 141–54
   exhibitions 146–7
   and music 118

assessment:
   art 145, 152–3
   English 36, 38–9, 43
   geography 81, 85, 87, 91–2, 94,
     99–101
   history 198–200, 202
   IT 167, 169–70
   maths 55, 60, 62
   music 113, 119–20
   PE 129–30, 134–5
   reading 21, 26–7
   religious education 210–11, 217
   science 69, 78–9
   technology 178
attainment 17
   geography 100, 101
   maths 58–9, 62
   music 120
   PE 128–9, 134
   reading 19, 26–7, 32
   technology 176
attainment targets 15
   art 142
   English 38–9, 43
   geography 86, 103–4
   maths 60
   music 111–13
   PE 127
   religious education 210–11
   science 69, 76, 78
   technology 175–7, 179–81
attitude:
   of child 57, 69, 82, 87, 98, 127, 210,
     212, 217
   of teacher 6, 35, 55, 58–9, 61, 159
audience awareness 40, 156
audit of resources 35–6, 70, 72, 90,
   130–1, 149

background, social 59
Barber, M. 2, 11
Belbin, R. Meridith 3

225